AF251799

DOLOS AND DIKE IN SOPHOKLES' ELEKTRA

MNEMOSYNE

BIBLIOTHECA CLASSICA BATAVA

COLLEGERUNT

H. PINKSTER · H. W. PLEKET

C.J. RUIJGH · D.M. SCHENKEVELD · P.H. SCHRIJVERS

BIBLIOTHECAE FASCICULOS EDENDOS CURAVIT

C.J. RUIJGH, KLASSIEK SEMINARIUM, OUDE TURFMARKT 129, AMSTERDAM

SUPPLEMENTUM DUCENTESIMUM DECIMUM NONUM

LEONA MACLEOD

DOLOS AND DIKE IN SOPHOKLES' ELEKTRA

DOLOS AND DIKE
IN
SOPHOKLES' ELEKTRA

BY

LEONA MACLEOD

BRILL

LEIDEN · BOSTON · KÖLN

2001

Library of Congress Cataloging-in-Publication Data

MacLeod, Leona.
   Dolos and Dikê in Sophokles' Elektra / by Leona MacLeod.
      p.   cm. — (Mnemosyne, bibliotheca classica Batava.
  Supplementum, ISSN 0169-8958; 219)
  Originally presented as author's thesis (Ph. D)—Dalhousie University.
  Includes bibliographical references (p.) and index.
  ISBN 9004118985 (alk. paper)
  1. Sophocles. Electra. 2. Electra (Greek mythology) in literature. I. Title.
  II. Series.

PA4413.E5 M33 2001
882'.01—dc21
                                          2001025589

Die Deutsche Bibliothek - CIP-Einheitsaufnahme

[Mnemosyne / Supplementum]
Mnemosyne : bibliotheca classica Batava. Supplementum. – Leiden ;
Boston ; Köln : Brill
  Früher Schriftenreihe
  Teilw. u.d.T.: Mnemosyne / Supplements
  Reihe Supplementum zu: Mnemosyne
  219. MacLeod, Leona : Dolos and Dikê in Sophokles ' Elektra

Dolos and Dikê in Sophokles ' Elektra / by Leona MacLeod. – Leiden ;
Boston ; Köln : Brill, 2001
  (Mnemosyne : Supplementum ; 219)
  ISBN 90–04–11898–5

ISSN 0169-8958
ISBN 90 04 11898 5

CONTENTS

ABBREVIATIONS AND EDITIONS

The following abbreviations are used in the bibliography:

A & A	*Antike und Abendland*
AC	*Acta Classica*
AJP	*American Journal of Philology*
BICS	*Bulletin of the Institute of Classical Studies of the University of London*
BCH	*Bulletin de Correspondence Hellenique*
BMCR	*Bryn Mawr Classical Review*
CA	*Classical Antiquity*
CJ	*Classical Journal*
C & M	*Classica & Mediaevalia*
CP	*Classical Philology*
CQ	*Classical Quarterly*
CR	*Classical Review*
CW	*Classical World*
G & R	*Greece and Rome*
GRBS	*Greek, Roman, and Byzantine Studies*
HSCP	*Harvard Studies in Classical Philology*
ICS	*Illinois Classical Studies*
JASO	*Journal of the Anthropological Society of Oxford*
JHS	*Journal of Hellenic Studies*
MH	*Museum Helveticum*
PCPS	*Proceedings of the Cambridge Philological Society*
RIDA	*Revue internationale des droits de l'Antiquité*
RhM	*Rheinisches Museum*
SO	*Symbolae Osloenses*
TAPA	*Transactions of the American Philological Association*
WS	*Wiener Studien*
UCPCP	*University of California Publications in Classical Philology*
YCS	*Yale Classical Studies*
YR	*Yale Review*

In addition the following abbreviations have been employed in the notes. Where there is a reference to a scholar (without date), it is to the relevant OCT or other named edition.

Campbell — L. Campbell, L. ed. 1881. *The Plays and Fragments of Sophocles Vol. II.* Oxford. Reprinted 1969.

Jebb — R.C. Jebb. 1907. *Sophocles: The Plays and Fragments Vol. VI Elektra.* Cambridge.

Kaibel — G. Kaibel. 1911. *Elektra.* Leipzig.

Kamerbeek — J.C. Kamerbeek. 1974. *The Plays of Sophokles. Commentaries, Part V: The Elektra.* Leiden.

Kells — J.H. Kells. 1973. *Sophocles' Electra.* Cambridge.

L-J & W — H. Lloyd-Jones and N.G. Wilson. 1990. *Sophoclis Fabulae.* Oxford.

L-J & W² — H. Lloyd-Jones and N.G. Wilson. 1990. *Sophoclea: Studies on the Text of Sophocles.* Oxford.

LSJ — H.G. Liddell, R. Scott, and H. Stuart-Jones. 1955. *A Greek-English Lexicon* (9th edition). Oxford

OCT — Oxford Classical Texts

Pearson — A.C. Pearson. 1928. *Sophoclis Fabulae.* Oxford.

Radt — S. Radt. (ed.) 1985. *Tragicorum Graecorum Fragmenta.* Vol. III: Aeschylus. 1977. Vol. IV: Sophocles. Göttingen.

West — M.L. West. 1972. *Iambi et Elegi Graeci ante Alexandrum Cantati.* Vol. 2. Oxford.

PREFACE

This study of the *Elektra* was originally a doctoral thesis prepared at Dalhousie University in Halifax, and accordingly, it owes much to the help and advice of many who read it and commented upon it at various stages. In particular thanks are due to the members of my thesis committee, Dennis House, Patrick Atherton, and Patricia Calkin, all of whom saved me from numerous errors. Special thanks as well are due to Desmond Conacher for his criticism and advice. The greatest debt, however, I owe to Professor Rainer Friedrich, who taught me as a graduate student, and has been unflagging in his support of me. I have benefited immensely from his scholarship, criticism, and advice, as has this study. Finally I would like to thank the external reader for E.J. Brill for his careful reading and suggestions. Any mistakes which remain are, of course, mine.

Unless otherwise indicated, the translations in this book are my own. They are entirely utilitarian and have no pretensions to either elegance or literary merit. I have transliterated the most important Greek terms, usually in their lexicon form, and I have left unmarked the long vowels in the transliterations, primarily for aesthetic reasons. My initial aim was to transliterate the Greek names directly, but as this procedure produced the expected problems, I have followed the Latinized forms in some cases. Thus the careful reader will note some inconsistencies here.

The text used for Sophokles' *Elektra* is that of Lloyd-Jones and Wilson, 1990, *Sophoclis Fabulae*, Oxford.

INTRODUCTION

Sophokles' *Elektra* deals with an old and familiar legend: the return and revenge of Orestes. It was a story mentioned by Homer, treated by lyric poets, and forming the basis of numerous tragedies. While Homer was able to avoid treating the morally questionable act of matricide, by fifth century this aspect of the legend had become so firmly established that no poet could omit it. As Aristotle says, Orestes always kills Klytaimnestra. And so he does in Sophokles' version, but in at least one important respect, his treatment represents a radical departure from his dramatic counterparts. In this version, and only in this version, there is no hesitation, no suggestion of remorse, and no punishment in store for the killers. Orestes and Elektra in Sophokles' play appear to get away with murder. That his *Elektra* seems to ignore the moral implications of the matricide has made it the most controversial and difficult play to interpret.[1] In this respect, the existence of Aischylos' *Oresteia* and Euripides' *Elektra* have accentuated the problematical nature of Sophokles' tragedy: neither author downplays the horror or criminality of the deed so that we are left with no doubt how either poet wishes us to view the vengeance. Sophokles' play, by contrast, appears to maintain a disconcerting silence on the matricide.

0.1   *The Legend in Poetry*

From the sources, it would appear that Homer was the only one to avoid all mention of the matricide.[2] Whether he was working from

---

[1] For an overview of the various treatments of this legend, see the introductions of Jebb and Kamerbeek; Garvie 1986: ix–xxvi; March 1987: 99–170; Easterling 1989: 10–16; Gantz 1993: 676–686. See McDonald 1994: 103–126 for a comparison of Sophokles' play and later operatic treatments. The question of the priority of Sophokles' play is not one which will be addressed here. For different views on the vexatious dates of these two plays, see Jebb's introduction (lii–lviii); Owen 1936: 145–157; Denniston 1939: xxxiii–xxxix; Whitman 1951: 51–55; Dale 1969: 227–229; Kamerbeek; Winnington-Ingram 1980: 342–343.

[2] There is no explicit mention of how Klytaimnestra met her end. Instead we

a different tradition or was aware of the killing of Klytaimnestra but simply chose to ignore it, is uncertain, but clearly matricide does not fit in with his portrayal of Orestes' revenge as a heroic deed worthy of everlasting glory.[3] The tale of Agamemnon's homecoming and murder at the hands of Aigisthos and the subsequent revenge of Orestes is not consistently presented in the *Odyssey*, but is referred to intermittently, with the House of Atreus operating as a contrasting parallel to Odysseus and his family.[4] It is first alluded to in Zeus' speech in the divine assembly which sets off the epic action (*Od.* 1.32–43) when Aigisthos' fate serves to illustrate Zeus' theodicy: man is responsible for suffering beyond his due and cannot blame the gods for it.[5] Aigisthos, who was warned by the gods not to kill Agamemnon and marry Klytaimnestra, persisted in his "reckless folly" and perished as a result. The story is referred to again when Athena, in the guise of Mentes, holds up Orestes' deed as a model of heroic action and filial devotion in an effort to stimulate Telemachos to take up his responsibilities to his *oikos*: "Have you not heard of the glory (*kleos*) great Orestes won among all men when he killed his father's murderer . . .?", Athena asks Telemachos. "Be bold, you also, so that in generations to come, men may praise you" (1.298–302). Later Telemachos hears the story from Nestor (3.193–98) and then again from Menelaos (4.514–47).[6] Each time the story ends with the mention of the revenge of Orestes, and each time it functions for Telemachos as a paradigm of heroic action and proper behaviour befitting a son. Throughout the epic the act is presented in a morally

---

have the rather elusive comment that after Orestes killed Aigisthos, he celebrated both their deaths: ἦ τοι ὁ κτείνας δαίνυ τάφον Ἀργείοισιν μητρός τε στυγερῆς καὶ ἀνάλκιδος Αἰγίσθοιο (3.309–10).

[3] Garvie 1986: xii mentions three possibilities: that there is a single tradition and Homer suppresses details immaterial to his purpose; that he actually invents details to suit his purpose; that they were different versions of the legend available and Homer simply chooses to suit his purpose.

[4] The legend of Orestes is referred to a number of times in the *Odyssey*: 1.35–43, 298–302; 3.193–8, 251–2, 256–75, 303–10; 4.92, 514–547; 11.428–434, 452–3; 23.383; 24.97, 199–201.

[5] For studies on how the legend of Orestes is treated by Homer, see D'Arms and Hulley 1946: 207–213; Gould 1983: 32–45; Alden 1987: 129–137.

[6] It is also related by the ghost of Agamemnon to Odysseus during his trip to the Underworld in Book 11 (423–434 and 451–453), but here the revenge of Orestes is not mentioned for the obvious reason that Agamemnon does not know the outcome of the story.

unambiguous fashion and its purpose is plain: just as Orestes avenged his father's murder and won glory and fame, so should Telemachos too assume his duty to his father and *oikos*. Any mention of the matricide would obviously destroy the parallels Homer wishes to draw between the members of the two families, and in this sense, the poet's silence is hardly surprising.[7]

What Homer fails to mention for the sake of representing Orestes' vengeance as heroic deed is precisely what the tragedians use to probe the problematic nature of revenge justice. Recognizing that the tragic essence of the story lies in the matricide, the dramatists make it the central issue. In the *Oresteia*, Aischylos focuses on the conflicting rights of competing claims to justice with the matricide presented as a necessary link in the chain of events leading to the establishment of a public form of justice based upon rational law. As necessary and justified as it is, Aischylos does not shy away from showing the horror and the criminal nature of the matricide. Despite the convergence of divine command, filial obligation, and his own wish to reclaim his patrimony, Orestes still hesitates when the moment comes. Urged on by the reminder of Apollo's words, Orestes brings himself to kill his mother, but he is fully aware that the justice which he extracts is at the same time a crime: "You killed whom you should not", he tells his mother, "now suffer what you should not" (*Ch.* 930). The Furies' pursuit of Orestes brings home the full horror of the crime and it requires a divinely instituted law court to acquit him of the stain of matricide.

Euripides takes a radically different approach to the legend with his portrayal of the matricide as an act of brutal violence. We see the barbaric nature of the whole affair through the psychologically devastating effect it has upon the offspring. Not only does Euripides question the morality of the human protagonists who would commit such a deed, but that of a god who would give such an order. "[Klytaimnestra's] punishment is just—but you did not work in justice", the Dioskouroi tell Orestes; "as for Apollo . . . he is wise but

---

[7] When we consider the function of the *Oresteia* story as a mythological parallel, his silence is not surprising, for the matricide is an issue completely irrelevant for Odysseus and his family. Mentioning it would destroy the parallels the poet wishes to draw between members of the two families, as Telemachos can hardly win fame as Orestes did by killing his mother, Penelope. More to the point, matricide is hardly a heroic deed, worthy of *kleos*.

he gave you unwise bidding" (*El.* 1244–46). For one poet, the problematic nature of the vengeance gives rise to the formation of a new type of justice: the public justice of the *polis*; for the other, the vengeance seems only to suggest its moral impossibility; both poets require divinities to absolve Orestes and neither is indifferent to the morally repellent nature of the matricide nor are their characters unaware of the criminality of their action.

In Sophokles' *Elektra*, however, no divinity appears on stage to effect a resolution, the explicit condemnation appears to be absent, and the avengers themselves show a disconcerting lack of awareness of the criminal nature of the deed. Instead Orestes speaks vaguely of winning glory by killing his enemies; mother and daughter hurl charges of shameful behaviour at one another; everyone claims to be acting in accordance with justice and no one mentions the matricide. The failure of Sophokles to bring about a clear resolution as Aischylos does, or condemn the deed outright, as Euripides does, is largely the cause of the controversy surrounding the play. Scholars have yet to come to an agreement over how precisely we are to understand the poet's attitude towards the matricide and the nature of the justice it represents, if indeed it does represent justice.

0.2 *Scholarship and Sophokles'* Elektra

Sophokles' *Elektra* is almost universally admired for its flawless dramatic structure and its exquisite technique, but its intense emotionalism and ambiguous ending often leave readers puzzled and disturbed. Grene expresses the ambivalent response of many critics to this tragedy with his judgement that it is "perhaps the best-constructed and most unpleasant play that Sophocles wrote."[8] The *Elektra* has generated such disparate responses and widely divergent interpretations that it has acquired the dubious status of a "problem play". Commentators cannot even agree on the overall mood of the play: one finds the pervading tone relentlessly sombre and dark, while another thinks it cheerfully bright and optimistic. Woodard may claim that *Elektra* offers "critics fewer toeholds"[9] than any other Sophoclean

---

[8] Grene 1957: 124.
[9] Woodard 1964: 163.

play, but judging from the range of interpretations it has generated, it would seem that it offers too many interpretative toeholds.

One persistent problem has continually dogged scholarship, reflected in the main interpretative approaches to this play: Sophokles' presentation of the vengeance. Some have placed the poet beside Homer in glorifying it as a heroic deed deserving of everlasting fame; some have adopted a more Aeschylean perspective in concentrating on the justice of the deed; and some have placed him alongside Euripides in condemning it as an act of wanton violence by morally bankrupt killers. Others have attempted to side-step the whole issue of the matricide, either by identifying themes which transcend this question or by arguing that the true focus of the play is not the killing of Klytaimnestra, but the character of Elektra. A simple, although crude division, however, can be made between two large interpretative camps: one with an "optimistic" or "affirmative" reading which sees the vengeance as unproblematical, and another with a "pessimistic" or "dark" reading which emphasizes the more disturbing aspects of the play. This is admittedly a very rough distinction which cannot do justice to the subtlety and complexity of many interpretations, but it provides a first orientation and a tentative guide to a diverse body of expository writing, without implying, as Kells' categories do, that all scholarship on this play has defined itself solely in relationship to the matricide.[10]

Those who offer an affirmative reading of this tragedy typically see the vengeance as a clear-cut case of just retribution, but do so with different arguments.[11] Earlier scholars, such as Jebb, saw the

---

[10] Kells divides scholarship into three main groups which he designates the amoral, the justificatory, and the ironic. I have reluctantly adopted the commonly used terms "optimistic" and "pessimistic" which, although not without their own problems, have the merit of leaving us free to make more refined distinctions within each group.

[11] Those with an affirmative reading include: Owen 1927: 51–52; Webster 1936; Bowra 1944: 212–260; Whitman 1951: 149–171; Adams, 1957: 59–80; Linforth 1963: 89–126; Woodard 1964: 163–205 and 1965: 195–233; Alexanderson 1966: 79–98; Waldock 1966: 169–195; Musurillo 1967: 94: 108; Stevens 1978: 11–20; Szlezak 1981: 1–21; Gardiner 1986:139–175; March 1987: 99–170 and 1996: 65–81; Burnett 1998: 119–141. These critics all argue, albeit with different emphases, that Sophokles justifies the deed. Some of these are specific responses to the ironic reading of the play (Alexanderson, Stevens, and Szlezak). Alexanderson's treatment is a response to Johansen 1964: 3–32; while he admits that Elektra is not a "stainless" heroine, he argues that her behaviour is justified. Stevens also attacks the ironic

drama as a return to the story as it appears in the *Odyssey*.[12] Sophokles, unconcerned with the deeper moral or ethical issues raised by the demand for revenge, retreats into an earlier and more archaic view which emphasizes the heroic nature of the affair. The play thus dramatizes Orestes' successful homecoming and revenge without Furies, moralizing judgements, or any other elements which might undermine the heroic character of the act. The stain of matricide is glossed over by making the death of Aigisthos the climax of the dramatic action. Others, while not explicitly adopting a Homeric framework, agree that Sophokles is uninterested in the moral and ethical issues raised by the act. Thus while it can hardly be said that he ignores the matricide, it is thought that he downplays it as much as possible. Waldock, for instance, argues that throughout the tragedy Sophokles engages in the "art of dramatic suppression" so that the effects of the matricide are "neutralised."[13] Not only are we not horrified by the killing of Klytaimnestra, but we fully sympathize with the killers. For Waldock, the play is best summed up as a combination of "mat-

---

interpretation on a number of points, but adds nothing new to the debate. Szlezak in his attack on the ironic reading of the play makes a number of good points about Sophoclean irony. For him, Orestes and Elektra are following conventional Greek morality in "helping friends/harming enemies". Of the more recent treatments, Gardiner in her study of the Sophoclean Chorus is critical of the psychological reading of the play, in particular, of Elektra's character. For her, Sophokles is concerned to show, contrary to conventional belief, that a female could take part in such an act and not be a monster. According to this view, Elektra remains in the end innocent of any wrongdoing, for tragic circumstances have forced her to such a position. This theme, Gardiner argues, is evident in Sophokles' other plays which all show crimes committed under "reasonable, humanly understandable circumstances, such as ignorance, desperation, or even moral conviction." March, who examines the treatment of the myth in literature and, more recently, focuses on the Chorus in the play, makes a strong case for the justificatory position. Burnett in her recent study on revenge argues that the death of Klytaimnestra is presented exclusively as the deed of Apollo. For her, the association of the deed with the god as well as the reunion scene function to diminish the impact of the matricide. The play ends in success and the spectator is made to feel that order and piety are restored.

[12] Jebb 1907: xl–xlii. Denniston 1939: xxiv-xxv also sees the moral issue of the matricide ignored: "Sophocles chose to treat his theme objectively, Homerically, archaically, deliberately shelving the moral issue, content with giving his audience a stirring play, lit up by the strength and tenderness of his heroine's character." Whitman 1951: 149–174 argues that the tragic focus of the play is not the matricide, which is assumed to be just and thus incidental, but the central character of Elektra. Whitman sees a vindication of her through the concentration on her heroic endurance and moral integrity.

[13] Waldock 1966: 186 and 178.

ricide and happy spirits".[14] Regardless whether they adopt the Homeric framework, as Jebb does, or the amoral approach, as Waldock does, for these critics, Sophokles has chosen to place his emphasis on other aspects of the story and his silence should serve as a warning against our desire to read the play in these moral terms.[15]

On the whole, few have been convinced by interpretations which minimize or eliminate the ethical problems of the vengeance as the readings of Jebb and Waldock do. The 'Homeric' reading of the play not only fails to account for the central role of Elektra, a figure not even mentioned in Homer, but as Jebb himself admitted, for an audience who was familiar with the *Oresteia*, it would appear to have failed to reach a "true conclusion."[16] Moreover, the instant that Apollo is introduced into the tragedy, the problem of matricide becomes almost impossible to ignore. Jebb was unable to offer anything other than the suggestion that Sophokles simply ignores Aischylos' version in favour of Homer's, a solution which even he seemed to find unconvincing. While Sophokles has always been recognized as the most Homeric of the poets, and his plays often recall specific themes and motifs from the epics, they tend to treat them in a far more complex and differentiated fashion than Jebb's approach suggests. By his reading, the vengeance poses no more problems than the killing of an enemy on the battlefield. Orestes may speak about the deed in the manner of the Homeric hero, but he does so in a context which implies something disturbingly inappropriate with this perception. Waldock's 'amoral' approach is equally unsatisfying. He may not go as far as Jebb does in suggesting that Sophokles ignores the *Oresteia*, but his refusal to see any conflict, moral or otherwise, deprives the play of its tragic nature.[17] Neither the explicit 'Homerizing' approach of Jebb nor the 'matricide and good cheer' approach of

---

[14] Waldock 1966: 174 n. 1 paraphrases Schlegel's description of the play in his *Lectures on dramatic art and literature* (Lecture IX) 1876: 122–133.

[15] Musurillo 1967: 94–108 is another who thinks that the moral issues are obscured and diminished by the focus on Elektra. The main conflict for him is the antagonism between mother and daughter. For him, the play shows the "destruction of Clytaimestra and the growth and glorification of Electra" (p. 95). Others have also argued that the matricide falls outside the central focus of the play, some in an affirmative reading (Whitman and Woodard); others in a dark reading (Segal and Johansen).

[16] Jebb *ad* §13 in Introduction.

[17] Waldock 1966: 195 suggests himself that the *Elektra* is "not a great tragedy . . . not even (in a deep way) a tragedy."

Waldock have ever been widely endorsed and are nowadays approaches largely abandoned.[18]

Much more influential has been the approach which argues that Sophokles, far from ignoring the moral problem of the vengeance, presents it as fully justified by the villainy of the tyrants. Bowra, one of the champions of this view, pointed out that Sophokles could hardly disregard the *Oresteia* or the matricide, as both had by this time become too closely associated with the legend. Bowra mounted his case for "justifiable homicide" primarily along historical lines. Sophokles is said to follow the beliefs of his time in seeing the vengeance demanded by the murdered man and justified by the conduct of Klytaimnestra and Aigisthos, who have contravened almost every law there is. In this way, the poet "builds up the religious, moral, and legal case for the matricide. The gods approve and human justice demands it."[19] Although Bowra has not been followed on every point, many have endorsed the overall tenor of his argument.[20] Generally, it is argued that Orestes has a duty and obligation to his father to avenge his death, and the oracle gives his cause divine sanction. Klytaimnestra, on the other hand, is portrayed as an adulteress as well as a murderess, and a μήτηρ ἀμήτωρ to boot. Against her criminality stand the Chorus of kind and sympathetic women and Elektra, who is portrayed as a model of heroic endurance and forbearance, faithful to the memory of her dead father and loyal to the cause of Orestes. While a few do concede that Elektra's grief appears excessive and her conduct to some extent objectionable, they argue that it is justified by the circumstances. Any lingering doubt about the wickedness of Klytaimnestra is dispelled by the portrayal of her reaction to her son's death. She makes a token gesture in the direction of motherhood, but her overwhelming emotion is one of

---

[18] There have been other attempts to connect Sophokles' tragedy, not with the specific Orestes' story in the *Odyssey*, but more generally with certain themes, motifs, or Homeric heroes. Woodard 1964: 170–174 for instance, suggests that the model for Orestes and Elektra is Odysseus; Davidson 1989: 45–72 on the other hand argues that the source of the figure of Elektra is Homer's Achilles and Penelope; he finds the model for Orestes in Telemachos and Odysseus. Davidson emphasizes similarities in plot and dramatic action between the *Odyssey* and Sophokles' *Elektra*, pointing to their similar situations. Ultimately Davidson sees the revenge pattern of the *Odyssey* and Homer's portrayal of honour and deceit as the direct antecedent to the *Elektra*.

[19] Bowra 1944: 229.

[20] See note 11 above.

joy and relief. Elektra's despair on the other hand attests to the depth of her grief while her decision to undertake the killing of Aigisthos reveals her heroic character and determination. Matricide is never mentioned and any reference to killing is left in the vaguest of terms or refers solely to Aigisthos. There is no dramatic confrontation between mother and son which might draw attention to the moral problem of kin-killing. Instead, Klytaimnestra is swiftly dispatched inside the palace and all the attention in the final part of the play falls upon Aigisthos, who throughout has been cast in the role of a tyrant. The reversal in the order of the killings downplays the matricide, making the appearance of the Furies unnecessary. Aigisthos is led off inside, and the Chorus ends the play on the optimistic note that Agamemnon's offspring have won their freedom and at last the chain of violence haunting this house has come to an end. The criminals have been punished; justice has been restored, and nothing suggests coming retribution or anything other than a bright and prosperous future for the siblings.

The justificatory approach has over the years attracted a considerable number of supporters and is perhaps the closest the play has come to having a conventional reading. The exegetic strategy usually adopted by these critics is to focus on the criminality of Klytaimnestra and Aigisthos in order to justify the actions of Orestes and Elektra. This is an effective strategy as far as it goes, supported by the fact that Klytaimnestra is one of Sophokles' most unsympathetic and repulsive creations, far more wicked than either her Aeschylean or Euripidean counterparts. In stripping her of the modicum of legitimacy that Aischylos granted his Klytaimnestra and according her none of the sympathetic qualities of Euripides', Sophokles gives us little reason to think that her death is anything but justified. Aigisthos, on the other hand, despite the bizarre assertion by one critic that he is a rather "decent" chap after all,[21] is never shown as anything but a villainous tyrant. In this respect, Bowra and others are surely right to argue that Klytaimnestra and Aigisthos are portrayed as criminals and that justice demands their punishment.

While this approach satisfies our sense of justice with respect to the killings of Klytaimnestra and Aigisthos, it is less convincing in its treatment of the two siblings who carry out the killings. This has

---

[21] Kells *ad* 1469.

always been one of the weakest aspects of any affirmative reading. There is a propensity amongst the optimists to ignore the extent to which Sophokles draws attention to parallels in the conduct of the tyrants and that of Elektra and Orestes. Both mother and son are willing to employ *dolos* in an effort to achieve their aims, and both see the death of the other as a personal gain. Equally significant is Elektra's own admissions of shameful behaviour to both the Chorus and her mother, an important element often ignored or downplayed by the optimists. Yet the personal nature of the quarrel between mother and daughter with the mutual accusations of shamelessness suggests a certain parallel between the two women and raises the issue of a shared *physis*. The 'messenger' speech itself rarely receives more than a passing tribute from these critics who prefer to concentrate on the effect it has on Elektra. Given that the speech is a lie, their response is hardly surprising, yet to gloss over eighty-four lines of poetry is unsatisfactory and lessens the validity of their readings.[22] As a number of commentators have observed, the use of deceit and trickery is behaviour not so very different from that of the tyrants; that the pursuit of justice in this play has its start in guile is enough for some to cast the whole enterprise in a dubious light. The final scene between Aigisthos and Orestes seems specifically designed to awaken us to the disturbing nature of the killing, when Orestes insists that it must take place inside the palace. All these elements seem to militate against the view that this is a clear-cut case of just retribution. In ending the play in violence, Sophokles seems to stop short of fully endorsing the deed and more than one critic has, with some justification, thought that he is drawing attention to the questionable nature of the enterprise to a greater degree than he is justifying it. While this approach has its adherents, its prominence has been on the decline for a number of years, and only a few critics currently hold a view which sees the vengeance as unproblematical.[23]

Over the last several decades, there has been a gradual shift in scholarship towards seeing the play as a much more critical treatment of the vengeance-killing than was previously acknowledged. If any approach could be said to dominate current scholarship, it would

---

[22] Winnington-Ingram 1980: 236.

[23] One recent work to take such a positive view of the vengeance is Burnett 1998: 119–141.

be, in most general terms, one which emphasizes the darker aspects of the vengeance.[24] Scholars who adopt this approach see the tragedy as being designed to raise questions and doubts about either the justice of the vengeance and/or the moral character of its agents. Generally they adopt an ironic reading of the play, but two clear positions are discernible here: the vengeance is just but shameful or harmful in some fashion; the vengeance is both unjust and harmful. The extreme position that the play expresses a clear disapproval of the matricide was first argued by Sheppard in the 1920's and later resumed by Kells. Wanting to rescue Sophokles from the charge of moral obtuseness which he saw implicit in the amoral or Homeric reading, Sheppard argued that, by reading between the lines and recognizing the irony of the play, we can detect the poet's condemnation of the deed.[25] His main argument revolved around the oracle of Apollo and more specifically Orestes' question of how best to avenge his father's death. Sheppard claimed that the oracle alone cast more than a shadow of doubt on Orestes and the act. He asked the wrong question of Apollo, who, in response, offers not sanction but words of encouragement, only to bring on his destruction all the more swiftly. Sheppard pointed to other places in the play, which he thought also cast the deed in a dubious light, most notably the ending where Aigisthos is led off to be killed inside the palace. His argument was not widely endorsed in his time but Kells took it up in his 1973 edition of the play. Expanding upon Sheppard's brief

---

[24] Those who have a dark or ironic reading of the play include: Sheppard 1918: 80–83; 1927: 2–9 and 163–5; Johansen 1964: 3–32; Segal 1966: 473–545 and 1981: 249–291; Minadeo 1967: 114–42 and 1994; Gellie 1972: 106–130; Kells; Kamerbeek; Winnington-Ingram 1980: 217–247; Schein 1982: 69–80; Seale 1982: 56–83; Seaford 1985: 315–323; Blundell 1989: 149–183; Kitzinger 1991: 298–327; Cairns 1991: 19–30 and 1993: 241–249; Hartigan 1996: 82–100; Rehm 1996: 49–59; Ringer 1996: 93–106.

[25] Sheppard 1918: 80–83, 1927a: 2–9 and 1927b: 163–65 was responding in part to critics such as Schlegel 1876: 132 who saw in the play a "heavenly serenity" and Jebb who saw the matricide "simply laudable and therefore final". Sheppard 1927a: 2–3 is rightly critical of the Homeric reading, pointing out that "in the *Odyssey* there is no oracle and therefore no religious problem: no Electra, and therefore no tragedy of Electra: no matricide, and therefore nothing relevant to our enquiry." He is also critical of Kaibel's view (a position more or less followed by Whitman) that the play marked the "triumph of Electra's loyalty to God's just will." This, for Sheppard, is tantamount to making Sophokles guilty of Murray's accusation of "moral bluntness" (Murray 1956: 239). Yet to assume irony when it is not explicit is always a hazardous exegetical practice; reading between the lines, as Sheppard has done, makes it even more so.

articles, he argues that, by means of ironic innuendo, Sophokles sub-
tlely reveals the heinous nature of the crime, and thus condemns the
matricide as much as Euripides does. Orestes is seen as devoid of
any morals and willing to employ any means of deception for gain
and profit; while Elektra, although a much more sympathetic character,
emerges as psychologically damaged by years of hatred and suffering.
The messenger's *rhesis* has an enormous effect in the *ethopoiia* of the
play: it reveals Klytaimnestra as a sympathetic and heart-broken
mother; and has Elektra, overwhelmed by grief, move gradually toward
madness, feverishly imagining herself as a tyrant-slayer first and then,
in her delirium, seeing her dead father rise from the grave. In the
end, she succumbs to her vengefulness becoming a fury that drives
Orestes on to the killing of their mother. In an act of cold-blooded
murder, he brutally slays his grief-stricken mother. Kell's interpretation turns the whole play into "a continuous exercise in dramatic
irony" so that Orestes and Elektra rather than Aigisthos and Klytaimnestra are condemned in the end as the villains of the piece.[26]

Although criticized in detail, the overall approach of Sheppard
and Kells has been enormously influential.[27] Thus, while many have
distanced themselves from the more eccentric aspects of these interpretations, they have been attracted by the ironic approach in general. It offered a way to account for the more disturbing elements
of the play, which, for many, were too prevalent to be ignored or
explained away as the justifiers did. Thus, they adopt a less extreme
version of Sheppard's and Kell's reading and concede the justice of
the vengeance, but argue that it is a grim or destructive form of justice, carried out in a dubious fashion, and driven by questionable
motives. This more moderate ironic approach is the impetus behind
many current readings, which, despite their diversity in perspectives,
reach remarkably similar conclusions. Blundell, for instance, reads
the play in terms of the ethical code of 'helping friends and harming enemies', in order to explore the moral questions raised by character and conduct of the offspring. Both mother and daughter are
guilty of using the same contradictory arguments, possessing similar

<hr>

[26] Kells (introduction p. 11).
[27] Many commentators, regardless of their approach, have strongly disagreed with
Sheppard's and Kells' interpretation of the oracle. For criticisms, see Bowra 1944:
215–218; Johansen 1964: 9; Segal 1966: 475; Gellie 1972: 107; Erbse 1978: 284–300;
Stevens 1978: 111–120; Horsley 1980: 20–21; Hester 1981: 15–25.

personal motives, and in the end, one is as bad as the other. Orestes, on the other hand, engages in behaviour that is as reprehensible as that of his mother and his morally questionable use of *dolos* is, for Blundell, just "another of those self-perpetuating evils that are only made 'right' in some sense by the *talio*."[28] The matricide may be justified by the law of *talio*, but it is a "grim and problematic form of justice."[29] Cairns, studying the play from the perspective of *aidos*, detects a similar pattern in the mutual recriminations between mother and daughter which reflect the continuing cycle of violent retribution haunting the House of Atreus. He, like Blundell, sees an emphasis on the shared *physis* between mother and daughter: they accuse one another of lacking *aidos*; both are preoccupied with their personal honour; and ultimately the character and conduct of Elektra is exposed as the image of her mother's.[30] Thus, unlike Kells, who redeems Klytaimnestra and Aigisthos, Blundell and Cairns willingly concede the reprehensible conduct of mother and lover and concentrate on exposing the ways in which Orestes and Elektra are guilty of the same behaviour as that of those they kill. For them, the irony of the play is that Orestes and Elektra are reduced to the moral level of the tyrants. The vengeance may be just, but it morally destroys its agents in the process.

Others seeing the vengeance as less central to the play have concentrated either on illuminating themes that transcend the dramatic action or on the central figure of Elektra. Segal, for instance, sees the play shifting between the polarities of appearance and reality; life and death; love and hate.[31] While the polarization is seemingly

---

[28] Blundell 1989: 174. Orestes' behaviour in this play has often been judged in a highly critical light. He has been accused of everything from unheroic behaviour to sophistry to a cold-blooded amorality. For critical remarks regarding Orestes, see Kirkwood 1958: 142; Segal 1966: 510–511 and 1981: 253; Horsley 1980: 21; Seale 1980: 57; Schein 1982: 72–79; Ewan 1984: 147; Grote 1988: 209–221; Blundell 1989: 173.

[29] Blundell 1989: 183.

[30] Cairns 1993: 241–249. Others who have drawn attention to the correspondence between Elektra and her mother include Johansen 1964: 17; North 1966: 65; Segal 1966: 525–526; Winnington-Ingram 1980: 246; Seaford 1985: 315–323.

[31] Others have similarly seen the play in terms of a shift between positive and negative action, reality and illusion, truth and lies, life and death and so on. Woodard 1964: 163–205 and 1965: 195–233 suggests that Elektra and Orestes represent a division between *logos* and *ergon*, male and female, the passivity of thought and feeling as opposed to the activity of deeds and facts. For Woodard, however, there is a reconciliation between these two previously opposed elements. Most, however, who adopt such an approach have a view closer to that of Segal.

resolved in the end, it comes at a certain cost, for "something has been lost in the strain of deaths and rebirths to which the main characters have been subjected."[32] For Segal, the play shows the destruction of a character once capable of love. Johansen, on the other hand, approaches the tragedy in terms of a conflict between τὸ δίκαιον and τὸ αἰσχρόν. For him, the true tragic element in the play is not the matricide, but Elektra's sense of her own degradation that results from years of suffering and hatred. She does what is right, but suffers the consequences in the damage to her soul; justice has its price and the cost for Elektra is the loss of her personality.[33] In the end, for Johansen, "als letzte Folge des göttlichen Auftrages, sehen wir nur einen unsicher gewordenen Jungen, und eine innerlich gebrochene Frau."[34] Schein reads the play in a somewhat similar fashion seeing the tragedy as a mixture of heroic greatness and brutality of action.[35] We may feel that the cause is just but are appalled at the "savagery" of Elektra and the "obnoxious" values of Orestes.[36] Like Johansen, Schein sees the success of the venture coming at the cost of Elektra's "identity."[37] For all these critics,

---

[32] Segal 1966: 482.

[33] Johansen 1964: 31 writes: "aber Elektra opfert ihre Persönlichkeit." For criticisms of his argument, see Alexanderson 1966: 79–98 who explains Elektra's moral degradation (Johansen's focus) as shame at her undignified behaviour and conduct generally unsuited to a woman, especially one of Elektra's elevated status. Unlike Johansen, Alexanderson sees no moral breakdown; the vengeance Orestes exacts is unproblematic and if Sophokles had a problem with their actions, he kept it to himself. See also McDevitt 1983: 3–4 who criticizes the "achievement-cost disparity" of Johansen's reading. The Sophoclean heroine, McDevitt argues, does not usually sacrifice her moral standards in order to yield to external demands, but rather the reverse. She refuses to give into to external demands for an internal moral principle.

[34] Johansen 1964: 32.

[35] Schein 1982: 69–80 acknowledges his debt to the reading of Johansen and Segal.

[36] Schein 1982: 79.

[37] More recently, there have been attempts to treat the play more in terms of 'theatricality' or even 'metatheatre'. Kitzinger 1991: 298–327 approaches it as a "theatrical script . . . that takes into account the way meaning is created on stage"; yet she still sees a serious moral purpose. For her the play ends in darkness and obscurity with the questions raised by human action left unanswered. Batchelder 1995 on the other hand reads it as a self-referential drama, which refers to itself not just as Sophoclean drama, but as the theatre itself, and more particularly, the "State Theater of Athens." She argues that the seal of Orestes represents not only a visible sign of his authority as head of the state, but his control of the whole drama. The play concludes by showing the rival dramatists, Aigisthos and Orestes, competing for dramatic and poetic control. Ringer 1996: 93–100 also attempts (less successfully) a metatheatrical reading of the *Elektra*. For him, the empty urn is the

the tragedy of the play resides in the moral or psychological annihilation of the central character; however just the vengeance may be, its success is tainted. With a justice pervaded by doubt and uncertainty, the play ends on a dark and grim note.

To their credit, those who adopt a dark reading of the play have brought much needed attention to elements often glossed over by those who take an affirmative approach. Deception, for one, is a theme too prevalent to be ignored or explained away as acceptable behaviour given the circumstances; for another, Orestes' concern for glory and Elektra's admissions of shame highlight the more dubious aspects of their rationale and conduct. Moreover, Elektra's behaviour during the matricide and the exchange between Aigisthos and Orestes suggest that this is not the praiseworthy and unambiguously just deed that the affirmative readings often claim it is. At no point does the matricide or the killing of Aigisthos appear to be portrayed in an unequivocal fashion; both Elektra's words παῖσον, εἰ σθένεις, διπλῆν (1415) and Aigisthos' refusal to go quietly (1493–1503) seem designed precisely to suggest that something remains disturbing about the whole enterprise. Neither sibling appears to escape unscathed or untarnished by the affair.

These ironic readings, however, are fraught with problems. Ironic interpretation is a delicate and risky exegetical tool which one should use with circumspection and restraint; otherwise it passes, as it does in Sheppard's and especially Kell's extremist versions of the ironic reading of *Elektra*, into what Fraenkel has aptly called "the magic wand of irony":[38] it discovers irony behind every bush and under every stone and has us read ironic undertones and sinister foreboding into lines which are at most ambiguous, often bidding us ignore the obvious meaning of a passage in favour of hidden innuendoes so subtle that they would escape the notice of the audience. This, of course, would defeat the purpose: irony to be effective requires that the audience grasp it. The more moderate ironic approach avoids some of the pitfalls associated with the extremes of unqualified justification or complete condemnation. In this respect, it recognizes

---

central metaphor of the play. Its emptiness is reflected in the characters' actions and words and culminates in the emptiness of Elektra's status as a tragic hero. For Ringer, the play "seems to question the survival of tragic drama and maybe even the culture which had fostered it." See also Chapter 7 n. 10 below.

[38] Fraenkel 1950: 791.

a moral complexity in the play often absent in the affirmative reading, without relying on the "magic wand of irony" as Kells and Sheppard do; yet they too have their problems. The position of Blundell and Cairns is far more defensible than Kells' is, for instance, in that they accept the villainy of the tyrants and the necessity for vengeance. Yet in focusing fixedly on the reprehensible aspects of the conduct of Orestes and Elektra, they become guilty of the same error as those they argue against: overemphasizing certain aspects of the play to the exclusion of others. The concentration on the exposure of the similarities between mother and offspring means that they fail to note the ways in which Sophokles distinguishes Elektra and Orestes from Klytaimnestra and Aigisthos. Johansen and Segal on the other hand come closest to striking a balance between justification and condemnation with the focus on contrary elements such as life and death, love and hate, or in Johansen's case, the *dikaion* and the *aischron*. With the shift in emphasis from the matricide to the destruction of the central character, however, the balance is lost, and the scale comes down solidly on the dark side of death, hate, and the *aischron*; ultimately we are left with a justice undermined by uncertainty and doubt. Moreover, the reading which sees the tragic element of the play in terms of the psychological, moral or spiritual destruction of a figure once capable of love relies heavily upon interpreting two or three lines in the text in certain ways, lines which are at best ambiguous. Too often those who see the disintegration of the central character support their views by reference to modern ideas of morality foreign to the Greeks. That Elektra is a figure who has suffered some sort of permanent damage to her personality or soul through her suffering is an interpretation which is informed by modern psychology, but there is little in the play to suggest that we are meant to see her in this way.[39] All ironic approaches, however,

---

[39] Many speak about Elektra in this fashion: Johansen 1964: 32 calls her "eine innerlich gebrochene Frau"; Segal 1966: 543 wonders whether Elektra has "suffered a maiming—an inner disfigurement...."; Kamerbeek in his introduction (p. 20) speaks of the "harm to her soul"; Horsley 1980: 27 speaks of the "ruin of her personality"; Schein 1982: 71 sees her "twisted by years of pure, unrelenting hatred"; Scodel 1984: 86 calls her a "damaged personality"; Kells is the most extreme in this regard seeing Elektra as moving towards "madness". For critical response to such views, see Stevens 1978: 119 who points out that "there is some danger of being influenced by the Christian (and Platonic) notion that prolonged hatred ending in revenge poisons and corrupts the mind of the hater, whereas it seems that

suffer from one common problem: the alleged grim irony by which Elektra and Orestes are reduced to the level of their enemies remains unresolved in that both are left unaware of it. This would be a highly uncharacteristic use of irony by Sophokles whose heroes all come to recognize the tragic irony that informed their self-destructive actions.[40] Orestes and Elektra do not; and it seems unlikely that the audience is expected to see the situation in such a diametrically opposed way to the characters without some strong suggestion to this effect in the text. In the end, the ironic reading leaves us with the sense that something has gone dreadfully awry in the whole enterprise. We may want Orestes and Elektra to succeed and we may recognize the justice of their cause, but we are urged to be repelled by their arguments and the brutality of their attitudes and actions. Even Euripides, with his clear condemnation of the deed, puts the ultimate blame for the matricide on Apollo in the end. The

---

in fifth-century Athens hatred for an enemy was more openly avowed and retaliation with interest regarded as natural and satisfying." Alexanderson 1966: 98 also warns against giving in "to the temptation of viewing the drama in the light of our own ideas about a deed as horrible as matricide and of forcibly remodelling the play in order to make it fit with more modern ideas of psychology, morals and justice." Hester 1981: 24 also speaks of the Christian ethos whose code is certainly far from helping one's friends and harming one's enemies. "To a Christian", Hester writes, "the revenge ethos is unacceptable; doubly so when it involves matricide. But why should Sophokles be expected to follow the Christian ethos?" For Hester, to register Elektra's moral degradation is to ascribe to Sophokles a "moral sensitivity" modern rather than ancient.

[40] This type of irony, sometimes called "tragic" or "dramatic" irony, is described by Kirkwood 1958: 249 as "the exploitation by the playwright of situations, natural or artificial, in which one or more characters are unaware of the true state of things; the exploitation may, but need not, involve the use of language with double meaning." In an article often overlooked, Szlezak 1981: 1–21 identifies some of the problems associated with an ironic reading of this play. With reference to other plays such as *Aias* and *Oidipous Tyrannos*, Szlezak points out that theses characters always recognize in the end the tragic irony in their fate. Hester 1981: 18 as well observes that in Sophoclean tragedy "*in every case* the spectators are in the know . . . in every case the further course of the play reveals the truth to the deluded person without any possible ambiguity." Stevens 1978: 112 makes the important observation that irony "never contradicts the natural impression of the play as a whole." See also the sensible remarks of Stinton 1986: 67–99 and March 1987: 104 n. 116 regarding the tendencies of some scholars to overwork the irony. That this tragic irony is always resolved in Sophoclean drama is a point to which none of the ironic readings has ever responded (to my knowledge). For other studies on irony in Sophokles or more generally in Greek tragedy, see Johnson 1928: 209–14; Rosenmeyer 1977: 31–44; Markantonatos 1977: 79–84, 1979: 59–72, 1980: 367–373; Hester 1995: 14–44.

ironic readings do not allow any such resolution for Sophokles' version. Not only do they bid us accept that Elektra and Orestes are
morally bankrupt, but also that the reasons by which they justify
their actions have no ethical ground.

Yet the concluding anapaests of the Chorus centering on the key-
word *eleutheria* tell against such a bleak and depressing account of
the outcome of Sophokles' *Elektra*. It reminds us of the continuum
that exists in Greek thought between the ethical and the political,
most manifest in the last paragraph of Aristotle's *Nicomachean Ethics*
(1181b12–23) which provides the transition to the *Politics*. This is
what almost all interpretations of the *Elektra*, whether they are of the
affirmative or the darkly ironic persuasion, have in common: they
all agree that the basic institution around which this play revolves
is the *oikos*. That the *polis* has only a "shadowy existence" as Segal
puts it, is an assumption widely held by many critics who see the
blood-ties and family loyalties of the *oikos* as the primary focal point.[41]
Knox argues this most forcefully, claiming that the characters in this
play speak and behave as if the *polis* does not exist.[42] This has never
been a controversial point and is perhaps the one aspect of the *Elektra*
which has not engendered any debate. There is much in the play
to warrant such an assumption, in particular, the shift in focus from
Orestes to Elektra. Given her dominant stage presence and the intense
focus on the conflict between the female members of this family, it
is not surprising that many critics have seen the play exclusively in
terms of blood-ties and family loyalties. Moreover, Elektra seems to
spend much of the play engaged in the ritual of mourning, often
considered a "passive" activity belonging primarily to the domestic
sphere of the female. Her intense filial devotion to her father which
is balanced by an equally intense hatred of her mother only seems
to underscore the domestic nature of the play. Thirdly, the type of

---

41 Segal 1981: 251.
42 Knox 1983: 1–27 is the strongest proponent of this view, but many hold a
similar view: Woodard 1964: 166–67 and Winnington-Ingram 1980; Bouvrie 1990:
261. For the most recent statement of this position, see Griffin 1999: 78–82. While
Griffen does not offer anything substantially new in his reading of the play, his article provides a useful restatement of the long-standing view of the non-political nature
of the *Elektra*. Despite the variety of interpretations this play has generated, a sustained treatment in terms of the civic ethics of the *polis* is still absent. The article
of Juffras 1991: 99–108 is a welcome exception in this regard, but its focus is limited to Elektra's 'vision of glory'.

justice represented in this play seems to be the principle of retaliation, the *lex talionis*, or blood vengeance most often associated with
the *oikos*.[43] That there seems to be no attempt to provide a solution
to the problem of revenge justice as Aischylos did in the *Oresteia* in
terms of civic institutions only confirms for many critics that Sophokles for whatever reason wished to ignore the political aspect of the
action.[44]

The very point on which all interpretations more or less agree,
that the dramatic action focuses solely on the domestic sphere to the
exclusion of the *polis*, is one of the weaknesses of scholarship. Once
we overcome this limitation, it will be possible to incorporate and
reconcile into a balanced synthesis the insights and rival truths of
each side in order to illuminate this most difficult play of Sophokles.
As we shall see, throughout the play, there are unmistakable signs
that we are to understand the action in more broadly political terms.
It is, however, the more subtle but pervasive sense of *polis* 'consciousness' evident in the ethical language of Elektra which is most
revealing. The virtues of *eusebeia* and *sophrosyne* but also the concept
of *eleutheria* and what it is to be *sophron* are all important for understanding Elektra's conduct. Yet these are all bound up in the broader
concept of *aidos*, and only by recognizing the relationship between
aidos and the ethical codes of behaviour which accompany mem-
bership in an *oikos* and the larger community of the *polis* can we
understand the nature of Elektra's moral dilemma and reasons for
her continued lamentation. One of the questions which this play asks
is whether the exercise of justice may be at times at odds with other
codes of conduct.

Grasping the nature of *dike* then is crucial for understanding the
play as a whole. One of the chief difficulties for critics, as we have
seen, has centred precisely on this problem: how we are to judge

---

[43] Blundell 1989: 149–183; Winnington-Ingram 1980: 222. Blundell certainly recognizes political elements in the action, but sees the ties of blood as the most
signficant element.

[44] Knox 1983: 37 has offered two possible reasons for the exclusion of any political element: Sophokles' desire to write a play that was obviously different from
Aischylos' *Choephoroi* and/or his wish to concentrate on the "hatreds of the family".
Neither suggestion is all that compelling, for the shift in focus from Orestes to
Elektra is in itself enough to distinguish Sophokles' treatment from that of Aischylos,
while his second proposal ignores the fact that this is a royal *oikos* whose members
rule the *polis*; their destructive vengeful acts would naturally impinge upon the *polis*.

the type of justice represented by the vengeance. Generally, most critics have seen it in terms of the *lex talionis*, the 'eye for an eye' justice in which crime is repaid by the imposition of the original act, or as in this case, blood for blood. Yet before we can understand the nature of *dike* we must realize the significance of its association with *dolos*. Those who have paid any attention to the theme of *dolos* tend to interpret it either as a means to highlight similarities in the character and conduct of those who use it or as a way to draw attention to the sophistry and moral relativism of Orestes and the *paidagogos*. In either case, the morally questionable use of *dolos* is thought to call into doubt the legitimacy of the justice exacted by its use. There is some validity to the suggestion that the use of deception is discreditable, and *dolos* is associated with the actions of Klytaimnestra as it is with those of Orestes. But it also is sanctioned and aligned with *dike* by the oracle of Apollo; and without recognizing the nature of this alliance, our grasp of *dike* remains incomplete. This makes the messenger *rhesis* much more important than previously acknowledged, for it is the dramatic actualization of the *dolos* sanctioned by Apollo, and as we shall see it is intimately related to the operation of *dike* in this play. Finally and most important is the connection between the oracle and the reunion of the siblings, as this is where Orestes is faced with the decision whether to follow the oracular command or not. In other words we have to approach the theme of *dolos* in the broader context of the whole play to understand its association with *dike*. This, together with the ethical arguments of Elektra, will allow us to recognize the significance of Elektra's behaviour during the matricide and Orestes' handling of the vengeance at the end of the play. As we shall see, the tension between *dolos* and *dike* in the oracle and the messenger *rhesis* and that between the *dikaion* and the *aischron* in Elektra's conduct are sustained throughout the play: in some circumstances *dike* will of necessity include an *aischron* act. The *Elektra* is a study of the tragic potential of that necessity.

CHAPTER ONE

PROLOGOS: ORESTES AND ELEKTRA

1.1 *Preliminary Remarks*

The play opens with the arrival of Orestes, his *paidagogos*, and Pylades at Mykenai. The *paidagogos* describes the scene before them, Argos, the city from which Orestes has been exiled since the death of his father. He bids the young man take counsel, and from Orestes we hear of his consultation of the oracle and its response to carry out his vengeance alone, using stealth and deception. They rehearse the plan to have the *paidagogos* appear at the palace with the story of Orestes' death in a chariot race. The young men will appear later disguised as Phocians bearing the urn containing the ashes of Orestes. They are about to retire to make the proper libations over Agamemnon's grave when they are interrupted by a cry from inside the palace. Urged on by the *paidagogos* to obey Apollo's commands, the men depart for the tomb, and Elektra appears alone on stage lamenting the death of her father. This θρῆνος ἀπὸ σκηνῆς gives us a glimpse of life inside the palace since the death of Agamemnon and the grim circumstances of Elektra.

One of the most striking features of this *prologos* is its diptych-like structure. Divided between the two siblings, it seems to contain two separate introductions to the play: one which introduces us to Orestes and the situation at hand, giving us an overview of how the dramatic action will unfold (1–85); and a second part which introduces us to the suffering of Elektra (86–120). Many commentators take this structure as the poet's way of drawing attention to the radically different circumstances and character of brother and sister.[1] The one appears in the bright light of day with the help and support of his tutor and trusty companion. Exuding confidence and full of plans, he is often described as the active, rational, and practical-minded

---

[1] Bowra 1944: 246–247; Whitman 1951: 154–155; Woodard 1964: 164–168; Kells *ad* 77–120; Segal 1981: 250; Seale 1982: 59; Burnett 1998: 121.

sibling who has been trained for this day.[2] Elektra, on the other hand, appears on stage alone, and her lamentation seems to introduce us to a world dominated by the dark emotions of grief and anger. Her life, bound by the walls of the *oikos*, is said to represent the interior, passive, emotional realm of a female who lives for revenge. There is something to be said for the obvious contrariety between them, but we should be careful not to let these differences pass into the rigid dichotomies of active/passive, male/female, rational/emotional, exterior/interior. Given the dominance of Elektra in the subsequent action, such a perspective would distort our view of her role and we would be left with a drama revolving almost exclusively around the blood-ties of the *oikos* and the emotional suffering of the protagonist. Elektra's lamentation is neither a sign of passivity as some assume nor can it be understood solely with reference to the *oikos*. Orestes, on the other hand, despite all the hope and confidence he is thought to exude, is not free from doubt and his hesitation serves as important preparation for later developments.

If we approach the *prologos* in terms of its primary function of exposing the plot rather than as a means to contrast brother with sister, we see how tightly integrated it is with the subsequent action. The speech of the *paidagogos*, as we shall see, grounds the action of the play in the *polis* and thus sets forth the basis for Elektra's arguments, which will be rooted largely in its ethical framework. Orestes' speech on the other hand introduces the main theme of the play, the restoration of order, accomplished by a *dike* that has explicit associations with *dolos*. His initial reticence over the use of deception as well as his momentary hesitation at his sister's voice serve to prepare two crucial turning points in the later dramatic action: the messenger speech which brings the theme of *dolos* into effect, and the reunion between brother and sister in which the *dolos* is revealed to Elektra. Orestes' appearance in the *prologos* thus looks ahead to the second half of the play when the *dolos* comes into operation. Elektra's monody serves as an introduction to the first half of the play and operates as a kind of bridge between the *prologos* and the *parodos*. We hear of the grimness of life within this *oikos*, but our first glimpse of

---

[2] Burton 1980: 189 points out that this is the only extant play of Sophokles which introduces the central figure with a monody before the entrance of the Chorus.

Elektra shows her *outside* the palace, engaged in a *public* display of mourning which protests the crimes of the rulers. At the same time, her appearance reinforces the sense that there is something inappropriate about Orestes' plan of action, for we see how utterly dependent she is upon his return and thus we gain some sense of how devastated she will be at the news of his death. Elektra is fully aware of her need for Orestes; what Orestes does not yet realize is how dependent he is upon her for his act to be carried out with justice. Sophokles, by juxtaposing the appearance of both siblings in the *prologos*, signals their interdependence and looks ahead to their reunion. For all their apparent disparity and differing circumstances, they are united by a common cause and ultimately one is as dependent upon the other for the restoration of order in *oikos* and *polis*.

1.2   *The Paidagogos and Orestes*

Commentators of the more traditional reading of the play as the successful restoration of order typically take this beginning at face value: the *paidagogos* and Orestes have returned to avenge Agamemnon's death.[3] Neither expresses any doubt or hesitation, but there is little reason for them to do so, as Orestes is duty-bound to restore his *oikos* and the oracle of Apollo has sanctioned his cause; the justice and legitimacy of the vengeance is taken for granted. For these critics, there is nothing in the opening of the play to suggest the slightest hint of conflict, moral or otherwise. On the other side are those with a "dark" or "pessimistic" reading of the play; for them, these very elements are evidence of the problematical nature of the revenge-plan.[4] Thus the single-mindedness of the *paidagogos* is a sign of his sinister and corrupt nature; Orestes' lack of scruples signals his 'moral bankruptcy'; and the oracle's association with *dolos* points to the dubious nature of their enterprise.

Neither side, however, has ever explained why Apollo specifically enjoins the use of *dolos*.[5] The association of *dolos* with *dike* in the

---

[3] See Introduction n. 11 above.

[4] See Introduction n. 24 above.

[5] For views of Apollo in the play, see Case 1902: 195–200; Horsley 1980: 18–29 and Hester 1981: 15–25 and Minadeo 1994. Generally the discussion of Apollo's role is restricted to his oracle at the beginning, but see both Horsley and Minadeo

oracle reflects a close connection between the two that suggests we cannot understand the nature of justice in this play without understanding its connection with deception and the reason why the god commends its use. The other element of significance is Orestes' hesitation, often downplayed by the "optimists" but important for understanding his perception of his endeavour at this point. Twice, Orestes displays doubt: once regarding the use of *dolos* and again when he hears his sister's voice. The first draws attention to a conflict between the heroic nature of the deed and the unheroic means by which it is to be carried out, deception; it looks ahead to the messenger speech and the response of Klytaimnestra to the *dolos*. The second intimates what Orestes' real conflict will be: between his duty to adhere to Apollo's instructions for the vengeance and the claim of blood-ties, foreshadowing the choice he will face later between maintaining the *dolos* as a strategy of vengeance or giving in to the urging of *philia*. The first suggests disturbing parallels with the behaviour of his mother, and the second points to what eventually will provide Orestes with the insight necessary to carry out his deed with justice: the grief of Elektra. At this stage, Orestes does not fully understand the nature of his undertaking, shown by his perception of it as a heroic deed worthy of *kleos* and *time*.

1.2.1 *The paidagogos*

The opening verses of any tragedy are generally important for setting the scene and tenor of the play. In Waldock's words, "they perform the all-important office of *stationing* us, of giving us a certain angle of vision."[6] In the *Elektra*, the opening verses are delivered by the *paidagogos* (1–22) and his speech orients us in the direction of the

---

for arguments which attribute a greater role to Apollo in this play. Horsley suggests that Orestes and the *paidagogos* are 'conscious agents' of Apollo, and that the victims of the *dolos* are not only Klytaimnestra and Aigisthos but also Elektra. The first two are physically destroyed while Elektra is psychologically destroyed by Apollo. For Horsley, the *dolos* theme is an attack, albeit a muted one, upon Apollo. Minadeo studies the play in terms of the themes of *dolos*, the antithesis of love and hate, and *logos* and *ergon*. Elektra, in representing the passionate and irrational force of emotion in opposition to the dispassionate reason of Apollo is his "absolute antithesis". The *dolos* mediates between the *logos of* Apollo and the *ergon* of the vengeance. The play then moves from *logos* to *ergon*; from divine to human; from reason to the emotions of love and hatred.

[5] Waldock 1966: 170.

polis with his detailed description of its defining features: the *agora* of Lycean Apollo (6–7), the famous temple of Hera (8) and finally the ruling palace of Mykenai itself (9). This identification of what Knox rightly remarks are the most salient characteristics of the *polis* of Argos serves to introduce Orestes to his city and give him a kind of lesson in its political structure.[7] Although Knox recognizes the heavy political note on which the play begins, he sees the play entirely in terms of blood-ties and family loyalties. That the tragedy focuses on the institution of the *oikos* and ignores the political aspect of Orestes' return has never been a highly controversial point and is one more often assumed than argued. Knox, however, overstates his case when he claims that the characters speak and behave as if the *polis* did not exist. As much as Elektra seems to exist for the *oikos* of Agamemnon, her actions and arguments will be shown to be deeply informed by a *polis* 'consciousness'. The firm embedding of the action in the topography of the *polis*, as evident from its prominence in the opening speech, will turn out to be programmatic for the play as a whole, as the *polis* will provide the frame for the moral arguments of Elektra, which will be based upon *polis*-ethics, manifest, for instance, in her alliance with the Chorus, who represent the citizenry opposed to the tyrants. Most important, it lays the foundation for the justice in the play which will be informed by communal ethics rather than the blood-based ties of the *oikos*.

Conspicuous though the *polis* is in the opening speech of the *paidagogos*, there is a suggestion of a heroic backdrop to the action as well. In the first line of the tragedy the *paidagogos* addresses his charge as ὦ τοῦ στρατηγήσαντος ἐν Τροίᾳ ποτὲ Ἀγαμέμνονος παῖ (1–2). The *hyperbaton* places the emphasis on στρατηγήσαντος, which in late fifth century Athens has strong political overtones. A *strategos* occupies a position of the highest civic and military authority in the *polis*; the word, however, appears here not in the context of the fifth century *polis*, but in that of the heroic world of the Trojan War: Orestes is

---

[7] Knox 1983: 1–27 in support of his claim points to the prevalence of familial terms such as πατήρ, μήτηρ, ἀδελφή, κασίγνητος, δόμος, δῶμα, and οἶκος and the almost complete absence of reference to πόλις or πολίτης (he cites 982, 1413 and πολίτιδες at 1227, but misses the occurrence of πόλις at 642). Certainly, blood-ties have a significant role in this play, but, as will be shown, Knox ignores the political significance of Elektra's lamentation and how much it is informed by the ethical framework of the *polis* rather than the *oikos*.

identified through his relationship to the leader of the expedition against Troy. As subtle as this allusion is, it acquires a greater significance when we see that Orestes conceives of his deed as a heroic feat worthy of honour and glory. Moreover, the *paidagogos'* allusion to a heroic backdrop looks ahead to his deceptive messenger speech in which he will present the 'death' of Orestes in terms strongly reminiscent of the Homeric hero, and again there will be an extended reference to Agamemnon's heroic expedition to Troy.[8] The marked presence of the *polis* together with the perceptible reference to the Trojan War serves to create a certain tension between two differing ethical codes: the heroic values of the Homeric warrior and the more communally oriented view of the fifth century *polis*, something which will have some significance in how we are to understand the nature of Orestes' undertaking.

The figure of the *paidagogos*, apparently an innovation on Sophokles' part, has caused some speculation about his role in the vengeance.[9] Uneasy as to the old tutor's unswerving devotion to the task at hand and his ready willingness to use deception, some suppose that we are to see him as an immoral sophist who has exerted an unhealthy influence on his young charge.[10] Certainly, there is a single-mindedness to the *paidagogos*, but this need not serve the sinister purpose some think that they have detected. When we take into account his status in the *oikos* of Agamemnon, his lack of qualms is evidence more of loyalty to his master than a sign of evil-mindedness or ruthlessness.[11] Historically, a *paidagogos* is a slave, generally appointed by the child's *kurios*, and in his absence, as Golden points out, he is considered "an instantiation of his interest and an extension of his authority."[12] His duty is to his master and his *oikos*; but because of the nature of a tutor's task, there is also a deep emotional attachment

---

[8] Haslam 1974: 166–174 rejects the opening line based on its association with Euripides' *Phoenissae* 1–2 and the "wretchedly feeble" nature of the verse. Haslam may find this line "insipid" and "dull", but it is closely integrated with the action of the play. See L-J & W[2] who defend these lines against Haslam's unconvincing arguments.

[9] A *paidagogos* appears also in Euripides' *Elektra*, and while there is no consensus in the dating of the two plays, such considerations do not affect the argument.

[10] As Sheppard 1927a: 4 does when he claims that "the youth's affections have been all his life exploited for the purpose of vengeance." Kells, taking his cue from Sheppard, calls him the "spirit of vengeance incarnate" (p. 11).

[11] See Horsley 1980: 20–21 and n. 14 for criticism of this view of the *paidagogos*.

[12] Golden 1990: 62.

to the *oikos*.[13] In this play, the *paidagogos'* duty and loyalty are to Agamemnon and with the latter's death he takes the role of father for the siblings and teacher to Orestes. Thus throughout the play, he is described in terms that suggest loyalty and faithfulness to the *oikos*: Elektra says that he was the only man faithful to her father (1351–52); she calls him the μόνος σωτὴρ δόμων (1354) and addresses him as father (1361). Orestes addresses him as φίλτατ᾽ ἀνδρῶν προσπόλων (23) and calls him ἐσθλός (24). To Elektra he appears as a father figure, and for Orestes he has the dual role of father/teacher. The *paidagogos* himself alludes to the important role he played in Orestes' life when he reminds him of how he rescued and raised him: ἤνεγκα κἀξέσωσα κἀξεθρεψάμην (13).[14] The choice of the verb ἐκτρέφω, which means "to rear up from childhood" is usually applied to the biological parent of the child and its use here draws attention to the parental aspect of his role.[15] The *paidagogos* carries out his obligation to Agamemnon by educating his son in his duty to restore the *oikos* to its legitimate heir.

With the introduction of the *paidagogos* into the drama, Sophokles has a figure whose status suggests unquestioning obedience. As a slave, he should naturally be expected to carry out his duty to the *oikos* of Agamemnon as well as be obedient to the words of the

---

[13] Hall 1997: 115 (citing Synodinou 1977: 62) refers to the loyalty slaves such as nurses and *paidagogoi* have to their households as a "vertical allegiance", that is, they are loyal to their masters rather to members of their own class.

[14] Orestes' age at this time has sparked a modest debate with some arguing that he was little more than a 'babe in arms' and while others (Jebb *ad* 13f), following traditional chronology, argue that he must have been older than ten (Orestes born before Agamemnon went off to Troy). Aigisthos was killed in the eighth year of his reign (*Od.* 3.303 ff.) making Orestes now about nineteen or twenty. Others, however, suggest that Orestes was little more than a small child, citing the use of the verb ἤνεγκα. So argues the scholiast, and Adams 1957: 63 and Kitto 1958: 5 follow suit. Such things are difficult to decide with any certainty, for poets seem free to dispense with such technical considerations as chronology. In this case, Sophokles seems unconcerned with suggesting anything more than the fact that Orestes is now a young man. Such insignificant details only become important when one wishes to construct an argument whose cogency is dependent upon such factors as age, as Grote 1988: 210–221 does. He argues at great length that Orestes was a 'babe in arms', as he wishes to emphasize the strong element of sophistic education in the *paidagogos'* raising of Orestes. For Grote, the longer Orestes was under his control, the greater his detrimental influence.

[15] ἐκτρέφω and τροφή have the same root. The prefix here may emphasize the length of time, that is "to raise up from childhood", while the use of the middle voice suggests the interest of the τροφός, i.e., the *paidagogos*.

oracle. Moreover, as a slave, he has no blood-ties to Klytaimnestra and thus is free to see her simply as the killer of Agamemnon. Not only would it be surprising for him to express doubts about this mission, but it would be a dereliction of his duty to do so. Yet for all the supposed control the *paidagogos* is thought to exert over his ward, and despite his final exhortation to him (ὡς ἐνταῦθ᾽ ἐμὲν ἵν᾽ οὐκέτ᾽ ὀκνεῖν καιρός, ἀλλ᾽ ἔργων ἀκμή 21–22), Orestes will hesitate. The absence of any conflict on the part of the *paidagogos* then draws attention to Orestes and his hesitation, for he is neither as single-minded nor as free from doubt as his tutor is. Moreover, that he is the one to urge Orestes to the task at hand, thus preventing the meeting between the two siblings, associates him with Apollo, something which gains a certain significance when we recognize the importance of the use of *dolos*.[16]

1.2.2 *Orestes and the oracle of Apollo*

The oracle has long been a matter of some controversy and scholars have read everything into it from divine sanction to explicit condemnation of the revenge.[17] Those who understand the tragedy as presenting the matricide as necessary and justified tend to argue that the oracle provides Orestes with divine sanction for his actions. For those who espouse an ironic reading, the oracle provides one of the play's more explicit condemnations of the matricide. Sheppard was the first to adopt this approach, arguing that Orestes asked the wrong question. Instead of asking, "should I be avenged?", he asked, "how

---

[16] There is at different times in the play a strong suggestion of a connection between him and Apollo so much so that he has been called the "agent of Apollo" or "incarnation of Apollo" (see Chapter 5 n. 19). The role of the *paidagogos* is rather ambiguous in this regard: while his unquestioning obedience may be explained by his status, he also seems to recognize how important the use of *dolos* is. Regardless of whether we see him simply as the faithful servant of Agamemnon or an agent of Apollo, the *paidagogos* prevents the meeting of brother and sister before the *dolos* comes into operation.

[17] Owen 1927: 52; Bowra 1944: 217; Adams 1957: 59–60; Gellie 1972: 107 see a clear endorsement of the deed. Case 1902: 197 sees the justification of Apollo's oracle as "tacitly assumed." Alexanderson 1966: 80–81 thinks the oracle unproblematical. On the other side stand those who find the oracle deliberately vague and ambiguous (Sheppard 1927, Kells, Segal 1981: 280). Erbse 1978: 293 suggests that Sophokles is not as concerned with justifying Apollo as portraying the spiritual greatness of Elektra. See Horsley 1980: 18–29 for brief summary of the various interpretations of Apollo's oracle.

should I be avenged?"[18] His mistake was to assume the justice of the vengeance; hence, the reply of the oracle only urges him headlong down the path of destruction. This reading of Sheppard, enthusiastically embraced by Kells, has rightly come under fire in recent years. As Hester, amongst others, points out, a son not only has a right to avenge the death of his father and reclaim his patrimony, but a duty and obligation to do so.[19] In none of the treatments of this legend is the duty itself ever questioned; indeed in the *Odyssey*, Orestes is held up as a heroic model worthy of imitation. There is no consultation of the oracle, but there is little need, for the justice of the vengeance is presumed and its heroic nature emphasized. Needless to say, Homer must also avoid all mention of the matricide. It is with the tragedians that this element becomes such an important issue. The obligation to avenge his father is not at stake, however, but only the conflict that arises from it; to a large extent it is the oracle that brings this issue into sharp relief. In the *Oresteia*, Aischylos overcomes the problem by having the matricide explicitly commanded by a god and then acquitting Orestes for his involvement in a court of law established by Athena. In other words, there is both divine command and divine acquittal. Euripides has Apollo order the matricide, but then condemns the god for doing so. Sophokles' treatment is different again, but for Sheppard and Kells to assume that Orestes should question his duty is to expect from him a moral sensitivity that radically alters the ethical framework of the play. That Orestes asks 'how' rather than 'if' is simply a reflection of his awareness of his obligation to his father.[20]

---

[18] Sheppard 1927a: 4. See the Introduction n. 27 as well as Hester 1981: 19 n. 15 for references to criticisms of the interpretation of Sheppard and Kells.

[19] Hester 1981: 23 states that the duty and not just the right to vengeance was part of the Athenian law code. See Plato's *Laws* 9.872–3, which, as Hester notes, prescribes death for the killing of a kinsman as well as civic stoning and the casting out of the body unburied. See Bowra 1944: 218–222 on this point as well and the references he cites there.

[20] Hester 1981: 22 makes the point that if Sophokles wished to raise questions about the morality of the act, he could have reverted to the Homeric version that has Orestes undertake the act without consulting the god. The absence of Apollo would be (especially in light of Aischylos' treatment) a striking omission and suggestive of an act done in the absence of any divine support. Hester is critical of Sheppard's thesis and refutes it by examining the three oracles from Herodotos which Sheppard cites as his support. Hester shows that these are all irrelevant to the play and that the most we can conclude from them is that it is best not to consult oracles at all. As he remarks, "If Sheppard's general assumptions are right,

There are, however, other aspects of the oracle apart from Orestes' specific question which should rightly be examined. First, the recommendation to use *dolos* in itself raises questions; what kind of justice endorses trickery and lies? Loath to see even a muted criticism of Apollo by the poet here, many take it as Sophokles' subtle way of casting Orestes' character and his vengeance in a dubious light. Equally problematical is Orestes' own endorsement of verbal deception (56) if it brings profit (61). Some, struck by the apparent sophistic character of these words, accuse him of unheroic behaviour, moral relativism, and even immorality.[21] Many who are troubled by his acceptance of *dolos* are equally bothered by what they perceive to be his cold, military-like manner; consequently, he has been called a blank, a symbol, flat, and *une machine à tuer*.[22] In their view Orestes' behaviour at the beginning of the play is not so different from that of those he has returned to kill. Some of these characterizations of Orestes are clearly off the mark, but critics are right to focus on the use of *dolos*. In the other treatments of this myth Apollo orders the killing and the oracle operates as the external necessity which compels Orestes to choose between killing his mother or disobeying divine command. Sophokles' shift in the oracle from ordering matricide to ordering deception is a radical departure from the accepted story. Not only does it change the nature of Orestes' choice, but with the emphasis falling on *dolos*, clearly it has a role of some significance in the play. Most important, however, is that Apollo prescribes *dolos* in order to carry out *just* slaughters (ἐνδίκους σφαγάς 37):[23] this asso-

---

it is hard to tell why Sophokles brings in the oracle at all, harder to tell why he lets the word "just" appear in what is (as far as the audience knows) the authentic text of the oracle."

[21] These charges made against Orestes often spring from an inappropriate comparison with other Sophoclean dramas in which *dolos* plays a large role such as the *Philoktetes*. However, in that play there is a clear expression of disapproval of *dolos* as indicated by Neoptolemos' ultimate rejection of it and the sympathetic portrayal of Philoktetes. Many critics see these words as reflecting badly upon Orestes: Kirkwood 1958: 142; Segal 1966: 510 and 1981: 253; Seale 1980: 57; Schein 1982: 72–72; Blundell 1989: 173 all make various charges against Orestes.

[22] Linforth 1963: 89; Whitman 1951: 155; Gellie 1972: 106; Ronnet 1961: 208–9.

[23] L-J & W follow the emendation of Lange (ἐνδίκου σφαγάς) in order to make ἐνδίκου agree with χειρὸς σφαγάς. There is nothing that demands such a change and the MSS all have ἐνδίκους σφαγάς; thus I have followed Pearson's text here. Moreover, by this reading we see a hint of a separation between the deed of the vengeance and the hand which carries it out. The justice of the deed is not at question, but Orestes will still have blood of kin on his hands (the Chorus will

ciates *dolos* expressly with *dike*; and therefore should make us determine its relationship to the vengeance.

Orestes recounts his visit to the oracle of Apollo as follows:

ἐγὼ γὰρ ἡνίχ' ἱκόμην τὸ Πυθικὸν
μαντεῖον, ὡς μάθοιμ' ὅτῳ τρόπῳ πατρὶ
δίκας ἀροίμην τῶν φονευσάντων πάρα,
χρῇ μοι τοιαῦθ' ὁ Φοῖβος ὧν πεύσῃ τάχα·
ἄσκευον αὐτὸν ἀσπίδων τε καὶ στρατοῦ
δόλοισι κλέψαι χειρὸς ἐνδίκους σφαγάς. (32–37)

When I came to the Pythian oracle, so that
I might learn in what way I could exact justice
for my father from his murderers,
Phoibos proclaimed to me such things which you will soon learn;
I, myself, unequipped with shields and army should carry
out stealthily the just slaughters of my hand through deceptions.

The oracle of Apollo establishes under what conditions Orestes is able to carry out a just vengeance: he should act alone ("without shields or army") and second, he should employ *dolos*.[24] Both are underscored, the first by *hendiadys*, and the latter by the use of the verb κλέπτω coupled with δόλος. Critics have generally focused almost exclusively on the oracular endorsement of *dolos* while ignoring that it also explicitly states that Orestes should act without military support. While the advice to return without army may be thought less significant than the counsel to use *dolos*, it is important for understanding the nature of Orestes' deed and the type of *dike* it represents. When Orestes returns to Argos, he is a *phugas*, an exile, thought to be one of the worst fates to befall a person, as it meant the loss of all civic rights and property as well as the estrangement from family, friends, and the tombs of one's ancestors. The word *phugas* is the conventional fifth century term for exile and generally means

---

assert the same sentiment after the vengeance, but it will also proclaim its justice). In other words, *endikous* with *sphagas* only attests to the justice of the deed without saying anything about the rightness of a son killing a mother.

[24] There have been attempts to question the validity of the oracle since we have only Orestes' words, but there is nothing to suggest that we are to doubt that he reports them correctly. Kells *ad* 35ff tries to argue that the sentence structure is deliberately ambiguous, so that we are meant to question whether these are the actual words of the oracle or only Orestes' estimation of the meaning. Segal 1981: 280 as well says we are unsure which words are Apollo's and which are Orestes'. See Kamerbeek *ad* 33 who sensibly calls this argument sophistic, as does Bowra 1944: 215–17.

'one who flees from his country'. It may refer to fugitives escaping
the law or those who leave for political reasons, but as Juffras points
out, in Sophoclean tragedy it is used almost exclusively to "describe
someone unwillingly exiled from his city by adverse political conditions."[25] The *paidagogos* refers to the cause of Orestes' exile when he
reminds him of how he rescued him after the murder of his father,
receiving him from the arms of his sister (11–12). He is sent away
to protect him from suffering the same fate as Agamemnon; as the
rightful heir to the kingdom Orestes is a political rival and a threat
to the new regime of Klytaimnestra and Aigisthos. In this sense he
is a political exile, but his circumstances are doubly difficult, as he
has been sent away from his city to protect him from his own kin.
Friendship and enmity cut across blood lines. In other words, Orestes'
deed cannot be treated solely as a family affair nor entirely as a
political one.

It is to the difficult circumstances of Orestes' situation that the
order to return without military support specifically addresses itself.
As Juffras points out, an exile exists in a somewhat uneasy relationship with his city, for there is the possibility of friendship or
enmity, reflected in the possible conditions of his return: under
amnesty or under arms.[26] That Orestes will come back under amnesty
is unlikely given the current state of affairs in Argos, and to return
under arms would place him in the undesirable position of march-
ing against his own city.[27] Polyneikes' actions in *Antigone* show well
the difficulties of an exile, for although he has a certain claim to
justice in that he was deprived of his right to rule, he places his
own desire to rule above the good of the city. In attacking his own

---

[25] Juffras 1988: 83 and 186 observes that it appears ten times in Sophokles' plays
and in nine of those occurrences, it is used in this sense. Both Klytaimnestra and
Elektra (776 and 1136) use it to describe Orestes.

[26] Juffras 1988: 80.

[27] In *Against Agoratos* Lysias argues that the one who harms his city is akin to the
son who beats his father and both are worthy of death (13.91). There are numerous examples from tragedy, comedy, and the Attic orators which point to the strong
demand for loyalty to one's *polis* and suggest that the nurture of the city produces
a reciprocal political obligation on the citizen. This theme appears as early as
Hesiod's *Works and Days* where the poet draws a parallel between the prosperity of
the city and the individual as an argument for just behaviour (225–47). In *Oidipous
Tyrannos* Oidipous accuses Teiresias of not being προσφιλής to the city which raised
him (322–23). The speeches of Pericles as well point to the strong demand for loyalty to one's *polis* as well. See Knox 1981: 1–27 on this theme.

city with a foreign army, he becomes a traitor, and Kreon rightly refuses him burial on these grounds. Orestes in this play would be guilty of a similar crime, for, no matter how legitimate his claim is, to lead an army against his city would be an act of betrayal which would make him an enemy. As much as Orestes has a right, and even a duty to his *oikos*, to avenge his father's death, he has a duty and obligation to consider the safety and security of his *polis*. The advice to return "without shields and army" thus protects the *polis* from the dangers of an invading army and Orestes from being a traitor.[28] Divine sanction of his deed then comes with certain restrictions or limitations: for Orestes to carry out ἐνδίκους σφαγάς, he must act within the confines and best interests of the *polis*. This is our first hint that *dike* in this play cannot be separated from the *polis*.

The association of Orestes' deed with *dolos*, however, is a serious concern; for many commentators it points to the dubious and unheroic nature of his enterprise. First, there is the disturbing parallel with the behaviour of Klytaimnestra, who is repeatedly condemned for her use of *dolos*. The Chorus and Elektra identify *dolos* as the contriver of Klytaimnestra's killing of Agamemnon (δόλος ἦν ὁ φράσας, ἔρος ὁ κτείνας 197; πατέρα τὸν ἀμὸν ἐκ δόλου κατέκτανεν 279). Moreover, she herself expresses a fear in her prayer to Apollo lest she be brought down by *dolos* (649). As Segal puts it, Orestes comes "dangerously close to those he would punish, for Agamemnon's murderers, like himself in 59–61, are repeatedly described as using trickery, lies, concealment."[29] Others point out that the attribution of *dolos* to both sides is indicative of the operation of the *lex talionis* and of the reciprocal nature of the killing.[30] *Dolos* is repaid by *dolos* as murder is by murder. However, we should remember that, while both may employ *dolos*, Orestes' use of it is consistently connected with *dike*

---

[28] Minadeo 1994: 113 sees an additional implication in the order to act alone which is meant to exclude Elektra from the plan and vengeance ("Electra's very participation in the *ergon* violates the spirit of the god's oracle"). If we are to understand the oracle as implicitly excluding Elektra, this would serve to intensify the nature of Orestes' conflict over whether to reveal himself to his sister or not; that he does eventually do so, according to my argument, suggests that he frees himself from the conflict between *philia* and vengeance, and carries out the deed as an act of justice rather than reciprocal violence.

[29] Segal 1981: 254.

[30] Horsley 1980: 21 draws attention to the connection between Orestes and Klytaimnestra through the use of *dolos*.

while Klytaimnestra's is not.[31] Moreover, while the oracle explicitly orders the use of *dolos*, this is not a blanket endorsement of deceit, but qualified as one which will bring about ἐνδίκους σφαγάς. That is, *dolos* is limited by its association with *dike*, something which will prove to have some significance in how we understand the actual *dolos* of the messenger *rhesis*. The unheroic nature of *dolos* on the other hand is certainly a legitimate concern, as the use of deception or trickery, at least in tragedy, carries with it certain unsavory associations.[32] In the *Philoktetes*, a play with which the *Elektra* is often compared, Odysseus' pragmatic promotion of deception to the earnest young Neoptolemos (107) is usually thought to reflect unfavourably on his character and to make his actions appear all the more questionable. In this play, however, Orestes' employment of *dolos* is sanctioned by Apollo, and its association with *dike* should warn against any outright blanket condemnation of the deed without first considering the relationship between the two. An unheroic action is not necessarily an unjust action.

The other disconcerting element is Orestes' apparent lack of moral conflict in regard to the grave violation of blood-ties his deed requires. That he seems to be unconcerned by the fact that one of the persons he is about to kill is his mother—the precise issue which preoccupies the other tragedians—has led some to see him as a cold-blooded killer. However, it is not as if Orestes is a stranger to inner conflict: twice he hesitates, once over the use of *dolos* (59–60), and again when he hears his sister's voice (80–81). The first points to a conflict between the heroic values which inform Orestes' outlook and the unheroic means (*dolos*) required to carry it out; the second is triggered by the presence of Elektra and points to a potential conflict

---

[31] Klytaimnestra's *dolos* is linked with *eros* by the Chorus while Orestes' use of *dolos* is linked with Apollo and *dike*. The Chorus foretells how *dike* will overtake Klytaimnestra and Aigisthos, a *dike* that is explicitly linked with stealth and ambush (490, 1439–41); and *dolos* is referred to just prior to the killing of Klytaimnestra (1392, 1396).

[32] This is more valid for tragedy than epic, where, for instance, Odysseus' ability to lie is not perceived as a flaw, moral or otherwise. Indeed he is the model hero of *dolos*, always willing to use his cunning and wits, but he is not presented as unheroic for doing so. See Segal 1983: 22–47 for a treatment of the association between *kleos* and *dolos* in Odysseus' behaviour; and Stanford 1954: 19–22 for a discussion of Odysseus' use of lies. He divides all lies into three types: lies told for entertainment; lies told in furtherance of a good end; and purely malicious lies. Stanford seems relieved to discover that Odysseus' lies all fall into the first two types.

between duty to vengeance and his feelings for his sister. Let us consider these in some detail.

We see the first hint of conflict in Orestes when he shows some hesitancy over the use of *dolos*:

τί γάρ με λυπεῖ τοῦθ᾽, ὅταν λόγῳ θανὼν
ἔργοισι σωθῶ κἀξενέγκωμαι κλέος;
δοκῶ μέν, οὐδὲν ῥῆμα σὺν κέρδει κακόν.
ἤδη γὰρ εἶδον πολλάκις καὶ τοὺς σοφοὺς
λόγῳ μάτην θνῄσκοντας· εἶθ᾽, ὅταν δόμους
ἔλθωσιν αὖθις, ἐκτετίμηνται πλέον·
ὡς κἄμ᾽ ἐπαυχῶ τῆσδε τῆς φήμης ἄπο
δεδορκότ᾽ ἐχθροῖς ἄστρον ὣς λάμψειν ἔτι. (59–66)

Why does this pain me, when after a reported death,
I shall be saved in deeds and win fame?
I suppose that nothing said is bad which brings profit.
For I have often seen that even clever men are
falsely reported dead; then when they come home
again they are honoured more.
So I boast that I too, being alive, will yet
shine forth to my enemies like a star.

Most commentators focus on Orestes' endorsement of *dolos* and his apparent willingness to employ any means, however immoral, for his own ends.[33] A few have attempted to defend Orestes, suggesting that his words simply refer to slight unease at reporting himself dead,

---

[33] The suggestion that the *paidagogos* add a false oath (47) is often interpreted as additional evidence of Orestes' sophistic nature. See Sheppard 1927a: 5; Schein 1982: 72–73 writes that these words have seemed so "unbelievable" that some scholars have emended them. For him, the whole point is that Orestes' words leave us with a "morally unpleasant taste in our mouths." Grote 1980: 232 thinks that ease with which Orestes violates religious oaths exposes how "unaristocratic his personal values are". Blundell 1989: 173 is equally outraged by Orestes' suggestion, claiming that it is "uncalled for and arguably reprehensible." The text itself is problematic here as the construction demands an accusative but the MSS have ὅρκῳ. It is usually emended to ὅρκον, but this still leaves us with a rather odd construction as Kells, Kamerbeek, and Jebb *ad loc.* all point out. Moreover, the *paidagogos* does not in fact add an oath when he reports Orestes' death. Many have thus found Musgrave's emendation of ὄγκον very attractive; not only does it rid Orestes of the charge of violating the sanctity of the oath, but he would now be saying "add *bulk* to my story", which is of course precisely what the *paidagogos* does with his elaborate messenger speech. We should, however, be wary of changing the text to suit our ideas. Kamerbeek prefers the slight correction of ὅρκον over the more radical introduction of ἔργῳ or ὄγκον into the text as do L-J &W. Moreover, as I argue below, the failure of the *paidagogos* to add an oath has some significance in understanding the function of the messenger *rhesis*. See section 5.2.2 below on this point.

something which was thought to be a bad omen.[34] There may be something to this, but as Winnington-Ingram points out, eight lines to suggest that there is nothing really "sinister" about the false report of his death seems "gratuitous" and, as he reminds us, Sophokles is not one to "waste lines".[35] Though Winnington-Ingram may be correct to see a dark cloud on the horizon here, we cannot judge Orestes and his behaviour until the end of the play. What we have here is a dubious rationale which has the potential to turn into discreditable behaviour. It will turn out as an important preparation for the development in the understanding of his task.

One of the most significant aspects of this speech is the sense we gain of Orestes' perception of his undertaking; at this stage, his view does bear a striking resemblance to that of his mother. While Orestes initially feels uneasy about reporting himself dead, he reassures himself by imagining the fame (*kleos*) and honour (*time*) he will win and by the thought that nothing said for *kerdos* can be *kakon*.[36] He overcomes any lingering doubts by the thought that other wise men have done the same and won even greater honour. Bolstered by his own arguments, he ends his speech with the heroic boast that "I, being alive, will yet shine forth to my enemies like a star" (65–66).[37] Orestes thus conceives of his deed as a glorious act that will win him fame and honour; the *kerdos* it brings him seems more important than anything that might seem *kakon* in the use of *dolos*. Yet the Homeric hero won his *kleos* performing brave deeds on the battlefield. Killing one's mother by the use of *dolos* hardly seems an act worthy of *kleos*. What is so disconcerting about this speech is that Orestes seems unaware that in his case the defeat of his enemies involves the killing

---

[34] Scodel 1984: 81.

[35] Winnington-Ingram 1980: 236.

[36] There is some debate how precisely we are to understand *kakon* here. Kamerbeek *ad* 61 suggests that it has no moral overtones; that is, we are to understand it as ill-omened rather than morally bad. So too argues Jebb 1907: 15 citing *Oidipous at Kolonos* 1433 and *Antigone* 1001. Given the nature of Orestes' task, however, it would be surprising if there were not moral overtones here.

[37] This sentiment has strong Homeric overtones and parallels are often drawn between this speech and 22.26–31 in the *Iliad* (so notes Kamerbeek and Jebb, who also adduces 11.62). Davidson 1988: 60 suggests in addition 6.295 and 19.381 although he notes that the context of Sophokles' play suggest the more developed star similies involving Achilles (22.26ff) and Hektor (11.62). Whether Sophokles has any particular speech in mind here is less important than the Homeric tone of the language which suggests the splendour and glory of the hero.

of his mother, an act which, for all its justice, should not be perceived as a heroic deed worthy of boasting of fame and glory. Orestes may claim to be returning with justice on his side (69–70), but at this stage he betrays a concern more for individual *kleos* and *time* than *dike*. His words are similar to those of his mother, for she too will attempt to justify her actions by reference to *dike* and will initially display some doubt over how to react to the death of her son, wondering whether to see it as "fortunate or terrible but a *kerdos*" (766–67). Klytaimnestra quickly overcomes her inhibitions and goes on to celebrate it as the death of an enemy, behaviour that will characterize her as a *hybristes* and morally condemn her. Mother and son (at least initially) thus conceive of each other's death as a *kerdos* and both seem unaware that the death of kin is not something in which to exult.

Orestes' words here may strike us as morally questionable, but we should remember that they are prospective and thus only potentially discreditable. That he feels some unease about his planned action, describing it as a kind of pain, implies that he senses something wrong with it and that he is not the immoral sophist some have seen. Others too will respond to the *dolos* and proceed to act in ways which will reveal their character and motivation, but Orestes' doubt is separated from his subsequent action by almost one thousand lines and by the occurrence of an event which will provide him with an insight into the nature of his undertaking. At this point, concerned only with vengeance and the benefits it will bring him, he, like his mother, places his own success above everything else. Critics thus are correct to describe certain aspects of his behaviour as questionable; but we should recognize that Sophokles prepares the way for a development in Orestes' understanding by focusing on his doubt and hesitation. What Orestes will come to recognize is exactly what Sophokles hints at with the association of *dolos* and *dike*: that his action must be understood as a form of justice rather than an heroic deed worthy of *kleos*. Justice will distinguish it from Klytaimnestra's murder of Agamemnon.

Orestes' second moment of hesitation occurs at the sound of his sister's voice. This foreshadows what will be the true conflict the *dolos* will pose for him: duty to his vengeance versus the ties of *philia*. When Orestes finishes rehearsing his plans with the *paidagogos*, remembering the importance of *kairos*, he suggests they withdraw. At that moment, a cry of lamentation from inside the palace interrupts their plans. The *paidagogos* suggests that it is a servant girl, but Orestes immediately thinks of Elektra. Wavering from his earlier resolution, he suggests that they stay and listen to his sister's voice. At this hesitation, the *paidagogos* reminds him of the instructions of Apollo: they are to go and make the proper libations to his father. Unquestioning in his obedience both to Agamemnon's *oikos* and to the commands of the god, the *paidagogos* does not admit any delay or deviation from their plans. Orestes' hesitation, however, identifies a potential conflict between his duty to his vengeance and his natural affection for his sister. With the *paidagogos* present to urge him forward, Orestes overcomes his hesitation, but that simply the sound of his sister's voice is enough to make him risk their plans shows that he is not without feelings or scruples. More significantly, his uncertainty looks ahead to the reunion scene and foreshadows Orestes' inability to carry through with the *dolos* out of pity for his sister.

When we consider Orestes' two expressions of doubt, we see that both involve conduct which seems morally questionable in some respects. In the first case, he overcomes his scruples about using *dolos* with the thought of *kerdos* (*kleos* and *time*), an attitude similar to that of his mother. In the second case, urged on by the *paidagogos*, Orestes places his duty to Apollo before his feelings for his sister. Both expressions of doubt have some reference to his blood-kin, one who is an enemy and one who is a friend. Orestes' plan at this point, however, makes no distinction between *echthroi* and *philoi*. Everyone, including Elektra, will be deceived by the news of his 'death'. In Orestes' situation, blood-ties cannot distinguish between friendship and enmity, and we can begin to discern the reason for Apollo's recommendation of *dolos*: it will make a distinction between *philos* and *echthros*, based not upon blood, but upon the capacity for pity, an emotion which more than anything else reflects one's understanding of the ties which should exist between members of the same community. In this sense the *dolos* operates as an agent of *dike*, for it will be the means by which every character in this play, including Orestes himself, will be tested. His deed will be carried out with justice, only if he understands the proper use of *dolos*. At this stage, Orestes has still a partial understanding of the nature of his task, but his doubt points to a potential development: his reaction to his sister's grief, as we shall see, will reveal his character. Ultimately, Orestes will be dependent on his sister for his deed to be carried out with justice, as she will be on him for justice to be restored.

1.3 *Elektra's Monody*

After the departure of Orestes and the *paidagogos* for the tomb of Agamemnon, Elektra appears on stage alone, engaged in the ritual of mourning. This is the only extant play of Sophokles to have a monody by the central character before the entrance of the Chorus. It draws attention to Elektra's isolation from those inside the palace and thus sets the stage for an alliance between her and those who represent the *polis* in this play, the Chorus. As often pointed out, her lyrical lament contrasts sharply with the spoken dialogue of the earlier scene, but her mourning need not mean that Elektra is governed solely by her passions. True, she hates the rulers and deeply grieves her father's murder, but there is an ethical basis to her lamentation. For all the suffering and pain evident from her ritual lament, we shall see that Elektra mourns not out of any morbid attachment to the dead, as sometimes suggested, but to make a public gesture designed to draw attention to the crimes of the rulers. Her passions contain an ethical truth.

Of the two anapestic systems of monody, the first one (86–102) is retrospective and the second (103–120) prospective.[38] This structure of her song points to one of the purposes of her ritual lamentation: it is the link between the past crime and a future in which the murder will have been punished and order restored. The first part of her song (86–102) describes in graphic detail the brutal killing of her father at the hands of Klytaimnestra and her lover, Aigisthos, likening the death blow to that of a woodcutter cleaving an oak tree (97–99). Alone in her loyalty to her dead father, she has been the only one to mourn his death (100–101). Elektra's lamentation is a way to maintain a vestige of the proper order of the *oikos* in the absence of its legitimate heir by keeping alive the memory of the crime against her father. The second part of her song (103–20) looks to the future as she declares her intention never to cease lamenting until the crime is atoned for. She ends her dirge with an appeal to the divinities of the underworld, Hades, Persephone, Hermes, and the Erinyes to avenge the murder of her father and send home her brother. Her mourning thus aims at bringing about a future in which murder is punished and justice accomplished. Death ritual thus

---

[38] See Campbell *ad* 86–250.

becomes the mediating force between past and future, and has as its *telos* the restoration and re-establishment of order in the same fashion as Orestes' carefully laid plans.

All this, Elektra recognizes, is utterly dependent upon Orestes' return and thus her appeal for justice is made in the form of an appeal to send her brother home (115–17). From the very beginning, we see that Elektra has placed everything, her own fate and the fate of the *oikos*, upon his return. She may appear to be at the end of her tether and her pain and suffering are readily apparent, but this is less a reflection of emotional instability than it is an indication of her complete dependence upon Orestes and thus of the devastating effect his reported death will have on her. In this respect, her appearance in the *prologos* directly after her brother's reinforces the sense that there is something terribly inappropriate in Orestes' perception of the vengeance as a heroic deed which will bring him glory.

Elektra's lamentation has often been considered a "passive" activity which does no more than fulfil the traditional female duty of mourning;[39] however, its context suggests that it serves a far broader function in this play. Elektra appears outside the gates of the palace, mourning the death of her father. In other words, lamentation has been separated from its normal ritual context, appearing not in its traditional setting of the funeral procession or over a tomb as in the *Choephoroi*, but in front of the palace and directed externally to the community (πρὸ θυρῶν ἠχὼ πᾶσι προφωνεῖν 109). Her lamentation is not directed to the dead, but is aimed at the living in an attempt to bring about *dike*. It is a protest, directed towards the community, a public declaration about the breach in the proper order of the *oikos* and *polis*, which is why its site—outside the royal household, in front of the palace—is so important. Fittingly, it will be answered by those who represent the community in this play, the Chorus of noble women.

---

[39] See Woodard 1964: 166–167, for instance, who overemphasizes the passivity and emotionalism of Elektra. A more recent example is Burnett 1998: 121–123 who also refers to her lamentation in these terms; she does, however, see Elektra moving towards a more aggressive form of action in the unfolding of the drama. For a useful corrective to the tendency of commentators to view mourning as "passive" activity reflecting the women's tie to the *oikos*, see Foley 1993: 101–43.

CHAPTER TWO

ELEKTRA AND THE CHORUS:
THE FOUNDATIONS OF THE COMMUNITY

2.1 *Preliminary Remarks*

Elektra's monody in the *prologos* is answered by the women of Argos
who make up the Chorus in this play. It enters singing a lyrical
response to her lament and the *parodos* takes the form of a *kommos*.
This is the first of three confrontations which structure the first half
of the play and, like the two which follow, it begins on a critical
note with the Chorus questioning the reason for Elektra's continual
lamentation exceeding the limits of custom. By the end of the *parodos*,
however, the Chorus declares its loyalty to her cause, and an alliance
is formed between the women of the city and Elektra. In the dialogue following the *parodos*, Elektra expresses her shame at her behaviour, but seeks to justify her actions through reference to the virtues
of *aidos* and *eusebeia*.

Elektra's behaviour has always posed a problem for critics and
although many readily acknowledge the justice of her cause, they
are troubled by the manner in which she pursues it. Some take a
psychological approach, interpreting her excessive lamentation as the
product of an obsessive personality which has become warped by
years of suffering.[1] Others, as we shall see, adopting a more ethical
approach, focus on what they perceive as Elektra's contradictory relationship to the concepts of *eusebeia* and *sophrosyne*, interpreting it as
evidence of her lack of self-awareness.[2] Regardless of whether her
actions are explained in psychological or in moral terms, generally
Elektra's expression of shame is taken as one of the strongest indi-
cations of the problematic nature of her conduct. This is a valid
point, but it addresses only one aspect of her *aidos*; too often critics
have concentrated on the shameful nature of her behaviour, while

---

[1] Kells' view of Elektra is the most extreme in this regard, but many take such
a 'psychological' approach to her behaviour. See Introduction n. 39 above.
[2] See note 28 below.

ignoring how much her lamentation is equally an expression of *aidos*
and of her attempt to uphold the fundamental beliefs of the community. The concept of *aidos* is crucial not only for the understanding
of Elektra's justification and the nature of her moral dilemma, but
it also forms a theme which runs through the whole play and ultimately has some role to play in how we are to judge the vengeance.

Douglas Cairns' recent book, *Aidos: The Psychology and Ethics of
Honour and Shame*, is important in this respect, as it is the most comprehensive treatment of this concept in decades.[3] While Cairns conveys very well the conventional understanding of *aidos* as "the cement
of society", he departs from this tradition with his rather controversial claim of *aidos* as the source of conscience. In his examination of the role of *aidos* in the tragedies of Sophokles, Cairns falls in
line with the now prevailing viewpoint of the Sophoclean hero as a
figure deeply opposed to society. Such a perspective accords well
with Cairn's thesis which emphasizes the self-regarding aspects of
aidos, yet it is open to criticism for its overemphasis on the individualism and uniqueness of the hero.[4] What is particularly questionable in Cairn's argument is that in order to support his view of *aidos*
as the source of a personal moral conscience, he must concentrate
almost exclusively on the self-regarding aspect of it and thus disregards the extent to which, at least in the *Elektra*, it is far more representative of communal ethics than of individual conscience. In what
follows, I shall argue that Elektra's behaviour is deeply informed by
communality and has its source in the ethical framework of the *polis*
rather than in any personal ideas of right and wrong.

2.2   *The Status and Function of the Chorus*

A poet's choice of Chorus is always highly significant since he is
able to suggest a great deal simply through the designation of such
things as its sex, age, and social status. In *Antigone*, for instance,
Sophokles uses the Chorus to intensify the isolation of his heroine.
By virtue of her sex and age she is alienated from the Chorus of

---

[3] Cairns 1993.
[4] Gill 1995: 48 and 1996: 153 is one of the few scholars critical of this viewpoint.

elderly male citizens who represent the interests of Creon's *polis*. In the *Trachiniae*, on the other hand, the Chorus is closely bound to Deianeira, having a natural bond with her due to their shared sex. In the *Elektra*, the age, sex, and, status of the Chorus are all significant in identifying its role and function in the play as representatives of the *polis* who are allied with Elektra in opposition to those inside the palace.

It is sometimes suggested that the choice of a Chorus of women underscores the non-political nature of the play. Strictly speaking, women did not participate in the running of the *polis*, but a female Chorus does not prevent a more broadly political element from entering its role in the dramatic action of the play. In one respect, it is essential that the Chorus is female, as Elektra is engaged in primarily a female activity, the mourning ritual. A Chorus of men would be highly artificial and would only heighten her isolation, suggesting not only her estrangement from her family but the *polis*. Their status as noble women of the community is alluded to early on in the play when they enter in response to Elektra's lamentation.[5] She addresses the women as γενέθλα γενναίων (129), an indication of their noble birth and later, as πολίτιδες (1227), a word which more strongly suggests a relationship to the state. By choosing free-born citizen women, Sophokles broadens the focus of the action to include the *polis* while still creating an environment in which Elektra, assured of a natural sympathy due to their common sex, is free to express her feelings. The presence of the Chorus is thus a constant reminder of the public sphere in which Elektra's actions take place.

As the representatives of the community, the Chorus offers a view of the royal *oikos* and the tyranny of Aigisthos and Klytaimnestra from the perspective of the *polis*. Not only does it often provide important confirmation of the validity of Elektra's accusations against

---

[5] Burton 1980: 186 brings out well the political overtones of the Chorus' role here. He remarks that their status as noble women indicates that they hold a position of some significance in the community and may even well be wives of citizens opposed to the rule of Aigisthos and Klytaimnestra. As he puts it, that "they are free-born women of Argos and not members of the household living in the palace gives a wider background to the play and suggests that there are political undertones." Gardiner 1986: 162 on the other hand thinks that Sophokles is able to suggest that the Chorus represents the people without implying any actual participation in the political reality of the state. See also Ierulli 1993: 217–229 on the role of the Chorus.

the tyrants, it does so from a more objective standpoint, unbiased because free from the personal hardships of living within an *oikos* controlled by tyrants. At the same time, the attitude of the Chorus to the tyrants, one of fear, points to the oppressive nature of their rule and identifies the broader consequences of Agamemnon's death for the *polis*. That the Chorus shares a view of Klytaimnestra and Aigisthos similar to Elektra's suggests a common suffering and establishes a bond between them. An alliance is thus formed between Elektra and the community against those inside the palace.

The age of the Chorus members also has some significance, for, being older than Elektra, they have certain authority over her, lending credence to their judgements and advice. The difference in age also suggests a mother/daughter relationship with the Chorus often appearing to function as a surrogate mother to her, addressing her as παῖ and τέκνον. Its kindness and support contrast sharply with Klytaimnestra's harsh and cruel treatment of her daughter. Thus the warm relationship between Elektra and the Chorus highlights the abnormal relationship between mother and daughter. As much as the Chorus is sympathetic to Elektra, sharing her hatred of the rulers, it is not blindly loyal in its devotion to her. Its words of comfort are mingled with critical remarks regarding what appears as excessive and futile in her behaviour, but it is through this criticism that we understand the basis of Elektra's lamentation. Burton may argue that the Chorus represents the "norm of balance" against the "obsessive" behaviour of Elektra, but 'this norm of balance', composed of fifteen practical and sensible citizen women, is ultimately tipped by the arguments of Elektra so that in the end the Chorus comes to declare its loyalty to her cause.[6]

2.3   *The Parodos*

The public nature of Elektra's mourning is underlined by the *parodos*, for the Chorus enters in response to her public cries. The form of *kommos* which the *parodos* takes, strongly suggests a basic alliance between the women of the *polis* and Elektra, as their shared song prevents any emotional gap which a division into lyrics and spoken

---

[6] Burton 1980: 192.

dialogue might have produced.[7] The *parodos* is made up of three strophic pairs, divided between Elektra and the Chorus, followed by an epode. In the first two strophes, the Chorus mixes words of comfort with slightly critical remarks, which prompt Elektra to defend herself. By the end of the *parodos*, the Chorus, while fearing for her safety, affirms its solidarity with Elektra.[8] These three strophic pairs which structure the *parodos* show the gradual movement of the women over to Elektra's side.

The Chorus begins by questioning her as to her continual lamentation (121–27) and, as many have pointed out, there is a hint of rebuke in its words. To the Chorus, her behaviour seems excessive and futile, and at the beginning it assumes that her lamentation has its source in purely personal reasons, grief for Agamemnon. This misunderstanding underlies the Chorus' initial criticism; for although it is sympathetic and filled with kindly intentions, the women do not understand why she continues to lament for a father now long dead. Elektra acknowledges its concern, but declares her intention not to cease lamenting. The Chorus, assuming she must be trying to raise the dead with her continual mourning (137–39), sees her as the author of her own misfortune and counsel moderation. This provokes a rather emotional response from Elektra that the one who forgets the pitiful death of a parent is νήπιος, foolish. The Chorus reminds her that she is not the only one to suffer misfortune for she has other siblings—Chrysothemis, Iphianassa and Orestes (153–54).[9]

---

[7] Burton 1980: 190 points out that this fully lyrical exchange is the only one of this kind in the extant plays of Sophokles.

[8] The suggestion of Ierulli 1993: 221 that Chorus and Elektra are separated metrically, as "the lines of the Chorus respond metrically only to other lines of the Chorus, and Elektra's only to Elektra's, reflecting the differences in their positions is overly subtle in this context.

[9] The reference to Iphianassa, who apparently also lives in the palace, has caused some scholars a slight discomfort, for there is no other reference to her in the play. Kaibel thinks that the mention of two other daughters more moderate in their behaviour than Elektra make the criticism of the Chorus much stronger. Winnington-Ingram 1980: 224 n. 26 and 336 suggests that the reference to Iphianassa is designed to bring to mind Iphigenia. He takes this subtle allusion as further evidence of the 'dark' nature of the play. Davidson 1990a: 407–409 argues that Iphianissa is actually the sacrificed daughter mentioned in the *agon* between Elektra and her mother rather than Iphigenia. *Contra* Winnington-Ingram, Davidson points out that Sophokles may have been trying to avoid the sacrifice motif from Aischylos and thus went out of his way to avoid mentioning the name Iphigenia. The difficulty with this interpretation, as Davidson himself notes, is that the expression "those inside" suggests that all these daughters are *living* in the palace.

This prompts a second defence from Elektra in which she points to her isolation: she has no offspring, no husband, and her brother has not seen fit to return yet (169–72). The Chorus attempts to console her, this time reminding her of the existence of Zeus and the healing remedy of time. Still faintly critical at what it sees as excessive anger and grief, it advises her to yield (176–77). In reply, Elektra points out what waiting has given her: no husband and no children; instead, she serves in the palace dressed in rags (187–92). She has been denied the basic social and biological role of a woman as wife and mother and deprived of the status befitting the daughter of Agamemnon; in short, she has been reduced to something closely resembling a lowborn slave (191–92). In the early part of the exchange, Elektra identifies the crimes of the rulers, the lack of any male to protect her or the interests of the *oikos*. Being the only sibling to mourn Agamemnon's death, she has been isolated from those in the palace by her loyalty to her father. In this respect, the introductory part of the *parodos* is essential for identifying Elektra as the sole representative of Agamemnon's *oikos* in the absence of any male and thus the necessity for and the validity of her actions. By her lamentation she keeps alive the memory of her father and the task of restoring the legitimate order of his *oikos*.

The Chorus responds to this outburst not with further advice to moderate her grief or with another attempt to comfort her; instead it offers its own understanding of the murder as a crime driven by passion and carried out with deceit: δόλος ἦν ὁ φράσας, ἔρος ὁ κτείνας (197). *Eros* and *dolos* are explicitly tied to Klytaimnestra's murder of Agamemnon and her motive is identified not as punishment for the sacrifice of Iphigenia but as sexual passion for Aigisthos. That the first mention of Klytaimnestra's motivation for killing Agamemnon comes from the Chorus is telling, for it suggests that her motives were commonly known to those outside the palace, i.e., to the *polis*, and it provides important external confirmation of Elektra's later accusations that Klytaimnestra acted not, as she claims, according to *dike* but out of an illicit desire for Aigisthos.

The association of *dolos* and *eros* with Klytaimnestra strongly recalls Orestes' own plans to use *dolos* against his enemies. Although Apollo commends *dolos* to Orestes, linking it with *dike*, Orestes justifies his use of *dolos* not by reference to its association with *dike* but by the prospect of winning *kleos*. Not only is there a similarity in their use of *dolos* but also in their motivations, for Klytaimnestra's *eros*, like

Orestes' *kleos*, involves the elevation of a personal desire over a tie of *philos*: in her case, to satisfy her passion; and in his case, to win glory. Each may claim to act in accordance with justice, but both apparently have strong personal motives. In both cases, Elektra will have some role to play in revealing who acts with justice, for she will unmask her mother's claims to *dike*; ultimately her grief will serve to awaken Orestes' compassion and show his capacity for pity.

The Chorus' description of the murder of Agamemnon prompts an outburst from Elektra; she appeals to the "great god of Olympus" (209) to bring down punishment on the murderers. The outspokenness and the public nature of this call frighten the Chorus and now it speaks to her with more force, advising her to yield:

> φράζου μὴ πόρσω φωνεῖν.
> οὐ γνώμαν ἴσχεις ἐξ οἵων
> τὰ παρόντ'; οἰκείας εἰς ἄτας
> ἐμπίπτεις οὕτως αἰκῶς;
> πολὺ γάρ τι κακῶν ὑπερεκτήσω,
> σᾷ δυσθύμῳ τίκτουσ' αἰεὶ
> ψυχᾷ πολέμους· τάδε—τοῖς δυνατοῖς
> οὐκ ἐριστά—τλάθι. (213–20)

> Consider, don't lament further.
> Don't you understand the present
> situation that comes from such things?
> That you fall into misfortunes of your own making
> in this way? For you have acquired a great measure
> of troubles always producing strife in your dispirited
> soul; but these things are not to be contested with
> the powerful—endure.

Some commentators suppose that the Chorus is criticizing Elektra for self-destructive and abnormal behaviour. Woodard, for instance, claims that the Chorus sees Elektra engaged in "shameful polemics and reproaches", and is accusing her of "self-engendered ruin"; Kells suggests that to the Chorus her behaviour appears "hybristic"; while Burton sees the conventional and moderate sentiments of the Chorus as designed to highlight by contrast the obsessive behaviour of Elektra.[10] Gardiner offers a more balanced view which recognizes the dramatic context; the Chorus is responding to the dangers of speaking so openly against the rulers:

---

[10] Woodard 1964: 179–180; Kells *ad* 153ff; Burton 1980: 192.

> Their admonition to speak no further has a tone of urgency and sug-
> gests conspirators' fear of being overheard . . . They do not say that
> Elektra's behaviour is "abnormal" or "hubristic", but that it is dan-
> gerous. By not keeping silent, by openly defying the ruling powers, she
> has got herself into terrible trouble.[11]

The Chorus, aware of the character of the present rule and therefore of the dangerous nature of her activity, is afraid for Elektra,
and it advises her to submit to those in power. This advice to yield
only provokes Elektra to defend herself again, this time by reference
to the traditional beliefs of *aidos* and *eusebeia*. It is her claim to protect and uphold principles basic to communal life which finally causes
the Chorus to declares its full solidarity with her (252–53).

2.4   *The Theme of Aidos*

Aidos is a theme which permeates this play. It has particular significance
for Elektra's arguments and thus it is necessary to understand its
role in order to recognize the moral dilemma in which she finds
herself. *Aidos* is a concept difficult to grasp and almost impossible to
translate. We have no precise parallel and the stock translation,
'shame', captures only a limited aspect of it. It has been described
as a 'respect or regard for the honour of others', a form of 'public
conscience' and a 'fear of disgrace'.[12] In any society dominated by
the standards of honour and reputation to the extent Greek society
was, 'what people say' or 'how things appear' is important. Yet *aidos*
is not mere conformity to public opinion or the simple adjustment
of one's actions to accord with popular sentiment. Rather it is the
awareness of and the respect for the proper treatment of others; a
sensitivity to the stated and unstated beliefs of society or, as James
Redfield puts it, "a vulnerability to the expressed ideal norm of the

---

[11] Gardiner 1986: 144 in response to what Kells *ad* 153, 213, and 221 says
regarding the remarks of the Chorus.

[12] Verdenius 1945: 48 speaks of *aidos* as a kind of public conscience ("Öffentlichkeit
des Gewissens"); Dodds 1951: 18 calls it "respect for public opinion"; Parker 1983:
189 defines it as the "self-restraint expressed through respect for recognized values"; Lloyd-Jones 1987: 256 describes it as "the respect that one owes to another
or oneself in virtue of the τιμή belonging to that other or oneself". For other treatments of *aidos* see Erffa 1937: 4–43; Cheyns 1967: 3–33; Dover 1974: 226–42;
Redfield 1994: 115–119; Scott 1980: 13–35; Williams 1993: Chapter 4 passim.

society."[13] *Aidos* has the ability both to inhibit actions that may be judged disgraceful or conversely, to propel one forward on a course of action to avoid disgrace. It thus operates as a forceful sanction against wrongdoing as well as powerful incentive to virtuous behaviour. It is perhaps best thought of as a kind of social virtue, the principle which makes communal life possible. By the fifth century, it had also acquired an additional but rather limited use that involved the retrospective sense of shame which accompanies the recognition of wrongdoing or disgrace.[14]

Cairns defines *aidos* as "an inhibitory emotion based on sensitivity to and protectiveness of one's self-image."[15] It includes the honour of both self and others, an inclusivity that is mirrored in the honour code itself, "which integrates self-regarding and other-regarding, competitive and co-operative standards, into a remarkably unified whole."[16] Where Cairns differs from the more traditional view of *aidos* is, as mentioned, with his focus on the self-regarding aspect of it, that is, how it looks towards the self and reflects the individual's own values, character, and ideas.[17] Unlike Redfield who argues that

---

[13] Redfield 1994: 116.

[14] The word *aischunomai* is usually used to indicate this aspect of *aidos*. This 'retrospective' aspect of *aidos* is often thought to be a later development of the term, although Cairns claims that we can see an example of this use of *aidos* as early as the *Iliad* (22.104–7). Erffa 1937: 62–3 on the other hand argues that the first use of the verb *aideomai* in a retrospective way occurs in Solon (fr. 32 West).

[15] Cairns 1993: 2–3 draws a distinction between the noun *aidos* and the verb *aideomai* arguing that the verb conveys a recognition that one's self-image is vulnerable in some way, a reaction in which one focuses on the conspicuousness of the self. He proposes that the verb be translated as "I am abashed".

[16] Cairns 1993: 14.

[17] Cairns has a number of arguments he is concerned with refuting in his book, something which may be partially responsible for his emphasis on the self-regarding aspect of this term. He is rightly critical of the tendency to speak about *aidos* in terms of the anthropological classification of societies into shame-cultures and guilt-cultures. Dodds 1951: 17–18 (see also 26 n. 100 and Chapter 2 *passim*) was the first to apply the term shame-culture to Homeric society, and since then it has become commonplace. Shame-cultures are distinguished by their reliance on external sanctions for good behaviour, while guilt-cultures are said to rely upon internalized standards. Thus, in a shame-culture, the worth of a person or action is determined by the judgement of others, while in a guilt-culture, the individual conscience governs ideas of right and wrong. According to this model, shame is a reaction to other people's criticism and requires an audience or at least an imagined audience while guilt does not (see Benedict 1946: 223 for the classic statement of the difference between the two societies). There are certainly parallels between Homeric society and what anthropologists call shame-cultures, and *aidos* and shame correspond at least to some degree. Nevertheless, this is a crude distinction which

aidos is nothing like conscience, Cairns posits *aidos* as the source of conscience.[18] He acknowledges that this may not be identical to our modern concept of conscience as based on a set of principles personal to the individual, and involving reflection, deliberation, and even, at times, opposition to society. Instead, the Homeric conscience is based on standards, which, internalized early in life, operate instinctively and automatically. Cairns recognizes that these may be identical to the standards of society, but he argues that they must still be regarded as the individual's own principles which operate on him as inner sanctions against inappropriate conduct.[19] Therefore, we are not yet at the stage where there is any opposition between the inner

results in a distorted view of the hero as one who simply adjusts his actions to accord with public opinion. Even those who use this antithesis often feel compelled to qualify it by pointing out that it is unlikely any society could function without some degree of internalization of its sanctions (Cairns 1993: introduction and 139–146, especially 142; Bryant 1996: 32. See Hooker 1987: 121–5 for another critical view of Homeric society as a shame-culture). Cairns collapses the distinctions between shame/guilt, external and internal sanctions as well as the notion that shame requires a viewer, real or imaginary. The anthropological model is not Cairn's only target; he is also critical of arguments typically associated with Snell (1928: 24–5; 1930: 141–58; 1975: ch. 1 & 2) and others (Voigt 1972; Fränkel 1975: 75–85; Scott 1982: 13–35) who have claimed that Homeric man has no internal standards and no independent sense of his own worth distinct from society's judgement of him. In other words, he is thought to lack a personal moral conscience in our sense of the term. Snell's claim that Homeric man is unable to reach a decision because of the absence of a concept of self has drawn much criticism in recent years (see Gill 1996 for a recent treatment of this debate). One of the underlying aims of Cairns' discussion of *aidos* in Homeric society is the identification of something he can call 'conscience'. Williams 1993 is also critical of this dichotomy although he approaches the subject from a slightly different perspective. He wants to rescue the Greeks from the 'progressivist' view which tends to see them as moral 'primitives', and shame as a more superficial type of morality (in that it depends on the reactions and evaluations of others). Williams points out that those who see guilt as a more sophisticated and/or superior concept of morality are approaching it in terms of a Kantian morality which sees the will as autonomous and motivated solely by duty. He, like Cairns, disputes the notion that shame relies solely upon external sanctions and face-to-face interaction and offers in its place a model of an 'internalized other'. Unlike Cairns, however, Williams finds the distinction between shame and guilt useful and, with some important qualifications, is content to retain it.

[18] Cairns 1993: 141–144 is critical of the argument of Redfield 1994: 116 that "the ideal norm is directly experienced within the self, as a man internalizes the anticipated judgements of others on himself." Cairns claims that this is incoherent. Redfield, he argues, supposes that judgements can be internalized and yet remain those of others. For Cairns, as soon as someone internalizes a standard, it becomes his own. He goes on to claim that Homeric man quite clearly does possess standards of his own.

[19] Cairns 1993: 142–143.

sanctions of the individual and those of society; that is, there could be no conscientious objectors in Homer. Yet clearly the argument of Cairns goes some distance in paving the way for them. He suggests that we see examples of individuals who disregard public opinion in order to stand by their own ideas of right and wrong in the tragedies of Sophokles and Euripides.[20] Thus Cairns, with his identification of a minimal sort of conscience in Homer, from which *aidos* springs, can now claim, without positing any new development in the concept, that *aidos* has become closely associated with "the internalized self-regulatory mechanism that we call conscience."[21] This argument that *aidos* springs from some inner sanction is very much a moot point and while I do not intend to enter into the problem of identifying a 'self' or 'conscience' in Homer, I think it is Cairns' quest to identify *aidos* with conscience which results in a slightly distorted view of the Sophoclean hero. To support such an argument Cairns must continually emphasize the individualistic aspect of *aidos* and the consequence of this is that it escapes him how much it is bound up with the political and ethical framework of the *polis*.

For Cairns, one of the characteristic traits of Sophoclean tragedy is the opposition between two types of *aidos* played out in the "contrast between limited, personal and self-assertive aspects of the conglomerate of traditional, honour-based values and wider aspects, which to a large extent limit the self-assertion of individuals."[22] Two aspects of *aidos* which were united in Homer—regard for self and

---

[20] Cairns 1993: 221 and 240 argues that Sophokles' Antigone and Odysseus (in *Aias*) are examples of figures who act according to their own personal conscience.

[21] Cairns 1993: 343. Cairns does not want to argue that there has been any development in the concept of *aidos*. He opposes himself to Snell who had argued that there is a new element found in Aeschylean tragedy (fr. 132c Radt). This, he claims, is a tendency towards the subjective evaluation of one's own account without reference to the universal standards of society—an indication of a personal moral conscience. Erffa 1937 also sees a development in the concept of *aidos*. He argues that *aidos* is closely bound up with the duties of the Homeric warrior whose first duty is battle courage; it may also be felt toward one's social superior as well as those who are weaker. In this sense, it is closely connected to pity. As the *polis* developed, Erffa argues, *aidos* became more political; in Aischylos it has close connections with justice; in *Aias* it is closely connected with fear and is the opposite of *hybris*. Ultimately, for Erffa, it is the glue which holds society together and prevents wrongdoing. Cairns however, by establishing that *aidos* relates strongly to self as early as Homer, can posit this as the constant unchanging aspect of the concept.

[22] Cairns 1993: 249.

regard for others—have been set at variance in Sophokles. The individualistic values of the hero, such as the preoccupation with his or her honour, the impulse to dishonour others or retaliate for dishonour suffered, are set in opposition to the more traditional values of society. The hero, in his quest to maintain his honour, is forced into a position in which his actions become a violation of the honour code. Elektra conforms to this pattern, Cairns claims, as she is a figure motivated by a deep sense of personal injury and thus "lives and acts as she does in order to annoy her enemies."[23] Her need to retaliate drives her to lament endlessly, disobey authority, and abuse her mother. Regard for her personal honour has led Elektra to act in a disgraceful manner and her expressions of shame function to underscore the morally dubious nature of her behaviour, the contradictory aspects of her argument, and ultimately only emphasize the similarities between mother and daughter.

Cairns follows the current trend to see the Sophoclean hero as a figure in conflict with society. One of the strongest champions of this view is Bernard Knox with his portrait of the Sophoclean protagonist in *The Heroic Temper*.[24] With its commanding portrayal of the lonely, self-willed tragic hero who acts in accordance with the demands of his own temperament and finds himself isolated from society, Knox's book had a powerful impact on Sophoclean scholarship, and it has continued to exert an influence on many critics. For Knox, these heroic figures are all "exquisitely conscious of their own uniqueness. Abandoned and unsupported by everyone, including the gods, they have nothing to fall back upon but a belief in themselves and their own destiny."[25] For Knox, Elektra is not any different; she is as self-determined, unyielding, stubborn, alienated, and insistent upon revenge as any other Sophoclean figure. Her avowal never to cease lamenting is for Knox evidence of her heroic nature and is comparable to the decision the hero makes that stems from "the deepest layer of his individual nature, his *physis*."[26] Knox's portrait certainly captures the common traits which characters as diverse as Antigone, Aias, Philoktetes, and Elektra share. They are all figures who adopt a stance and hold fast onto it. What is troublesome with this for-

---

[23] Cairns 1993: 241.
[24] Knox 1964.
[25] Knox 1964: 36.
[26] Knox 1964: 10.

mulation is its concentration on the overwhelming uniqueness and individualism of the hero to the exclusion of all else. In focusing on the hero's individual will and his ability to sustain his decision in the face of opposition, without addressing the broader ethical issues, Knox leaves us with a rather unbalanced portrait of them as iconoclastic figures who stand apart from the communal framework. Christopher Gill identifies the main weakness of Knox's argument when he writes:

> [Knox] does not provide an understanding of the way in which the heroes appeal . . . to ethical principles which they regard as basic to their society. Thus, although Knox does not present these figures as ethical individualists or 'outsiders' in quite the way that Whitman does, they take on something of that character by default.[27]

As we shall see, Elektra is not as opposed to society as the arguments of Knox and Cairns seem to suggest, and it is her expression of *aidos* that will show how deeply representative her arguments are of principles fundamental to society. She may oppose herself to those who surround her, but these are all figures who themselves transgress some of the most fundamental beliefs of the community.

2.4.1 *Aidos and eusebeia*

The Chorus has suggested to Elektra that given the circumstances it is best to yield to authority (219–20). In reply, Elektra says:

φέρε,
πῶς ἐπὶ τοῖς φθιμένοις ἀμελεῖν καλόν;
ἐν τίνι τοῦτ᾽ ἔβλαστ᾽ ἀνθρώπων;
μήτ᾽ εἴην ἔντιμος τούτοις
μήτ᾽, εἴ τῳ πρόσκειμαι χρηστῷ,
ξυνναίοιμ᾽ εὔκηλος, γονέων
ἐκτίμους ἴσχουσα πτέρυγας
ὀξυτόνων γόων.
εἰ γὰρ ὁ μὲν θανὼν γᾶ τε καὶ οὐδὲν ὢν
κείσεται τάλας, οἱ δὲ μὴ πάλιν / /
δώσουσ᾽ ἀντιφόνους δίκας,
ἔρροι τ᾽ ἂν αἰδὼς
ἁπάντων τ᾽ εὐσέβεια θνατῶν. (236–50)

---

[27] Gill 1996: 153. He goes on to point out that an exegesis along ethical lines would offer an altogether different interpretation of the plays from that which Knox suggests.

> Come, how can it be right to be forgetful of the dead?
> In whom does this flourish?
> May I never be honoured by such people,
> nor may I ever live free from care with any good
> thing I may have, if I restrain the wings of
> loud lamentation dishonouring my father.
> For if the dead man lies there being earth and
> nothingness, miserable man, and they are not to
> pay the penalty, killed in turn, *aidos* and
> *eusebeia* would disappear from all mankind.

Her answer reveals the basic motivation underlying her lamentation, namely, the traditional values of *aidos* and *eusebeia*, principles shared by everyone and fundamental to communal life. Simply put, shame and piety demand that she lament; and, in doing so, she safeguards and upholds these principles. At the same time Elektra is able to recognize how her behaviour must appear to others, and she expresses her shame:

> αἰσχύνομαι μέν, ὦ γυναῖκες, εἰ δοκῶ
> πολλοῖσι θρήνοις δυσφορεῖν ὑμῖν ἄγαν.
> ἀλλ᾽ ἡ βία γὰρ ταῦτ᾽ ἀναγκάζει με δρᾶν,
> σύγγνωτε. πῶς γὰρ, ἥτις εὐγενὴς γυνή,
> πατρῷ᾽ ὁρῶσα πήματ᾽, οὐ δρῴη τάδ᾽ ἄν . . . (254–58)

> I am ashamed, women if I seem to you
> to lament too much
> but force compels me to do this,
> forgive me; for how could any noble woman
> seeing the sufferings of her father's house not do this . . .

She then goes on to defend her behaviour on other grounds—the conditions in the palace. She is at odds with her mother (261–62); she must live with and be ruled by the murderers of her father (262–64); Aigisthos sits on Agamemnon's throne, wears his royal robes, and sleeps in his bed with her mother (267–74); her mother carries out monthly ritual sacrifices in celebration of Agamemnon's murder (277–81) and insults and abuses her daughter (287–98). In circumstances such as these, Elektra claims, moderation or piety is impossible; rather there is great necessity to practice evil in evil circumstances (ἐν οὖν τοιούτοις οὔτε σωφρονεῖν, φίλαι, οὔτ᾽ εὐσεβεῖν πάρεστιν· ἀλλ᾽ ἐν τοῖς κακοῖς πολλή 'στ᾽ ἀνάγκη κἀπιτηδεύειν κακά. 307–9). The problem for commentators has always been that her relationship to piety seems somewhat contradictory, for having earlier claimed *eusebeia* as a basis for her actions (250) she then goes on to deny this possibility and many interpret this as Elektra's lack of awareness or her attempt to redefine the concept according to her own terms.[28] Cairns sees a similar paradox in Elektra's claim to maintain *aidos* and *eusebeia* and her acknowledgement that in doing so, she has been forced to act in ways that *aidos* should prevent. Elektra, he argues, "recognizes that she is not behaving as a noble woman should in normal circumstances", but justifies her conduct in terms of her own honour and the need to retaliate. motivations

---

[28] North 1966: 52; 65. See also Blundell 1989: 159. Kirkwood 1942: 86 sees the contradiction between Elektra's various claims of piety and shame ("it is not possible to *sophronein* or to *eusebein*" [307–8]; "shame holds me" [616]; "I know my conduct is unseemly" [618] and later her claim that that would win praise for piety [967–8]) as evidence of Elektra's lack of self-knowledge. She deceives herself as to the true nature of the matricide. Kirkwood may be right to see in Elektra's failure to mention the name of her mother a sign that she is deceiving herself, but he fails to acknowledge that this is at a point in which Elektra is ignorant of the true nature of her circumstances, something which changes when the *dolos* is revealed to her. Burton 1980: 195 adopts a more psychological interpretation of her behaviour, arguing that in Elektra's contradictory claims we see evidence of a psychological disorder: "It is as if she were regarding herself from two points of view, both as the just avenger of her father and therefore εὐσεβής, and also as a woman whose natural instincts are so warped that she feels incapable of either σωφροσύνη or εὐσέβεια in her daily conduct. A psychological 'split' of this type indicates that the mind is obsessed and the judgement confused." Burton ignores how *aidos* works here and interprets her reaction in a too psychological fashion. If Elektra's natural instincts were as warped as Burton believes, one doubts whether she would even recognize her own transgressions. Others (Johansen 1964: 8–32) have interpreted Elektra's numerous confessions of shame at her behaviour as pointing to the tension between what is *dikaion* and what is both *aischron* and *kalon* on the other. The question is not whether the matricide is just; that is assumed, but given that it is just and necessary, is it not also shameful? Justice then comes at the cost of Elektra's moral disintegration. While I agree with Johansen on the tension between the *dikaion* and the *aischron* evident in the matricide, there is little to suggest Elektra's moral breakdown. McDevitt 1983: 3–4 also agrees with Johansen on the just but shameful aspect of the matricide but disagrees with the conclusion Johansen draws. For McDevitt, Elektra feels no shame at the matricide, but only at the life she is forced to lead. Elektra acts according to an inner moral truth, which, "contrary to public opinion", makes it shameful not to carry out the vengeance. The audience on the other hand is forced by Sophokles' presentation of her to judge the matricide as shameful. McDevitt attempts to show how Sophokles invites us to view the matricide as shameful by the allusion to the discreditable history of the house in the *epode* and messenger speech. The violence is marked by the reference to the chariot race between Pelops and Oinomaos and is connected with the chariot race in which Orestes supposedly dies. We are meant to judge both as shameful and thus the whole vengeance of which this story is part. It seems unlikely that Sophokles would leave something so crucial to our understanding of the play (the judgement that the matricide is shameful) to such a subtle allusion (see critical remarks of Stinton 1986: 79 regarding the allusion to the chariot race).

that are compelling only to her.[29] Cairns has certainly identified an important conflict, but when we examine Elektra's arguments, we shall see that the opposition is more between the blood-based ties of the *oikos* and the broader ethical framework of the *polis* than in any conflict between Elektra's values and those of society.

There are two aspects of *aidos* in operation here: that which compels Elektra to continue lamenting even in excess of customary measure in order to uphold what she perceives to be the basic beliefs of society; and her sense of shame that in doing so she has failed to live up to other codes of conduct. That is, we have one action which, in one aspect, is praiseworthy and, in another, disgraceful. Cairns claims, like others, that Elektra's "pursuit of *eusebeia* necessitates its negation."[30] Yet her failure to be pious, which Cairns rightly identifies as her lack of respect for her mother, is only a breach of one aspect of *eusebeia*. Usually translated as piety, *eusebeia* involves a regard and respect for authority and as such was not restricted to the gods, but was felt towards one's *polis* and for one's parents.[31] In this sense, then, it includes both a respect for the laws and the principles of order within the community and a respect for parental authority and proper behaviour within the *oikos*. It is a regard for power, but is properly only felt for power which is legitimate.[32] More than anything else, *eusebeia* means upholding ancestral custom (*patrios nomos*) and to be *eusebes* is, as Zaidman says, "to believe in the efficacy of the symbolic system that the city had established for the purpose of managing relations between gods and men, and to participate in it, in the most vigorously active manner possible."[33]

Elektra's dilemma is that she is forced to breach *eusebeia* in one or another form no matter what she does. She may be respectful towards her mother, but that would mean dishonouring her father,

---

[29] Cairns 1993: 248.

[30] Cairns 1993: 249.

[31] See Cairns 1993: 207. The common translation of *eusebeia* as "pious" is best avoided because of its heavy religious overtones. Kells *ad* 245ff suggests that at lines 245 & 308 *eusebeia* means something closer to law-abidingness or respect for the law than piety. The gods are assumed as they have an interest in order and the standards of human conduct. See Bremmer 1994: 4–5 and Zaidman and Schmitt Pantel 1992: 13–15 for discussions of piety and impiety.

[32] Its root *seb* and the related forms *sebas* or *sebein* mean literally 'to retreat in awe'. *Eusebeia* or a related form of it occurs at lines 250, 308, 464, 589 and 968.

[33] Zaidman and Schmitt Pantel 1992: 15.

abandoning the dead, justice, and ultimately, the principles of *eusebeia* and *aidos*. Alternatively, she may honour her father with her lamentation, which means she has to disobey her mother. In the realm of the *oikos*, Elektra's dilemma is insoluble—no matter whom she chooses, she will betray a parent. Within the broader ethical framework of the *polis*, however, the choice is clear. Aigisthos' and Klytaimnestra's rule claims the authority which resides in power, but it is power without legitimacy or justice—it was accomplished by murder and is sustained by tyranny. The decision to honour her father over her mother then is not driven solely by some need to retaliate against her mother, but by her sense of *aidos* or respect for the ideals of *eusebeia* within the broader sphere of the *polis*. That this forces her to breach a narrower form of *eusebeia*, respect for her mother, she is all too aware of, hence her shame.

In focusing upon the individualistic aspect of *aidos*, Cairns takes what is only a welcome by-product of her lamentation—that she irritates her enemies—and makes it her primary aim, thus ignoring the broader ethical motivations in favour of the personal and subjective. In elevating one above the other, Cairns creates a deeply subjective heroine driven solely by a compulsion to act that is understandable only to her. Such an argument ignores the fact that her claim to uphold *eusebeia* and *aidos* wins the support of the Chorus (251–53), and it further ignores the fact that, in claiming to do what any noble woman would do (257–58), Elektra operates not according to her personal set of values, as Cairns argues, but those which she perceives to be the fundamental laws of the community. For her, this is what it is to be noble.[34]

2.4.2 *Aidos and sophrosyne*

Elektra's sense of shame also involves her recognition that she breaches a form of *sophrosyne*. *Sophrosyne* generally means something akin to 'moderation', 'soundness of mind', 'self-limitation' or 'observance of limits' and is often translated as 'prudence' or 'self-restraint'.[35] When

---

[34] Elektra's understanding of nobility emerges more clearly in the confrontation with Chrysothemis. Cairns ignores this exchange, but it is important for establishing the radically different motivations of the two sisters. See Chapter 3 below.

[35] *Sophrosyne* derives from the verb *sophronein* which itself is composed of '*sos*' (safe) and '*phren*' (mind). The noun *sophrosyne* is absent in both Aischylos and Sophokles.

applied specifically to the female, this term has a narrower meaning of 'chastity', 'modesty', 'obedience', and 'inconspicuous behaviour'.[36] Helen North, who provides the most comprehensive treatment of this term, traces its development from Homeric times to later fifth century. She points out that in the epics *sophrosyne* means basically 'soundness of mind' and appears to be of little importance alongside the heroic virtues of courage and skill in fighting. With the rise of the *polis*, it moved beyond its original meaning and developed the moral sense evident in Aischylos' use of it. In Sophokles, North argues that *sophrosyne* has a more intellectual force than moral and is used primarily to refer to the ability to recognize reality and thus it is closely tied to self-knowledge.[37]

North's discussion of the theme of *sophrosyne* in Sophokles' tragedies reveals a perspective similar to that of Knox, Cairns, and others in that she sees its characteristic plot pattern revolving around a hero in conflict with society. He is, as she puts it, a figure who "carries his individualism to some extreme incompatible with the apparent welfare of the community."[38] For North, the Sophoclean protagonist is an example of a "failure in *sophrosyne*".[39] With regard to the *Elektra*, North argues that in Elektra's rejection of moderation, she betrays a lack of self-awareness which makes her resemble her mother. She exults in every excess of emotion, rejects τὸ μέτρον (236) and declares that in her circumstances, *sophrosyne* is impossible (ἐν οὖν τοιούτοις οὔτε σωφρονεῖν, φίλαι, οὔτ' εὐσεβεῖν πάρεστιν· 307–8).[40] Elektra, North argues, follows her own independent standards of behaviour, taking familiar ethical terms such as *aidos*, *eusebeia*, and *sophrosyne* and filling them with new meaning.

Elektra does break all rules of decorum with her outspoken and public lamentation. This is behaviour which is immodest and con-

---

The more commonly used terms in this play are forms of the root φρων mind and thus *euphronein*, *phronein*, occur frequently. The adverb *sophronos* occurs once; the adjective four times and the verb eight times (See North 1966: 50 n. 39 and Ellendt 1872). The following forms are found in the *Elektra*: σωφρονεῖν (307); σώφρων (365); εὖ φρονεῖν (394); σωφρονήσεις (465).

[36] North 1966: 1 n. 2 points out that throughout Greek history the idea of feminine *sophrosyne* remained the same in these four aspects.

[37] North 1966: 32–33.

[38] North 1966: 12.

[39] North 1966: 51.

[40] North 1966: 65 sees an intended echo of the *Choephoroi* suggesting that Elektra's

spicuous and thus a clear violation of *sophrosyne*, but it is a breach of a conventional form of *sophrosyne*; in other words, Elektra contravenes the behaviour befitting a woman in her conventional role.[41] There is no evidence to suggest that her claim—*sophrosyne* is impossible in her circumstances—involves a wholesale rejection of the concept or that it reflects her lack of self-awareness, as North claims.[42] Rather, Elektra recognizes that her behaviour is not suitable for a woman and is ashamed that her public lamentation has made her act in such an unseemly fashion. In this respect, her breach of *sophrosyne* is analogous to her breach of *eusebeia*, that is, it is a violation of one aspect of it. Greater support for this argument is found in the following confrontation with her sister, for their debate is essentially over what constitutes *sophron* behaviour. There we shall see that Elektra's breach of *sophrosyne* is only a violation of a restricted form of *sophrosyne*, the type embodied in the behaviour of her sister. While Chrysothemis would seem to be the living refutation of Elektra's claim that every noble woman would act as she does, ultimately the exchange vindicates Elektra's behaviour by showing she acts more in line with communal standards than does her sister, Chrysothemis. In other words, Elektra's understanding of *sophrosyne* is not unique to her, but one fully informed by the civic ethics of the *polis*.

---

nature is revealed through a contrast with her Aeschylean counterpart: The Elektra of Aischylos' tragedy "who was genuinely different from her mother, could pray sincerely for *sophrosyne* and piety; this Electra, although chaste where her mother is wanton, is like Clytemestra in rejecting moderation, and both mother and daughter lack self-knowledge."

[41] Others have argued that her breach of *sophrosyne* here is less significant than her breach of *eusebeia*. Alexanderson 1966: 79–98 for one takes this view, arguing that her expressions of shame refer to only minor breaches of decorum. He suggests that it reflects Elektra's recognition that she does not conform to the traditional view of a young woman's behaviour and does not feel happy about it, in spite of her hard attitude." Cairns 1993: 248 as well claims that her *aischune* here refers only to embarrassment regarding conduct unfitting in a woman of her status. Johansen 1964: 8–32 attaches far more significance to Elektra's expressions of shame, arguing that they indicate the evil realm into which she has been forced.

[42] North's argument regarding the rejection of *sophrosyne* and the delusion of the hero is more applicable to the later scene with Chrysothemis in which Elektra presents her with a vision of glory and fame they will win if they kill Aigisthos. This could be seen as Elektra's delusion, especially because it is connected with a failure to see the truth of the ritual evidence her sister brings (see Chapter 6). As North points out, "[o]ften the theme of delusion is connected with a misunderstood oracle or prophecy." But this is a direct result of the messenger speech of the *paidagogos* and is only temporary; the delusion vanishes once the *dolos* is revealed to Elektra.

Both instances of Elektra's transgressions, that is, her failure to uphold one aspect of the familial form of *eusebeia* as well as her rejection of a conventional form of *sophrosyne* are at the same time examples of Elektra's maintenance of and loyalty to other standards of behaviour. This is to a large degree what constitutes her moral dilemma: her conduct is right by some standards, but wrong by others. Yet Elektra herself realizes this conflict and thus her *aidos* betrays a stronger sensitivity to the conventions regarding behaviour suitable for a noble person rather than the lack of awareness many have seen. Most important, Elektra reveals a capacity for recognizing a hierarchy amongst the virtues and various aspects of them, which rank some as more important than others.

CHAPTER THREE

ELEKTRA AND CHRYSOTHEMIS I: THE SOPHRON CITIZEN VERSUS FEMALE SOPHROSYNE

3.1 *Preliminary Remarks*

The Chorus, who has just finished reassuring Elektra that Orestes will come, now warns her to speak no further, as her sister is approaching. Chrysothemis enters, apparently on the way to Agamemnon's grave with ritual offerings from Klytaimnestra. When she comes upon Elektra outside the gates of the palace, the two sisters become engaged in a lengthy debate. Chrysothemis is openly critical of her sister's public lamentation while Elektra has nothing but contempt for her weak-willed acquiescence in tyranny. Neither is convinced by the arguments of the other and, just as Chrysothemis is about to depart, she reveals to her sister the report of Klytaimnestra's dream. Elektra, who immediately recognizes its significance, is emboldened by the vision and tells her sister to throw the ritual offerings away and replace them by their own gifts to their father. Persuaded by her sister, Chrysothemis leaves to carry out her request.

Chrysothemis is often thought to function as a 'foil' to Elektra.[1] With her modest demeanor and respectful obedience, she seems the model of conventional female *sophrosyne*. Elektra, on the other hand, outspoken and defiant, seems to reject every manner of *sophrosyne* as a pretext for cowardice and weakness. Many critics have thus concentrated on Elektra's alleged rejection of *sophrosyne*. North's argument in this regard is typical, as she, like others, claims, as we have seen, that in contrast to Chrysothemis' more conventional form of *sophrosyne*, Elektra has her own private interpretation of this concept, in line with her *agathe physis*.[2] Although Chrysothemis appears to be governed by a code of behaviour limited to the subordinate position

---

[1] Kitto 1959: 160; Stevens 1978: 117; Schein 1982: 74; Minadeo 1994: 119.
[2] North 1966: 65; Blundell 1989: 159 makes a similar argument. See 2.4.2 above.

of women, while Elektra repudiates this code of conduct, the quarrel between the sisters is never over how a female *qua* female should behave; rather it is over what constitutes *sophron* behaviour in their circumstances.[3] Each sister makes a claim to 'right thinking' in order to justify her decision and each accuses the other of being 'without sense'. Their speeches are full of references to honour, nobility and freedom; and the way in which the two siblings interpret these terms reveals much about their understanding of *sophron* thinking. Chrysothemis' failure to acknowledge any larger ethical framework exposes her actions as driven more by a narrow form of self-interest concerned exclusively with material comfort and physical safety than any specific concern with proper behaviour for a woman. Elektra, on the other hand, has an awareness of honour and freedom that embraces a moral dimension absent in her sister. She may violate certain codes of behaviour, but the source of her defiant behaviour lies not in a private understanding of *sophrosyne* unique to her, but in the civic beliefs of the fifth century *polis*. Finally, while neither sister makes any specific mention of *aidos*, apparent in Elektra's actions is an acute sensitivity as to 'how things appear'. Chrysothemis is more openly critical of her sister's behaviour than the Chorus, but unlike that earlier exchange, her words do not provoke any expression of shame in Elektra. This suggests that this scene is designed to justify Elektra's breach of familial piety and conventional female *sophrosyne* in contrast to a sister who rigidly adheres to these concepts without reference to their context.

3.2 *Sophron Thinking versus Female Sophrosyne*

Chrysothemis' opening speech (328–40) betrays some of the limitations and weaknesses of her position. She begins by criticizing her sister for her public lamentation, thinking it futile and her anger pointless (328–31). Although she declares that she is similarly grieved

---

[3] North 1966: 65 claims that evidence for Elektra's "private interpretation of *sophrosyne*" may be found in the confrontation between her and Chrysothemis in which Elektra accuses her sister of χλιδή. Chrysothemis, Elektra argues, would not act in the manner she does if she were *sophron* (σώφρων γ' οὖσα 365). But the fact that the two sisters differ in their understanding of *sophrosyne* is hardly proof that Elektra has her own independent standards.

at their present situation, she thinks silent obedience is the best course
of action:

κ̓αίτοι τοσοῦτόν γ' οἶδα κἀμαυτήν, ὅτι
ἀλγῶ 'πὶ τοῖς παροῦσιν· ὥστ' ἄν, εἰ σθένος
λάβοιμι, δηλώσαιμ' ἂν οἷ' αὐτοῖς φρονῶ.
νῦν δ' ἐν κακοῖς μοι πλεῖν ὑφειμένῃ δοκεῖ,
καὶ μὴ δοκεῖν μὲν δρᾶν τι, πημαίνειν δὲ μή.
τοιαῦτα δ' ἄλλα καὶ σὲ βούλομαι ποεῖν. (332–37)

However, I know this much about myself, that
I grieve over the present situation; so that if I had the power
I should show them what I think about them.
Now in times of trouble, it seems best to me to sail with a
slackened sail and not seem to do something but do them no harm.
And I wish you also to do such things and others.

Despite the fact that Chrysothemis claims to share a view similar to
her sister, she thinks that since she is without power, it is best "to
sail with a slackened sail". Justice (*dikaion*) may not lie in these words,
Chrysothemis admits, but freedom does. She ends her speech with
the claim that if she is to live in freedom, she must obey those in
power in all things: εἰ δ' ἐλευθέραν με δεῖ ζῆν, τῶν κρατούντων ἐστὶ
πάντ' ἀκουστέα (339–40).

According to Chrysothemis, action requires *sthenos*, a word which
means 'might' or 'prowess' and is used primarily with reference to
males or masculine physical strength. Action then is defined entirely
in a physical sense and thus becomes the exclusive domain of males.
Being without *sthenos*, Chrysothemis thinks she has no ability to do
anything and thus to her, behaviour like Elektra's is senseless in that
it accomplishes nothing. Less concerned with justice than freedom,
she willingly sacrifices the one in order to obtain the other. Yet freedom for Chrysothemis is nothing more than being free to move
about the palace unhindered. Like action, freedom is defined by
Chrysothemis in an entirely physical sense. As Knox rightly remarks,
such a non-political use of the word *eleutheros* is startling in fifth century tragedy.[4] Freedom for the Greeks was a concept primarily political in nature. Having fought the Persians, they were all too aware

---

[4] Knox 1983: 8 takes this as further evidence of the non-political nature of the
play. Chrysothemis does have a strikingly narrow definition of freedom but this only
draws attention to Elektra's different understanding of freedom, which is not as
"personal" as Knox claims.

of their system of absolute monarchy which demanded the submission of one's will to the king. In contrast, the Greeks counted themselves free because they obeyed a magistrate whom they themselves had elected and a system of laws which they themselves had created. The Chorus in Aischylos' *Persai* expresses this well when it proclaims that to be an Athenian citizen was to be masterless, a servant to no mortal man (*Per.* 242). To submit oneself to the arbitrary will of an individual was for the Athenians nothing more than a form of slavery. By the democratic standards of fifth century Athens, Chrysothemis' claim that freedom requires obedience to οἱ κρατοῦντες in all things sounds remarkably servile. Only by the narrow conventions of female *sophrosyne* might it seem praiseworthy, as submission to authority was thought to be the prime *arete* of women. Yet Chrysothemis has justified her behaviour not by reference to how a woman should behave, but by the much weaker claim of a lack of physical strength and a desire for a rather limited form of freedom, in other words, by an argument that has no broader application beyond her own physical safety and comfort.

Elektra's speech (341–68) begins on an equally critical note that exposes the consequences of Chrysothemis' decision to follow a course of silent obedience. It means that she must forget her father and remain loyal to her mother (341–42). Their dispute is not simply a quarrel over family loyalties, for the opposition between the two sisters runs much deeper. We saw in the previous exchange that Elektra's motivations lie in her desire to care for the dead and thus the protection of the traditional beliefs of *aidos* and *eusebeia*. If the dead are neglected, Elektra points out, then the principles of *aidos* and *eusebeia* vanish. That is, her motivations have reference to reasons external to herself. Here, Chrysothemis' neglect of her father means that she denies one of the basic principles of both domestic and communal life, care for the dead. She may uphold a narrow and superficial form of familial piety in that she shows the respect a daughter should display to a mother, but she must also breach a form of familial piety as this means that she forgets her father. Equally unacceptable to Elektra is that Chrysothemis has tied herself to the will of the woman responsible for Agamemnon's death and thus can do nothing other than carry out her mother's commands (343–44). She may hate the rulers, but she does so only in words (λόγῳ 357), for in fact (ἔργῳ 358) she must keep company with them. Chrysothemis' code of behaviour thus places her in the position of being able to uphold concepts such as *sophrosyne* and *eusebeia* in only their narrowest form.

Elektra then goes on to demonstrate how limited and shallow Chrysothemis' view of action is by a comparison with her own:

> ἥτις λέγεις μὲν ἀρτίως, ὡς εἰ λάβοις
> σθένος τὸ τούτων μῖσος ἐκδείξειας ἄν·
> ἐμοῦ δὲ πατρὶ πάντα τιμωρουμένης
> οὔτε ξυνέρδεις τήν τε δρῶσαν ἐκτρέπεις.
> οὐ ταῦτα πρὸς κακοῖσι δειλίαν ἔχει; (347–51)

> You who said just now, that if you had the power
> you would show your hatred of them,
> but when I do everything to revenge my father,
> you do not help and you turn away the one who does act.
> Is this not cowardice in addition to the evils?

Chrysothemis, as stated earlier, thinks that she needs the physical strength of a male to show her hatred of the rulers; yet Elektra's form of action, lamentation, only requires the moral strength to maintain a set of beliefs in the face of suppression. Nor is it as futile and ineffective as Chrysothemis thinks, for by lamenting Elektra honours her father and thereby brings pain to the rulers (355–56). Although Chrysothemis has come to tell her sister that she will be put away unless she ceases her lamentation, she fails to grasp that this threat confirms Elektra's claim that her action has the power to harm the rulers. Chrysothemis, because of her limited perspective, is unaware that Elektra's lamentation acquires through its public nature a political power that makes it an effective form of action. Her restricted definition of action and freedom leaves her unable to comprehend anything in terms other than their physical consequences.

Each sister makes a claim to being *sophron* while accusing the other of being 'without sense'. As Elektra points out, Chrysothemis' form of honour allows her to live a life of privilege (360–62), but it also means that she must appear cowardly (351) and base (363). Elektra rejects her form of honour and tells her sister she would too if she 'thought rightly':

> τῆς σῆς δ' οὐκ ἐρῶ τιμῆς λαχεῖν.
> οὐδ' ἂν σύ, σώφρων γ' οὖσα. νῦν δ' ἐξὸν πατρὸς
> πάντων ἀρίστου παῖδα κεκλῆσθαι, καλοῦ
> τῆς μητρός. οὕτω γὰρ φανῇ πλείστοις κακή,
> θανόντα πατέρα καὶ φίλους προδοῦσα σούς. (364–68)

> I don't desire to obtain your honour,
> nor would you at least if you thought rightly. Now although it

> is possible to be called the child of the best father of all, be called
> after your mother. For in this way you appear base to most,
> having betrayed your dead father and your own.

The point is not that Elektra has her own personal understanding of *sophrosyne* or honour, which Chrysothemis fails to live up to, but that, when judged by the standards of the community, Chrysothemis would appear base to most (φανῇ πλείστοις κακή 366). *Pleistoi* here seems to have the force of 'public opinion', that is, Elektra defines 'right thinking' by reference to communal standards. The difference in their view of *sophron* behaviour is most apparent when Chrysothemis reveals the threat of the rulers to imprison Elektra unless she ceases her lamentation. Elektra's willingness to give up her physical freedom in order to maintain a set of beliefs seems to Chrysothemis a form of madness, and she tells her sister that it is high time that she show some sense (νῦν γὰρ ἐν καλῷ φρονεῖν 384).

To Chrysothemis, Elektra seems to have no concern for the kind of life she leads (392), but this is only a rejection of a life reduced to physical comforts. Elektra eschews all the material benefits of Chrysothemis' life, and willingly endures a miserable existence in servitude in order to uphold her idea of honour. For Elektra, honour includes her father's honour, the honour of the *oikos*, and a kind of communal honour, while for Chrysothemis honour means looking out for oneself and not acting foolishly (398), which is only another way of saying it means obedience to authority. Thus for her "thinking well" (εὖ φρονεῖν 394) is simply submitting to the powers-that-be (τοῖς κρατοῦσι δ' εἰκαθεῖν 396).

When we remember that Elektra sees herself as the representative of her *oikos* and the upholder of the traditional beliefs of *eusebeia* and *aidos*, her refusal to give way before the threats of the tyrants says much about the code of conduct she follows. The Athenian civic virtues of *sophrosyne* and *eusebeia* (as well *andreia* and *dikaiosyne*) all stress the citizen's subordination and duty to the *polis*. Unlike the modern concept of morality, which is based upon personal moral conscience and the individual's ideas of right and wrong, the ancient citizen was guided in his conduct and actions by ancestral custom (*patrios nomos*) and the laws of the *polis*. His freedom was the freedom to participate in the life of the *polis* through carrying out his duties and obligations to the state. Although, historically, women had no more active political freedom than metics, and Athenian democracy meant freedom for a select group of people, namely, male citizens entitled to vote and hold office, we should not expect tragedy to reflect with any degree of precision the historical and social realities of its time.[5] Therefore, we should not be unduly surprised that the female in Greek tragedy acts and behaves in a fashion never allowed to her historical counterpart.[6] Elektra appears so masculine to commentators precisely because she follows a code of behaviour more in line with the values associated with the notion of active citizenship in fifth-century Athens than with any conventional ideas of female *arete*.[7] What allows Elektra to sacrifice so willingly her physical freedom is her understanding of a duty and obligation beyond that of ensuring her own safety. That is, her behaviour is remarkably consistent with that demanded of one who has a share in the *polis*; and, in refusing to submit herself to the will of another, she acts in accordance with the Athenian concept of freedom. This is precisely why Chrysothemis is judged so harshly by Elektra. By the standards of fifth century society her sister's behaviour appears cowardly and base, unworthy of a free-born citizen. For the Athenians, to be accused of cowardice is to be guilty of one of the worst vices.

Those who argue, as North does, that Chrysothemis follows a conventional form of *sophrosyne* are formally correct. The problem is that Chrysothemis does not so much argue from this stance as from a concern for herself; because she has more regard for her own comfort than anything else, her behaviour appears less than admirable.

---

[5] The discrepancy between the behaviour of the female in tragedy and her social status in fifth century society has become the focus of much feminist scholarship. For an idea of the range of views expressed over the years, see Gomme 1925:1–25; Kitto 1951; Pomeroy 1975; Shaw 1975: 235–66; Gould 1980: 38–59; Foley 1981b: 127–168; Blok and Mason 1984; Cohen 1989: 3–15; Seidensticker 1995: 151–73. See Katz 1995: 21–43 & 199 for a good historical overview of this subject and Zeitlin 1985: 63–94 for a recent attempt to move the debate beyond the status of women as represented in either their poetic context or their social and historical context.

[6] Hall 1997: 93–126 identifies a generic plot-pattern in regard to the female in tragedy. Women, she argues, break 'unwritten laws' only in the physical absence of a legitimate husband or *kurios*. Elektra follows a pattern of behaviour similar to many other dominant female characters in that she acts in the absence of a husband or legitimate *kurios*.

[7] See, for instance, Vickers 1982: 587 n. 4; Cairns 1993: 241 n. 92; Vernant 1983: 136–8 who points out that the figure of Elektra herself is a strong and masculine one.

There is, however, as already pointed out, no evidence for the claim that Elektra acts in accordance with purely personal standards or that her breach of *sophrosyne* indicates her lack of self-knowledge. Hers is a different code of behaviour from Chrysothemis, but far from being a private code of conduct, it has turned out that its principles are more in line with the cardinal civic virtues rather than the conventional standards of female *arete*. The word *aidos* may not appear in the exchange, but it quite plainly governs Elektra's actions, as her ideas of honour and freedom show a sensitivity as to how these concepts are understood in the wider community. For Elektra, *sophron* behaviour should aim at fulfilling the duties and requirements of society, and in this respect it may be understood as a consequence of her *aidos*. Elektra has the ability to conceive of her situation in the context of the norms of society and act accordingly. Chrysothemis, having no such ability to see things in their broader context, rigidly adheres to a code of conduct that can only uphold concepts such as *sophrosyne* in their most restricted conventional form. What Chrysothemis promotes is good sense or good behaviour that has no wider reference to the community or even to the *oikos* of her father. She simply consults her own interests and acts accordingly.

One of the striking differences between this confrontation and the previous one is that although Chrysothemis criticizes Elektra, it does not evoke an expression of shame from her. Unlike the exchange between Elektra and the Chorus, and the later one with her mother, in which criticism forces Elektra to acknowledge wrongdoing, no such acknowledgement of shame appears here. There are at least two reasons for this. First, the Chorus and Klytaimnestra are in a position of authority while Chrysothemis is not. As Erffa points out, *aidos* is most often felt towards one's social superiors: rulers, elders, and parents.[8] It may be felt towards those who are weaker and then passes into *eleos*, but generally, *aidos* is expressed for what is higher and superior, and pity, for what is weaker and inferior. The Chorus and Klytaimnestra are both Elektra's superiors and in a position of some authority over her while Chrysothemis is not. A more important point is that both the Chorus and her mother make criticisms that have some validity. Elektra's expression of shame is in many ways an acknowledgement of their legitimacy. Chrysothemis' criti-

---

[8] Erffa 1937: 10–12.

cisms, however, have no such effect on her sister, suggesting that
the contrast between the two sisters is contrived to highlight the
questionable aspects of Chrysothemis' behaviour rather than those of
Elektra. Her rigid adherence to a strict and narrow form of female
sophrosyne in these circumstances forces her to act in a less than virtuous manner. This seems substantiated to a certain degree by
Chrysothemis' reaction to her sister's accusation of subservient behaviour, for she comes close to a recognition that her behaviour is in
some ways less than commendable:

> Χρ.   καλόν γε μέντοι μὴ 'ξ ἀβουλίας πεσεῖν.
> Ηλ.   πεσούμεθ᾽, εἰ χρή, πατρὶ τιμωρούμενοι.
> Χρ.   πατὴρ δὲ τούτων, οἶδα, συγγνώμην ἔχει.
> Ηλ.   ταῦτ᾽ ἐστὶ τἄπη πρὸς κακῶν ἐπαινέσαι. (398–401)

> Chr.   But honour means not to fall through foolishness.
> El.   I shall fall if I must avenging my father.
> Chr.   But our father, I know, has forgiveness for this (*sc.* behaviour)
> El.   Such words are for the base to approve of.

Chrysothemis' recognition that her behaviour requires forgiveness
implies a neglect of duty, and she seems at least dimly aware that
she is being disloyal to her father. This comes nowhere near Elektra's
deep expression of shame to the Chorus and later to her mother
which involves a clear recognition that she has been remiss. More
importantly, Chrysothemis tries to excuse her action by appealing to
the personal need for physical safety while Elektra justifies her breach
by reference to the principles of *aidos* and *eusebeia*, and the conditions in the palace.

This confrontation, coming so closely after Elektra's expressions
of shame to the Chorus, is designed to justify her breach of familial piety by contrasting it with a figure who strictly adheres to this
principle. Sophokles allows us to see the consequences of a rigid
adherence to a code of behaviour without reference to its broader
moral implications. That is, Chrysothemis' action in itself may be
right, but considered in its context is wrong. This is set against
Elektra's actions, which may contravene a code of conduct based on
lesser moral principles, but are justified given the circumstances. The
basic opposition then between the two sisters has its source in the
different spheres in which they move. Elektra has a deeper understanding of *sophron* behaviour, for she defines behaviour according to
the ethical framework of the larger community. Chrysothemis advocates strict obedience to certain codes of behaviour based upon her

subordinate position in the *oikos*, and failing to understand the ethical and moral implications of her actions, is free to pursue her own selfish interests.

3.3 *The Dream of Klytaimnestra*

The confrontation between the two sisters comes to an impasse, as neither sister is able to persuade the other. Although Chrysothemis displays a modest awareness that her behaviour is wrong, she refuses to join Elektra in any form of action. As Chrysothemis is leaving, she reveals to her sister the reason for her appearance: she has been sent by Klytaimnestra to make ritual offerings on Agamemnon's grave as her mother has been frightened by a dream. Chrysothemis recounts it as follows:

> λόγος τις αὐτήν ἐστιν εἰσιδεῖν πατρὸς
> τοῦ σοῦ τε κἀμοῦ δευτέραν ὁμιλίαν
> ἐλθόντος ἐς φῶς· εἶτα τόνδ᾽ ἐφέστιον
> πῆξαι λαβόντα σκῆπτρον οὑφόρει ποτὲ
> αὐτός, τανῦν δ᾽ Αἴγισθος· ἐκ τε τοῦδ᾽ ἄνω
> βλαστεῖν βρύοντα θαλλόν, ᾧ κατάσκιον
> πᾶσαν γενέσθαι τὴν Μυκηναίων χθόνα. (417–23)

> There is a story that she envisioned a second
> intercourse with my father and yours when
> he visited the light. Then he himself who was
> carrying the staff, which Aigisthos now carries,
> took it and fixed it in this hearth; and from it a
> branch burst forth luxuriant above by which
> all Mycenean land was overshadowed.

Dreams are always highly significant in ancient poetry, but we should be careful not to interpret them in a too psychological fashion. For moderns, dreams are generally thought to reflect the unconscious desires or wishes of characters; that is, the origins are sought within the person herself. For the ancients, however, dreams have an external, often divine, origin, and were usually thought to disclose the future.[9] The reactions of Elektra and Klytaimnestra are typical in this regard, as both see it as a portent; for the one it is a sign of

---

[9] See Kessels 1978: 10–11; Del Corno 1982: 55–62 for a discussion of dreams in Greek literature.

hope, and for the other a source of fear. For Elektra, the origin is clearly Agamemnon (459–60) and the dream heralds the return of legitimate rule. Klytaimnestra, on the other hand, is frightened enough by it to send her daughter with ritual offerings to placate Agamemnon, while Chrysothemis either has no ability or no need to interpret the dream; she simply carries out the wishes of her mother. The Chorus, like Elektra, is overjoyed at this news and in the following ode they take courage and hope from the dream, expressing the belief that *Dike* will arrive shortly. For the Chorus, the meaning is so obvious that for it to go unfulfilled would be enough to cast doubt on the efficacy of all prophecy for mankind (497–501).

In the dream Klytaimnestra envisions Agamemnon's return as a δευτέρα ὁμιλία, that is, as a "second intercourse". Earlier commentators such as Jebb have overlooked the sexual connotations of these words, perhaps from a sense of delicacy or prudery.[10] Later commentators, however, such as Kamerbeek and Kells, have no such qualms and see clear sexual connotations in the words. That we are to see a sexual meaning in *homilia* seems clear, as Klytaimnestra's crime is not just the murder of Agamemnon, but her adulterous union with Aigisthos. Symbolically then the dream functions to re-establish the proper and legitimate sexual relationship between Agamemnon and Klytaimnestra, thereby condemning the present sexual union between her and Aigisthos as a form of adultery. Moreover, it establishes the connection between the proper domestic relationship (Agamemnon and Klytaimnestra) and the true political order, for in the dream immediately after the act Agamemnon takes the symbol of political power (the sceptre) and plants it beside the hearth. From this planting of the sceptre springs a fruitful bough which covers all of Mykenai.

---

[10] Jebb *ad* 417 takes ὁμιλίαν to refer to social intercourse; Kamerbeek points out that *homilia* may mean nothing more than "at her side" but he also notes that ὁμιλία and ὁμιλέω are often used of sexual intercourse. Kells also thinks that sexual intercourse is meant. He goes on to ask what would be "more terrible for the guilty women than to dream that she had intercourse with the man she had murdered?" Kells is certainly correct in asserting the sexual meaning of the dream but his modern psychological reading of it as a reflection of Klytaimnestra's guilt is doubtful. Bowman 1997: 141 and n. 18 in a recent article oddly enough sees no sexual undertones in ὁμιλίαν but then goes on to argue that the sceptre is a metaphor for the phallus (Agamemnon's) which is planted in the hearth (Klytaimnestra's womb), and thus the dream sequence is a metaphor for the sexual act. This is dubious psychologising; it seems perverse to argue this way while refusing to see any sexual connotations in ὁμιλίαν, a word which was used to refer to the act itself.

Some have even seen sexual overtones in Agamemnon's planting of
the sceptre in the hearth which reinforce the sexual nature of *homilia*
so that the sceptre becomes a symbol not only of Agamemnon's
political power but of his virility as well.[11] The tree, often a symbol
of fertility and reproduction, which springs from this planting, then
represents Orestes, and its fruitful growth points to his future success and dominion in Mykenai. The meaning for Elektra is plain:
the dream was sent by her father and identifies the legitimate ruler
in the *polis* (σκῆπτρον) and *oikos* (ἐφέστιον) as the offspring of Agamemnon and Klytaimnestra.[12]

As in the *Choephoroi*, the dream serves as an omen to Klytaimnestra,
but the two poets have focused on entirely different elements. Aischylos'
Klytaimnestra dreams of giving birth to a snake, which, when she
suckles it, bites her breast; it has a threatening quality to it and
clearly points to the return and vengeance of Orestes. At its centre
stands the relationship between mother and son, and the unnatural
character of the dream reflects the unnaturalness of a son killing a
mother. Ultimately the dream works against Klytaimnestra, as it
prompts her to send libations to appease the dead man, which brings
about the reunion of Elektra and Orestes; together with the Chorus,
they invoke the spirit of their dead father to return to aid in the
vengeance. In Sophokles' version, the emphasis falls not upon the
matricide, but the re-establishment of the proper familial and political order. More important, it clearly points to the success and future
prosperity of the offspring. There is no need for any invocation of
the spirit of the dead man, for the dream is Agamemnon's endorsement of their deed. Equally significant, the dream provides important confirmation for Elektra's main accusation against her mother.
She is not obsessed with sex as some critics have argued;[13] rather
her claim has always been that Klytaimnestra's sexual alliance with
Aigisthos is a form of adultery, an act destructive of the *oikos* and
the political stability of the *polis*.

---

[11] Kamerbeek *ad* 419–421; Kells *ad* 417ff; Bouvrie 1990: 264 all see sexual undertones here.

[12] Bouvrie 1990: 264 has some sensible remarks to make on the significance of
the dream. She too sees strong sexual connotations in the dream and understands
it as representing the "reproduction of legitimate offspring, the continuity of the
oikos seen as an unbroken line of patrilineally connected generations. The dream
forebodes the restoration of the interrupted descent line."

[13] See Chapter 4 n. 37 below.

3.4 *Ritual Activity*

The performance of a ritual action in any tragedy is generally a highly significant action and careful attention should be paid to the diverse ways in which the poet is able to use ritual as a means to express the central theme or conflict of the play, to indicate the mood or character of dramatic personages, or simply as a way to draw attention to critical moments in the action of the drama.[14] As ritual touches on so many issues and beliefs central to the community, its performance (or lack of performance) may cause conflicts to develop between differing obligations, such as loyalty to family versus duty to the state. This makes ritual action a particularly effective way for the poet to raise complex and difficult moral issues. As Patricia Easterling points out, ritual "provides tragedy with a range of particularly potent metaphors . . . because it was intimately concerned with all the most important perceptions and experiences of the community."[15] Thus the corruption of ritual makes a powerful statement about the collapse or disintegration of the social or political order. Ritual action, however, is also a uniquely stabilizing activity; and, as one of its basic functions is to control and maintain order, especially in the face of disorder, it may just as often be a vehicle for the reintegration and restoration of order to the community.

---

[14] Some of the more important contributions to the study of ritual and tragedy include: Burkert 1966: 87–121; Friedrich 1983: 159–223 and 1996: 257–283 (and the response of Seaford 1996: 284–294); Easterling 1989: 97–109; Foley 1985 and 1993: 101–43; Seaford 1985: 315–323; 1987: 106–130; and 1993: 115–146; Segal 1982; Zeitlin 1965: 463–508. The most relevant works for this study are Foley 1993 and Seaford 1985 and 1994. Foley explores the political dimensions of mourning in tragedy showing how it often portrays the female manipulating and using her command over ritual to control or subvert male authority. By connecting lamentation with deception, resistance to authority, and vendetta, tragedy portrays the mourning woman not only as a socially disruptive force but as dangerous. Seaford takes a much broader approach to ritual, seeing it in connection with tragedy's "expression of the historical contradiction between *oikos* and *polis*." The autonomy of the *oikos* threatens the unity of the *polis* and it is only from its destruction that the commonality of the *polis* finds its survival. Tragedy reflects this conflict by dramatising the perversion of sacrificial ritual involving kin-killing as the vehicle through which the *oikos* is destroyed. Social order is restored not by the return of the disrupted ritual but by the establishment of a new ritual at the level of the *polis* and it, through its rejection of violence and vengeance, becomes the agent of social and political unity. For criticisms of Seaford's argument, see Friedrich 1996: 268–277 and 2000: 115–152. See also note 18 below for a summary of Seaford's argument on the *Elektra*.

[15] Easterling 1989: 108–109.

In the *Elektra*, every character in the play is portrayed with some relationship to ritual activity, from Elektra's continual mourning to the perverted rites and blasphemous prayers of her mother. In this respect, ritual reflects something of the character of the members of this family as well their relationship to the social and political order. Moreover, all the confrontations in the play come about through the performance of some ritual activity: Elektra's initial monody outside the palace gates answered by the Chorus; Chrysothemis' ritual task to bring her mother's offerings to Agamemnon's grave; Klytaimnestra's sacrifice and prayer to Apollo; Chrysothemis' report of Orestes' ritual offerings; the revelation of Orestes' identity motivated by his pity at the sight of his sister's lamentation for him; and the final confrontation between Orestes and Aigisthos prompted by the tyrant's hypocritical desire to lament his 'dead' relative.

In this confrontation, Chrysothemis' appearance on stage is prompted by her ritual mission on behalf of Klytaimnestra.[16] Frightened by her dream, Klytaimnestra has sent her daughter with offerings in an attempt to appease Agamemnon. Chrysothemis is momentarily delayed from carrying out the task by her encounter with Elektra, who is likewise engaged in her ritual of mourning. During their exchange, we see Chrysothemis justifying her acquiescence in tyranny as necessary for her safety and what she calls freedom. Morally weak and inordinately concerned with her own comfort, she is blindly obedient to the commands of her mother. Not only does she fail to recognize the significance of her mother's dream, but she seems only dimly aware of the obvious impropriety of bringing ritual offerings to her father from the woman responsible for his death. Ritual thus serves to underscore her lack of awareness, her moral weakness, and her submission to tyranny. Yet as obedient as Chrysothemis is to the will of her mother, she is still able to recognize the justice of Elektra's cause, and thus when her sister commands her to throw Klytaimnestra's offerings to the wind, she obeys. The ritual action which with this scene ends confirms the rightness of Elektra's position, and results in an alliance between the two sisters who join together to restore the proper ritual norm.

---

[16] Kitzinger 1991: 298–326 treats the ritual action of the play in a fairly detailed manner. See 310–11 for a good analysis of the significance of the ritual elements of this scene.

Although Klytaimnestra has yet to appear, a striking portrait of her emerges from the descriptions of her ritual activity. We have heard of her brutal killing of Agamemnon; her atavistic ritual of purification performed after the murder when she wiped off the bloodstains on Agamemnon's head as a form of ablution; and her mutilation of the body in which she severed his extremities and placed them under his armpits in an attempt to prevent the dead man from carrying out a revenge for his death (445–46). The grotesque perversion of a rite of purification as well as the horrific mutilation of the body emphasize both the barbarity of Klytaimnestra as well as her complete and utter contempt for the propriety of ritual norms. She does not simply neglect to perform the proper funerary rites for her husband; instead, she institutes a new monthly ritual sacrifice, which is nothing more than a celebration of her own crime. John Jones makes a good point about how this ritual act of Klytaimnestra serves to characterize her:

> While Aeschylus makes Clytemnestra's irreligion rest mainly on her parody or inversion of ritual forms, her Sophoclean counterpart is distinguished by the pressure of individual will thrusting her along a solitary course against the tide of traditional religious restraints. The tremendous impersonal blasphemies of the one must be contrasted with the outfacing of propriety which makes the defiance of the other so different, so keenly "personal", in its nature.[17]

The characteristic feature Jones identifies in Klytaimnestra's ritual activity, its deeply individualistic nature, is a quality apparent in all her actions. Motivated by a lust for Aigisthos, she murders her husband to gratify her desires and then continues to renew the original crime each month. Ritual action characterizes Klytaimnestra as someone driven solely by her own desires, who is willing to transgress all norms of behaviour, ritual or otherwise, in order to serve her own ends.

Elektra's ritual actions portray her as the sole character who remains faithful to Agamemnon in the face of all opposition. Mourning him since his death some years earlier, Elektra uses ritual to maintain the proper order of the *oikos*, to keep alive the memory of her father's brutal murder as well as to point to the breach in the

---

[17] Jones 1962: 153.

political and social order caused by the rule of the tyrants.[18] Ritual, for Elektra, is placed in the service of her *oikos*, as a way to maintain its order but, at the same time, it has an ethical basis derived from the communal framework of the *polis*. While her lamentation is the basis of the conflict between her and the other members of her family, it also forms the basis of Elektra's own moral conflict between performing an action which is by some standards right, and by others wrong.

In this confrontation, Elektra's ritual activity identifies her as the faithful upholder of proper ritual activity. Her response to the tainted ritual offerings from Klytaimnestra is to reassert the proper ritual order in the face of her mother's disruption and her sister's weakness. She tells Chrysothemis that it is not ὅσιον or θέμις to bring offerings to Agamemnon from the person who killed him. Klytaimnestra's original act of murder coupled with her barbaric act of mutilation and her continued ritual perversions cannot, Elektra asserts, be absolved by her ritual offerings. She commands her sister to toss them to the wind and gives her sister detailed instructions that reflect her understanding of the proper ritual action. Thus she prevents her mother's misuse of ritual and replaces it with proper rites.

---

[18] Seaford 1985: 315–323 has an argument almost diametrically opposed to my own; he identifies in Elektra's continued mourning a perversion of ritual that is equivalent to her mother's. Klytaimnestra's monthly celebrations of Agamemnon's death "both transgress the temporal limit set to the commemoration of the death and reverse the mood of mourning." Elektra's response—perpetual lamentation— as well subverts the death rites by equally violating their temporal limitation. Aigisthos and Klytaimnestra respond by threatening imprisonment, which is only an intensified form of the mourner's segregation. This reciprocal perversion continues with the murders: Klytaimnestra is killed while ordering the urn containing Orestes' ashes, and Aigisthos is entrapped when he arrives intending to lament Orestes. The final perversion comes with Elektra's declaration that Aigisthus be thrown to the gravediggers most fitting for him: dogs and birds. For Seaford, the *Elektra* is a play marked by a series of rituals, which, perverted by vengeance, finally become the means by which the household destroys itself. This play then, according to Seaford, falls into the pattern that he claims is common in Greek tragedy: the destruction of the royal household on behalf of the *polis*, expressed through the perversion of ritual. But this is far more than a conflict between mother and daughter. Elektra is directly resisting the city's illegitimate rulers and thus her opposition has political consequences. Seaford not only disregards the political implications of Elektra's behaviour, but in claiming that Elektra's lamentation is as perverse as Klytaimnestra's blasphemous ritual action is, he ignores that the two act with contrary purposes. What Seaford calls Elektra's perversion of ritual is at most a technical violation of the time limits imposed on mourning, necessitated by Klytaimnestra's continued perversion of ritual, and in effect to remain faithful to the purpose of the rites, she must continue mourning.

Elektra instructs her sister to cut a lock from her hair and place it on the tomb with a lock of her own. She also gives her sister her girdle and tells her to kneel and pray for help from the dead so that Orestes may return and restore his house. The detailed and precise manner in which she instructs her sister marks Elektra as the possessor of ritual knowledge and as one who uses ritual activity in the proper way and for the right reasons. Not only does the Chorus characterize Elektra's instructions as in accordance with piety (πρὸς εὐσέβειαν), but it suggests that Chrysothemis will show *sophrosyne* if she does as her sister asks:

> Xo. πρὸς εὐσέβειαν ἡ κόρη λέγει· σὺ δέ,
> εἰ σωφρονήσεις, ὦ φίλη, δράσεις τάδε.
> Xp. δράσω· τὸ γὰρ δίκαιον οὐκ ἔχει λόγον
> δυοῖν ἐρίζειν, ἀλλ᾽ ἐπισπεύδει τὸ δρᾶν.
> πειρωμένη δὲ τῶνδε τῶν ἔργων ἐμοὶ
> σιγὴ παρ᾽ ὑμῶν πρὸς θεῶν ἔστω, φίλαι·
> ὡς εἰ τάδ᾽ ἡ τεκοῦσα πεύσεται, πικρὰν
> δοκῶ με πεῖραν τήνδε τολμήσειν ἔτι. (464–71)

> CH. The girl instructs you in line with *eusebeia*; and if
> you are *sophron*, my dear, you will do this.
> CHR. I shall do it; for justice does not allow two
> people to dispute but urges action.
> Let there be silence, friends, by the gods,
> when I attempt the deed, since if mother hears of this,
> I think that I will dare a thing bitter still.

The Chorus' urging of Chrysothemis to follow Elektra's instructions and her willingness to do as her sister asks confirms that Elektra's form of *sophrosyne* is the proper one. Chrysothemis now performs an action that does not require the *sthenos*, the possession of which she had previously made a prerequisite for action, but the moral fortitude on which her sister bases action.[19] For the first time Chrysothemis is called upon to recognize something beyond a regard for safety and comfort, and, although she expresses a certain fear of what may happen if Klytaimnestra finds out, she has brought herself to perform at least what she perceives to be a daring gesture in alliance

---

[19] Blundell 1989: 160 argues that Chrysothemis' action here is not incompatible with her form of *sophrosyne*, as it is a deed that requires no strength, no personal risk and thus Chrysothemis can perform the deed without any danger. Yet lines 469–471 tell against this; Chrysothemis clearly is taking some risk and she does mention reprisal from her mother if she finds out.

with her sister Elektra. More important, her response explicitly vindicates Elektra's idea of justice and implicitly her own failure to live
up to it. With the Chorus' and Chrysothemis' expressed acknowledgement of the rightness of Elektra's actions comes the external
confirmation of her position. The Chorus and the two sisters are
briefly united in a shared act against the rulers of the *polis* on behalf
of their own *oikos*.

Ritual action thus confirms and validates the notions which have
emerged of these three women. In Chrysothemis' case, ritual activity reveals a characteristic moral weakness: she has submitted to
tyranny and thus willingly takes her mother's tainted offerings to
Agamemnon's grave. Her relationship to ritual activity thus reveals
her as one who has subjected her will to another because of fear,
moral cowardice, and self-interest. Yet she is still able to recognize
that Elektra has justice on her side and thus is persuaded by her
sister to make a gesture that acknowledges this. Klytaimnestra on
the other hand is portrayed as the source of the disorder and her
willingness to pervert every form of ritual is only a reflection of her
willingness to break every form of law. Elektra's interpretation of
Klytaimnestra's dream and her instructions to her sister on proper
ritual activity substantiate that her actions are in accordance with
eusebeia and *sophrosyne*.

CHAPTER FOUR

ELEKTRA AND KLYTAIMNESTRA: DIKE VS DIKE?

4.1 *Preliminary Remarks*

After the departure of Chrysothemis to the tomb of Agamemnon, Klytaimnestra comes out of the palace to perform a ritual action on her own behalf. Confronted with the spectacle of her daughter lamenting in public, she harshly rebukes Elektra for her disgraceful behaviour. The two become embroiled in a dispute over the nature of the two killings: the sacrifice of Iphigenia and the murder of Agamemnon. Klytaimnestra claims to have acted with justice while questioning Agamemnon's right to sacrifice Iphigenia. Elektra defends her father while accusing her mother of acting unjustly. Finally, Klytaimnestra asks for silence in order to carry out her sacrifice and prayer to Apollo, which is nothing more than an expression of her desire for her good fortune and a veiled wish for the death of her son.

Most commentators, regardless of their overall interpretation of the play, willingly acknowledge that Elektra emerges as winner of this '*agon*'.[1] For those with a darker reading of the play, it is a hollow victory which only draws attention to the grim irony of Elektra's moral defeat as she reveals herself to be no better than her mother. Those who promote this currently fashionable approach to the play concentrate on construing similarities between Klytaimnestra and Elektra. For them, the resemblance between mother and daughter mirrors the reciprocal nature of the revenge justice operating in the play.[2] On the other side are those with a more positive reading of

---

[1] Erbse 1978: 290 writes: "Elektra geht, vor allem mit diesem für die Mutter beschämenden Nachweis, als Siegerin aus dem Agon hervor." Burton 1980: 203 speaks of how Elektra "demolishes" the arguments of her mother; while Minadeo 1994: 116 calls it an "impeccable rebuttal". Others such as Gellie 1972: 115, while not entirely impressed by the arguments of Elektra, find them much more convincing than Klytaimnestra's. Even Kells *ad* 626f and Segal 1966: 536 who both have a darker reading of the play see Elektra as the winner. See Swart 1984: 23–29 for a good treatment of this scene as well as an overview of various interpretations.

[2] See, for example, Blundell 1989: 149–183; Cairns 1993: 241–249; Seaford 1985: 315–23.

the play, and, for the most part, they have generally seen Elektra's arguments as a convincing, even if somewhat artificial, refutation of her mother's.[3]

At the heart of this debate are the concepts of *dike* and *aidos*. Blundell has analyzed this confrontation and the question of *dike* in terms of the ethical code 'help friends/harm enemies'; while Cairns has treated it with reference to *aidos*. Their arguments are to some degree complementary and to a large extent representative of the current *communis opinio* and therefore I shall restrict myself primarily to addressing their points. With regard to the question of *dike*, most critics assume that it is the principle of revenge justice, the law of *talio* which we see operating (and being superseded) in the *Oresteia*.[4] Blundell argues that the debate between the two women is designed to bring out the irreconcilable conflict which arises when both sides simultaneously pursue the code of 'help friends/harm enemies'.[5] As Blundell points out, this code works best in a military context where it is clear who belongs to which group.[6] Outside this environment, the status of friend/enemy is much harder to determine, and more often than not is simply an arbitrary exercise in which each makes a subjective evaluation of who counts as a friend or enemy. What is lacking is any independent basis on which to judge character or action. Blundell argues that in the *Elektra* 'harm enemies' takes the form of the *lex talionis*, the law of revenge, which simply deals with injustice by the imposition of the original act of wrongdoing in recompense, that is, 'like in return for like' or 'an eye for an eye'. This sets in motion an endless cycle of revenge and retaliation, as each act of justice is at the same time a wrong that demands a similar response in turn. For Blundell, mother and daughter simultaneously

---

[3] Waldock 1966: 180–181 says that "the speech is not logical" and "the reasoning is flawed" but that it is "more than adequate for its purpose; it sweeps her opponent from the field." Burnett 1998: 138 also finds the exchange incoherent but suggests that this is because two angry women are quarrelling rather than "legal theorists". She thinks, however, that Elektra convincingly refutes Klytaimnestra's arguments.

[4] Winnington-Ingram 1980: 221, for instance, claims that the principle of retaliatory justice runs throughout the play. It is the "law which the Erinyes administer, on which Elektra and Orestes intend to act, and under which, if the law is generally valid, they will themselves by liable to retaliation."

[5] Blundell 1989: 149. See Chapter 2 and 261–273 in *Help Friends Harm Enemies* for a useful discussion of this ethical code and some of its limitations.

[6] Blundell 1989: 52–53.

pursue this code, each claiming to have justice on her side. Their arguments only expose the weakness of their cases: while both claim *philia* as the basis for their actions, both equally subvert it. Klytaimnestra places blood-ties to a daughter over marriage ties to a husband, who, as a king, has public obligations, while ignoring her own disruption of the kinship ties. Elektra acts on loyalty to her father while rejecting her mother. She further undermines her own position by her refusal to allow her mother her claim to *talio* justice while relying upon it herself. One argument is as contradictory as the other, but for Blundell this only emphasizes the retaliatory aspect of *dike*, the shared *physis* of mother and daughter and, in the end, the harsh and grim nature of revenge justice.[7]

Cairns, who studies the play in terms of the theme of *aidos*, argues along similar lines and ultimately reaches the same conclusion. Like Blundell, Cairns sees the entire debate between mother and daughter as "representative of a recurrent process of retaliation and mutual recrimination", which reflects the sequence of crime and vengeance haunting the house of Atreus.[8] Each displays a regard for her own *time*, and each sees the other as trying to implicate her in dishonour. When the exchange degenerates into personal abuse, their similarity in nature is all too evident. For Cairns, the theme of *aidos* functions to bring out the similarities and parallels between mother and daughter, thereby drawing attention to the morally dubious aspects of Elektra's behaviour and casting the vengeance in a questionable light.

Both Cairns and Blundell see the confrontation designed to expose the equally personal motives of mother and daughter. Like Klytaimnestra who hides hers behind a claim to justice, Elektra conceals hers behind seemingly rational arguments; she may have a just case to make, but she cannot conceal the fact that she is driven by a hatred and a desire for personal revenge. There is a limited validity to some of these contentions, for honour is a concern for Elektra, and she plainly despises her mother. Yet both Blundell and Cairns overlook the differences brought out in this *agon* between mother and daughter, and both ignore that this conflict is, at least for Elektra, far more than simply a quarrel over personal honour. What emerges

---

[7] Blundell 1989: 161ff.
[8] Cairns 1993: 242.

from this debate is not the tit-for-tat reciprocity of the *lex talionis*, but a *dike* that has clear reference to the motives and attitude of the offender.

4.2 *Dike*

One of the main points in dispute in this confrontation between Elektra and her mother is the question of *dike*. Klytaimnestra begins by openly admitting to the murder of Agamemnon, but claims a personified *Dike* as her accomplice: ἡ γὰρ Δίκη νιν εἷλεν, οὐκ ἐγὼ μόνη (528). Her appeal to justice is usually understood to refer to the principle of *lex talionis* which demands a spilling of blood in return for the original killing. The rest of her speech, however, is not so much a defense of her own actions as it is a condemnation of Agamemnon for his. She argues that he had less claim to Iphigenia as a father than she did as a mother because of her suffering in bearing her (532–33). Having established a greater claim to Iphigenia, Klytaimnestra then proceeds to question the grounds for Agamemnon's sacrifice of his daughter in a speech full of rhetorical flourishes contrived to deflect attention away from the weakness of her own case to the evil of Agamemnon's act.[9] She anticipates the possible defenses of Agamemnon and replies to each in turn, moving from point to point with a strategic swiftness designed to prevent close examination of her arguments. She begins with the question: for whose sake did Agamemnon sacrifice his daughter? If it was on behalf of the Argives, then they had no claim to what is hers (535–36). And if for Menelaos, did he not have two children of his own who ought to have died instead (537–41)? Perhaps, she asks sarcastically, Hades had some desire to feed on her children (542–43) or maybe Agamemnon felt sorrow for his brother's children but not his own (544–45)? The aim is to condemn Agamemnon by considering every possible motivation and then rejecting each in turn as the act of a "foolish and base father" (οὐ ταῦτ' ἀβούλου καὶ κακοῦ γνώμην πατρός 546).

---

[9] The figure she uses here is *hypophora*, a rhetorical device which consists of raising one or more questions and then proceeding to answer them. See Kells *ad* 534–545 for a discussion of it with reference to Klytaimnestra's argument.

Although Klytaimnestra has begun with the assertion of the cooperation of an impersonal and impartial *dike* in the killing of Agamemnon, she makes a case against him based entirely upon personal and
subjective considerations. Rather than buttressing her claim to justice by appealing to some higher principle such as the sanctity of
blood-ties, she supports it by the dubious suggestion that her pain
and suffering give her more right to Iphigenia. Agamemnon's sacrifice
is a crime not because it is an affront to the gods or a violation of
kinship ties, but only because it is an offense committed against her.[10]
The possessive nature of her language (536, 538) reflects, as Blundell
points out, the "proprietorial sense" from which she argues.[11] For
Klytaimnestra, Iphigenia was a possession to which Agamemnon had
no claim. Any sympathy which might be generated for the rights of
an aggrieved mother is thoroughly dispelled with her suggestion that
one of Menelaos' children should have been sacrificed instead of her
own. She never questions the legitimacy of or the necessity for the
sacrifice, but only the choice of victim. In other words, she does not
argue from the rights of a mother, but from a much narrower position: self-interest. There is no independent assessment of the deed;
no appeal to any higher authority independent of her own judgement; nothing to suggest that it was an act worthy of moral condemnation, but only a claim based upon her own personal concerns.
For Klytaimnestra, Agamemnon's act is more an affront to her personal honour than a breach of human or divine law.

As personal and subjective as this perspective is, by the principle
of retaliatory justice, Klytaimnestra would appear to have a valid
claim. *Talio* justice operates without regard to the intentions or motivations of the offender; a person is guilty simply based upon the results
of his act rather than through any examination of cause.[12] Klytaimnestra, however, does not argue from this principle in her consideration of Agamemnon's guilt; instead she argues that his motives
for sacrificing Iphigenia were unacceptable. Klytaimnestra thus implicitly recognizes the importance of intention and motive in deciding
guilt, but in raising the question of motive, she opens the door for

---

[10] Blundell 1989: 161–72 brings out very well the subjective and personal nature
of Klytaimnestra's arguments.

[11] Blundell 1989: 163.

[12] Blundell 1989: 29; see also MacKenzie 1981: 109–112. In *Agamemnon*, the
Chorus states this principle as παθεῖν τὸν ἔρξαντα (1564); see also *Choephoroi* 306–14.

the examination of her own. Elektra in her rejoinder to her mother does just that.

Elektra offers three different arguments in reply to her mother. Before she begins, however, she asserts that the killing of Agamemnon is shameful even if done with justice (558–60). This claim is crucial for establishing Klytaimnestra's lack of *aidos* and will therefore be treated in the section on *aidos* below. For now it is enough to note that Elektra's point here is that an act can be both shameful and just. Having claimed that the killing of Agamemnon was a shameful act, Elektra proceeds to address the question of its justice by challenging Klytaimnestra's motives. She exposes the falseness of her mother's claim to justice by pointing out that she killed her husband, not out of some sense of duty to Iphigenia, but for the sake of an illicit passion for Aigisthos (560–61). She then proceeds to defend her father by mentioning the one reason that Klytaimnestra left out: Artemis' demand for the sacrifice of Iphigenia. She recounts the story of how Agamemnon killed a stag in the grove of Artemis and in boasting about it offended the goddess. Artemis then held the Greeks back at Aulis so that they could sail neither to Troy nor home without the sacrifice of Iphigenia. Agamemnon, Elektra continues, performed the sacrifice against his will and under great constraint:

> κἀκ τοῦδε μηνίσασα Λητῴα κόρη
> κατεῖχ' Ἀχαιούς, ἕως πατὴρ ἀντίσταθμον
> τοῦ θηρὸς ἐκθύσειε τὴν αὐτοῦ κόρην.
> ὧδ' ἦν τὰ κείνης θύματ'· οὐ γὰρ ἦν λύσις
> ἄλλη στρατῷ πρὸς οἶκον οὐδ' ἐς Ἴλιον
> ἀνθ' ὧν, βιασθεὶς πολλὰ τ' ἀντιβὰς μόλις
> ἔθυσεν αὐτήν, οὐχὶ Μενέλεω χάριν. (570–76)

> Because of this, the daughter of Leto, angered
> held back the Greeks, until my father, as
> compensation for the beast, sacrificed his daughter.
> Such was her sacrifice; there was no
> other release for the army to go home or to Troy,
> for the sake of which, much constrained and after much resistance,
> he reluctantly sacrificed her, not for the sake of Menelaos.

Somewhat surprisingly, a number of critics have reacted to this account of the sacrifice with disbelief, ridiculing any suggestion that we are to take this version of events seriously.[13] Yet nothing in the

---

[13] Kells *ad* 566–633 relies more on rhetoric than argument when he suggests that

text substantiates such an accusation; no one disputes Elektra's story or suggests that it is false, and no one, not even Klytaimnestra, offers an alternative version.[14] At first glance, it might appear that we have two different accounts but upon a closer look, it turns out that Klytaimnestra has simply omitted a significant element of the story. Her account never actually states what happens; it only sarcastically enquires into Agamemnon's motives. Elektra, on the other hand, offers a complete rendering of the events at Aulis. Hers is the well known account which accords with the mythological tradition;[15] more important, however, it specifically refutes Klytaimnestra's claim that Agamemnon killed his daughter for the Argives or for Menelaos. He did neither, but acted solely out of necessity. As for the suggestion that it would have been reasonable for some other child to be sacrificed, Elektra's story establishes that it was Iphigenia's parentage which required her death rather than someone else's.[16]

That this is a "trivialization" of the sacrifice which deprives it of its tragic potential is a charge which stems from a misunderstanding of Sophokles' purpose and an inapposite comparison with the sacrifice in *Agamemnon*.[17] Aischylos works from a much broader perspective and has a purpose in mind far different from that of Sophokles.

---

no "intelligent" Greek would believe her version of events. If we are not to believe this story, whose do we believe? It is the only explanation offered and Klytaimnestra does not dispute it. See a recent article by Erp Taalman Kip 1996: 517–536 for good criticisms of Kell's argument and of Winnington-Ingram's charge of trivialization (see also notes 14 and 17 below).

[14] Kells tries to suggest that Elektra's words ὡς ἐγὼ κλύω (566) cast doubt on the veracity of her story. She has only *heard* this version (he points out that hearsay evidence was not admitted into Athenian courts) but this is a too subtle argument; if Sophokles wishes to cast doubt on her words, he could simply have someone challenge them. Moreover, Elektra could only have heard of the sacrifice as she was not there. Erp Taalman Tip 1996: 519 in reply to Kells points out that what Elektra says is 'as *I* am told' not 'as I am *told*', "implying that she is better informed than her mother or that Clytaemnestra is unwilling to accept the truth."

[15] It is similar, as Erp Taalman Kip 1996: 517 points out, to the story in *Cypria* with one important exception: in Sophokles' version, Agamemnon is unable to return home.

[16] This indirectly answers Klytaimnestra's question whether Hades had some desire to feast on her daughter rather than someone else, for, as Blundell points out, from a divine point of view Iphigenia must be sacrificed because of her relationship to her father. Klytaimnestra's argument is, as Blundell observes, nothing more than a "misleading rhetorical flourish" (165).

[17] Winnington-Ingram 1980: 220 argues that Sophokles trivializes the sacrifice so that we are not meant to take it seriously. It is hard to understand this accusation of trivialization unless Winnington-Ingram is comparing this version with the sacrifice in *Agamemnon*; there the focus was on his choice and his decision; here it is not;

He presents the sacrifice of Iphigenia as another link in a chain of events which reaches back into the violent history of the House of Atreus, suggesting the operation of a family curse and a hereditary guilt. At the same time, the focus on Agamemnon's moral dilemma of having to choose between disobeying divine command or violating the blood-ties of the *oikos* allows the element of personal motives to enter into the equation: although the deed is forced upon Agamemnon, he is also driven by the desire for glory and success at Troy. Thus once he dons the yoke strap of necessity and decides to sacrifice his daughter (*Ag.* 218–21), he becomes increasingly committed to this decision. As Martha Nussbaum puts it, Agamemnon "begins to cooperate inwardly with necessity, arranging his feelings to accord with his fortune."[18] In the end, what we watch is not a man acting against his will, but someone who has been convinced of the piety and rightness of the sacrifice, and thus carries it out with a passionate desire for it: παυσανέμου γὰρ θυσίας παρθενίου θ᾽ αἵματος ὀργᾷ περιοργῷ σ<φ>᾽ ἐπιθυμεῖν θέμις· (*Ag.* 214–17). The Chorus sings of the horror and impiety of the deed, clearly holding Agamemnon responsible for it. None of this exists in the Sophoclean version, but this hardly warrants the accusation of trivialization. Sophokles' focus in this play is not on the decision of Agamemnon, but on the guilt of Klytaimnestra. To explore the 'tragic potential' of his decision would require an extended and ultimately an entirely different treatment of this scene. The consequences of this would be the dissipation of all tension and conflict between mother and daughter whose debate is at least as much over the wrongs committed by Klytaimnestra as it is over those done by Agamemnon. Indeed, the force of Sophokles' version suggests that he wants his Agamemnon as little guilty as possible, for he presents him as a man entirely constrained by external circumstances to commit an act against his will: ἀνθ᾽ ὧν, βιασθεὶς πολλὰ τ᾽ ἀντιβὰς μόλις ἔθυσεν αὐτήν (575–76). Sophokles reinforces the necessity of Agamemnon's decision and the compelling circum-

---

this hardly trivializes it. Blundell 1989: 167 following Winnington-Ingram claims that Elektra "manipulates the events of Aulis so as to support the rhetoric of her own case, thereby belittling their tragic potential. It is unclear what version Elektra is supposed to be manipulating since nothing else is offered.

[18] Nussbaum 1986: 34. The question of the guilt of Agamemnon in Aischylos' *Oresteia* is a much debated topic. For a good treatment of this problem as well as a useful overview of the scholarship, see Conacher 1987: 12–15 and the more detailed treatment of this question at 85–96.

stances by refusing him any alternative: he can neither go home nor to Troy (οὐ γὰρ ἦν λύσις ἄλλη στρατῷ πρὸς οἶκον οὐδ᾽ ἐς Ἴλιον. 573–74).[19] As Erp Taalman Kip points out, "this considerably lessens Agamemnon's guilt, while Klytaimnestra is largely deprived of what might have been a righteous motive for her deed. The other motive, her adulterous love, now carries all the weight."[20]

As contrived as Elektra's account may strike some and as much as Winnington-Ingram reminds us that after all Agamemnon "did kill his daughter",[21] the story provides important information which speaks specifically to motivation. Apparently, Sophokles wants us to consider *why* Agamemnon killed Iphigenia, and thus has Elektra add οὐ . . . λύσις ἄλλη . . . πρὸς οἶκον οὐδ᾽ ἐς Ἴλιον. When we remember that the debate is in part about *why* Klytaimnestra killed Agamemnon, we see that the contrast in motives suggests that this is not murder for murder, but two separate incidents: a sacrifice demanded by a goddess and a killing driven by the adulterous passion for another man. Klytaimnestra may try to link the two, but she can only do so by hiding her own motives and imputing false ones to Agamemnon.

Elektra's second argument is a rhetorical move in which she grants the legitimacy of Klytaimnestra's defence in order to demonstrate to her that by the terms of her notion of justice, she should expect to die as well:

> εἰ δ᾽ οὖν, ἐρῶ γὰρ καὶ τὸ σόν, κεῖνον θέλων
> ἐπωφελῆσαι ταῦτ᾽ ἔδρα, τούτου θανεῖν
> χρῆν αὐτὸν οὕνεκ᾽ ἐκ σέθεν; ποίῳ νόμῳ;
> ὅρα τιθεῖσα τόνδε τὸν νόμον βροτοῖς
> μὴ πῆμα σαυτῇ καὶ μετάγνοιαν τίθης.
> εἰ γὰρ κτενοῦμεν ἄλλον ἀντ᾽ ἄλλου, σύ τοι
> πρώτη θάνοις ἄν, εἰ δίκης γε τυγχάνοις.
> ἀλλ᾽ εἰσόρα μὴ σκῆψιν οὐκ οὖσαν τίθης. (577–84)

---

[19] Jones 1962: 158 points out how Sophokles' version "gives the plight of the commander and his men a wholly new aspect, with the result that Agamemnon's status is no longer called upon to bear the full weight of his dilemma. He cannot disband his army, even if he wants to." The other important element in this account is that Iphigenia's sacrifice is presented as a punishment for Agamemnon's *hybris*. His crime was boasting about the killing of the stag of Artemis, making the sacrifice of Iphigenia Agamemnon's punishment; that it is a heavy punishment is suggested by his strong resistance to the deed.

[20] Erp Taalman Kip 1996: 517.

[21] Winnington-Ingram 1980: 220 n. 15 and 232.

> But even if he had done this to help him, for I
> shall state your version also, was it necessary
> for him to die on account this by your hand? By what principle?
> Take care that in establishing this law for mortals
> that you are not establishing pain and repentance for yourself.
> For if we are to take a life for a life, then you would, you know,
> be the first to die, if you were to receive justice.
> But see to it that you do not put forward an excuse
> which has no substance.

These words are often thought to carry ominous implications for her and Orestes.[22] Kells, for instance, writes:

> In these lines we have the crux of the whole ethical situation of the play: if retributive killing is wrong (δίκη in that sense), then Elektra's and Orestes' killing of their mother is going to be just as wrong as was Klytaimnestra's killing of Agamemnon. Elektra condemns herself out of her own mouth.[23]

Kells, however, misses the point. Elektra never says that retributive killing is wrong;[24] rather she adopts the rationale of Klytaimnestra in order to show that by her own argument, she would be the first to die.[25] This is not an argument against *talio* justice, but the exposure of a specious claim to it.[26] Those who argue that Elektra unwittingly condemns herself with these words assume that she fails to see the applicability of this law to herself. Yet she refers to the law as a general principle applicable to everyone, including herself using

---

[22] Blundell 1989: 168 argues that Elektra undermines her own case with her rhetorical concession. So too Gellie 1972: 110 who suggests that the *lex talionis* is "an awkward principle for a person intent on murder." Bowra 1944: 238 grasps the strategy much better when he writes that Elektra is concerned with refuting Klytaimnestra's argument here and thus "meets her on her own ground and shows her wrong even on that."

[23] Kells *ad* 582f. See also Winnington-Ingram 1980: 220–21.

[24] This point is also made by Swart 1984: 26 and Burnett 1998: 137 n. 57.

[25] See Swart 1984: 26 who criticizes the arguments of Kells and Johansen for overlooking the rhetorical nature of Elektra's argument. See also note 26 below.

[26] Heath 1987: 136–137 makes an important point when he remarks that too many critics overlook the function of rhetoric in tragedy with often "disastrous" results. He argues that rhetoric in tragedy has a "centrifugal, self-contained tendency". Heath takes particular issue with Kells' view of these lines, believing that they belong to a reading of the play that is "irretrievably faulty". As he says, "an audience used to the conventions of tragic rhetoric would receive them as making a case against Clytaemnestra, but would not be inclined to explore their implications beyond this limited context." See Cairns 1993: 247 n. 107 for his reply to Heath.

the first person plural (εἰ γὰρ κτενοῦμεν ἄλλον ἀντ᾽ ἄλλου 582).
Elektra does not see their conflict in terms of *talio* justice, evident
from her adoption of a strategy that demonstrates her mother's guilt
by reasons that are beyond the code of revenge justice; hence her
focus on Klytaimnestra's motives.

Elektra's third argument in reply to her mother is the most dam-
aging as it condemns her on grounds other than the killing of
Agamemnon and for crimes against which Klytaimnestra has no
defense, that is, her present behaviour:

> εἰ γὰρ θέλεις, δίδαξον ἀνθ᾽ ὅτου τανῦν
> αἴσχιστα πάντων ἔργα δρῶσα τυγχάνεις,
> ἥτις ξυνεύδεις τῷ παλαμναίῳ, μεθ᾽ οὗ
> πατέρα τὸν ἀμὸν πρόσθεν ἐξαπώλεσας,
> καὶ παιδοποιεῖς, τοὺς δὲ πρόσθεν εὐσεβεῖς
> κἀξ εὐσεβῶν βλαστόντας ἐκβαλοῦσ᾽ ἔχεις.
> πῶς ταῦτ᾽ ἐπαινέσαιμ᾽ ἄν; ἢ καὶ ταῦτ᾽ ἐρεῖς,
> ὡς τῆς θυγατρὸς ἀντίποινα λαμβάνεις;
> αἰσχρῶς δ᾽, ἐάν περ καὶ λέγῃς. οὐ γὰρ καλὸν
> ἐχθροῖς γαμεῖσθαι τῆς θυγατρὸς οὕνεκα. (585–94)

> Explain, if you will, why you are doing the most
> shameful thing of all, you who are sleeping
> with the murderer, with whom before
> you killed my father, and having children by him,
> while you have cast out your former children
> who are respectful and born of respectful
> parents. How could I approve of this?
> Or will you say that this too is taken in payment
> for your daughter? If you do say this, it will be
> a shameful thing to say; for it is not honourable
> to share the marriage bed with enemies for the sake of your daughter.

Elektra's point is simple but effective: her mother's present behaviour cannot be justified by the principle of *talio* justice, which does
not sanction sleeping with Aigisthos and replacing Agamemnon's children with his. We can now discern Elektra's strategy in her arguments against her mother and the reason for the recurring emphasis
on her mother's sexual behaviour. Only a consideration of motive
is able to expose the true nature of her mother's crimes. The Chorus
identified *eros* as the driving force behind the actions of Klytaimnestra
early on in the action (297), and Elektra's arguments here confirm
the validity of its judgement. This third argument clinches her case
against her mother and provides conclusive proof that her mother

did not act according to the *lex talionis*. Klytaimnestra's real crime
has always been her adulterous union with Aigisthos; from this act,
all other crimes emanate. By identifying, and focusing on, motivation, Elektra is able to condemn her mother and vindicate her father.[27]

Commentators have for the most part seen nothing other than
the principle of *talio* justice running through this scene and the play
as a whole.[28] Blundell makes the best case for this view in her discussion of the play. She argues that both Klytaimnestra and Elektra
apply in a personal fashion the law of *talio*. When there are no independent grounds upon which to judge character or action, there can
be no escape from the endless vendetta of retributive killing. Each
claims the justice of her position, while denying it to her opponent.
Blundell concludes then "if both rely on the same principle, while
each denying it to the other, then both claims to neutrality are undermined."[29] Yet Klytaimnestra's defence of *talio* justice is a mask designed
to hide her true motives while Elektra raises the question of revenge
only to dismiss her mother's claims to it as false. More important,
both the arguments of Klytaimnestra and Elektra acknowledge the
necessity of examining the motives of the offender in deciding guilt,
Klytaimnestra's implicitly and Elektra's explicitly. The consideration
of motive goes beyond *talio* justice and establishes an independent
basis on which to judge the actions of the offenders. The theme of
aidos will establish an independent basis on which to judge character and attitude, and we shall see here, as well, important differences
between Elektra and her mother.

4.3   *The Theme of Aidos*

The theme of *aidos* has already been raised in the exchange between
the Chorus and Elektra; there it had revealed the moral dilemma
in which Elektra is caught: no matter what she does, she will breach
a form of *eusebeia*. As we recall, she chose to show her *aidos* and *eusebeia* towards her father and community over a narrower form of

---

[27] The continual harping on Klytaimnestra's adultery is not evidence of Elektra's
obsession with sex, as so many critics allege, but part of her strategy in exposing
the true nature of her mother's crimes. See note 37 below on this point.

[28] Stinton 1986: 81 is one of the few exceptions in this regard.

[29] Blundell 1989: 267.

aidos: maternal authority. At the same time, her expression of shame showed her recognition that her behaviour was in some respect discreditable. In the current exchange, we see a similar pattern: Elektra's behaviour is simultaneously an example of her maintenance of communal standards and a breach of familial respect. While Elektra chooses one over the other, she recognizes that this choice does not free her from the authority of those ties which she now rejects. In other words, her *aidos* involves her in a moral conflict between what are now, because of her mother's actions, rival and incompatible ethical demands. Cairns may be correct in pointing to the bitter and at times personal nature of this quarrel, for there is a degree of hostility between mother and daughter unparalleled in Greek tragedy. This, however, does not reduce it to the battle over personal honour as Cairns alleges, for Elektra is defending more than her own honour and it is she who, at the most bitter moment in the quarrel, expresses her sense of shame. In focusing almost exclusively on Elektra's breach of *aidos*, Cairns ignores that her behaviour at the same time upholds other standards of behaviour; thus he fails to acknowledge the degree to which *aidos* serves in establishing important differences in the character and attitude of mother and daughter.

As Cairns rightly points out, mother and daughter accuse one another of shameful deeds. Klytaimnestra begins with the charge that Elektra shames her family by lamenting publicly outside the palace and showing no respect for her mother. With Aigisthos away, Klytaimnestra claims that her daughter fails to show her the respect she deserves; that is, Elektra breaches a familial form of *eusebeia*. She goes on to define precisely what this disrespect involves: Elektra publicly states that her mother is bold or insolent (θρασεῖα 521); that her mother's form of political rule is unjust (πέρα δίκης 521); and that she treats her daughter and what is hers (σὲ καὶ τὰ σά 522) in a hybristic fashion. Klytaimnestra only answers Elektra's final charge, claiming that she is innocent of *hybris*; she only responds in kind to the abuse she suffers at the hands of her daughter. In other words, Klytaimnestra, by interpreting Elektra's behaviour as a flagrant affront to her personal honour, justifies her own conduct by the need to retaliate. In ignoring Elektra's other charges, Klytaimnestra reveals the weakness of her position: she has no defense against her daughter's charges of political injustice. She thus tries to restrict the quarrel to a personal level where her claim has some legitimacy. At the level of personal honour, each has a valid accusation to make against the other: Elektra is guilty of acting disrespectfully to her mother, and Klytaimnestra shows no regard for Elektra's honour. In this respect, Cairn's argument has a limited validity, as each shows concern for personal honour and responds to the other's abuse of it. Elektra's accusations against her mother, however, involve more than simply the charge that her mother insults her honour and, for her, this is far more than a battle over personal honour. Klytaimnestra unwittingly reveals this when she identifies Elektra's reason (or "pretext"—πρόσχημα, as she calls it at 525) for making these accusations against her: her murder of Agamemnon (525–26). Not only do Klytaimnestra's words καθυβρίζουσα καὶ σὲ καὶ τὰ σά, as Campbell says, recognize "that Elektra's complaints were never for herself alone, but for her father",[30] but it is quite apparent from the various charges Elektra makes that she is responding to far more than her mother's mistreatment of her. In focusing on her mother's unjust rule and her insolence, Elektra elevates the debate beyond the level of personal grievances and individual retaliation. She attaches a greater moral significance to her mother's wrong-doing so that her actions are not just a violation of Elektra's personal honour but contravene, as we shall see, the ethical foundation of the κοινωνία πολιτική. A regard for personal honour then is not Elektra's exclusive or even primary motivation; even Klytaimnestra recognizes this (525).

Klytaimnestra has accused her daughter of shameful behaviour, but Elektra has her own charge of shamelessness to make. To her mother's admission that she killed Agamemnon, Elektra replies:

καὶ δὴ λέγω σοι. πατέρα φὴς κτεῖναι. τίς ἂν
τούτου λόγος γένοιτ' ἂν αἰσχίων ἔτι,
εἴτ' οὖν δικαίως εἴτε μή; λέξω δέ σοι,
ὡς οὐ δίκῃ γ' ἔκτεινας, ἀλλά σ' ἔσπασεν
πειθὼ κακοῦ πρὸς ἀνδρός, ᾧ τανῦν ξύνει. (558–62)

Well, I put it to you. You say that you killed father.
What statement could be more shameful than this,
whether it was justly done or not? And I will tell you
that you killed him not by justice but persuasion led
you on by that base man, with whom you now live.

Elektra's accusation that her mother's killing of Agamemnon was shameful even if it were done with justice has been interpreted in

---

a number of ways.[31] Cairns claims that Elektra's words here point to the fundamental problem lying at the heart of this family conflict:

> ... injustice, wrong, or insult against oneself or a member of one's family calls forth retribution (*dike*), and the requirement to pursue *dike* is a powerful one, but to pursue it within one's own family must inevitably involve an action which is *aischron*.[32]

This, to be sure, is at the root of Elektra's moral conflict, for *aidos* requires her to pursue *dike*, but it also leaves her in the position of breaching a form of familial *eusebeia*, behaviour which is *aischron*. Unfortunately for Cairns' argument, such a dilemma does not lie behind Klytaimnestra's behaviour. The whole point of Elektra's reply, as we saw earlier, was that her mother was never pursuing *dike* in her killing of Agamemnon, but was gratifying her own passion for Aigisthos. Cairns assumes that mother and daughter are both in pursuit of justice for entirely personal reasons and thus sees their motives as being of the same moral stamp. Blundell, on the other hand, thinks that Elektra's pronouncement "must mean that in virtue of their relationship a wife is never justified in killing her husband, even if the killing is just according to the *talio*", and goes on to argue that these

---

[31] Adkins 1960: 156 and 185 argues that this statement is "Sophocles' solution to the problem set by the crime in the family." He sees Elektra as upholding the traditional beliefs as found in Homer where an action that is *aischron* is worse than an action that is unjust: "to say that an action is *aischron* is to play the ace of trumps: to justify performing it, one cannot press the claim that it is *dikaion*, for this is of less importance, but must maintain that it is in fact not *aischron* at all." Johansen 1964: 18 argues similarly that *dikaion* is subordinated to *aischron* ("Das αἶσχος bleibt also bestehen ungeachtet Recht oder Unrecht. Die Frage des δίκαιον is in dieser Sache der des αἰσχρὸν untergeordnet"), which for him holds disturbing implications for the position of Elektra. For these two scholars then, to call an act *aischron* is to subject it to a higher standard than that of *dikaion*, the assumption being that *aischron* is a stronger term of moral condemnation that overrides the justice of the act. Yet there is nothing to suggest that *aischron* outranks *dikaion* on some moral scale of values; rather what we have here is the precise same ethical dilemma underlying Elektra's conduct: a single action which is by some standards just, and by another, shameful; we can only tip the scales in favour of one or the other when we take into account what these standards or codes of conduct are. Adkins' argument has been criticized by a number of commentators: see Stinton 1986: 77–78; Blundell 1989: 166–67 and Cairns 1993: 243–44. Blundell argues that Adkins is wrong to suggest a Sophoclean innovation here. That a deed can be both just and shameful is not the solution for Blundell, but part of the problem. Cairns points out that there are examples of people admitting that they have acted in a way which may be judged disgraceful but justify it by claiming some higher imperative (Sophokles fr. 352 Radt).

[32] Cairns 1993: 244.

words carry ill-omened connotations for Elektra, for if the conjugal tie overrules *talio* justice so should the kinship tie.[33] It is not altogether clear why Elektra's statement must mean what Blundell says, for Elektra does not say that a wife is never justified in killing her husband, she only says that to kill a husband, however justly, is a shameful act. That is, she recognizes that an act can be both just and shameful. This admission will have implications for Elektra later, as we shall see, but what she criticizes in this confrontation is her mother's attitude towards her offence and what this signifies. In openly admitting to killing Agamemnon without shame or regret, Klytaimnestra reveals her profound lack of respect for the ties which should exist between husband and wife (ἐγὼ μὲν οὖν οὐκ εἰμὶ τοῖς πεπραγμένοις δύσθυμος· 549–50). Underlying Blundell's argument is an assumption that at some point there was a conflict for Klytaimnestra between competing claims: blood-ties versus marriage ties. Elektra's point, however, is that her mother never acknowledged the authority of conjugal ties; in other words, for Klytaimnestra, there was never any struggle between rival claims with blood-ties in the end triumphing over marriage ties, but simply one over-riding concern: self-interest. Because Klytaimnestra's motivations do not have their source in any of the ties of the human community (either the natural or ethical ties of the *oikos* or the civic ties of the *polis*), but in her own desires, she is unable to recognize anything wrong with them. In not recognizing the shamefulness of the act, Klytaimnestra reveals she has no disposition for *aidos*, as one needs *aidos* to experience *aischune*.[34] In other words, what Elektra exposes is her mother's complete lack of *aidos*. If this were as far as she went, Klytaimnestra could be condemned for her lack of shame (while still admitting that the act was just) but Elektra goes on to show that it was not by justice either. In the end, as we shall see, Klytaimnestra will be condemned for a deed that is both *aischron* and *adikon*.

Elektra has called her mother's killing of Agamemnon *aischron* (559) but what some have found surprising is her designation of Klytaim-

---

[33] Blundell 1989: 166–67. Her argument is basically this: if it is unjust to break the marriage bond, it is unjust to break blood-ties. One could argue, however, that because marriage is based upon ethics and conscious choice, while blood-ties are based upon biology, it is a higher bond than blood-ties. Elektra's argument then would rest upon a hierarchy which recognizes that the conjugal tie is more important than the tie of blood.

[34] Cairns 1993: 417.

nestra's adulterous union as the most shameful act of all.[35] Surely murder is worse than adultery? This is the point at which to deal with Elektra's alleged obsessions with sex which some critics have seen in her words. Woodard, for instance, says that she "locates the source of the family ills in lust" and calls her "sex-ridden".[36] Segal thinks her hatred has its source not just in Klytaimnestra's "unmotherly and unwifely behaviour but also in a deep sexual rivalry and resentment";[37] while Cairns claims that Elektra sees her sexual union with Aigisthos as specifically designed to undermine her status, but in a footnote suggests that it may refer "to the distaste Elektra feels for the [sexual] acts themselves".[38] No doubt there is an intended contrast drawn between the sexual license of her mother and the enforced chastity of Elektra, but we should understand this with regard to the social and cultural context in which this occurs rather than with reference to modern psychology. Elektra is not expressing aversion to the sexual act nor should we imagine that she is envious of her mother's free-wheeling sexuality. Rather her chastity reflects Klytaimnestra's and Aigisthos' denial of her social and biological role in the community while her mother's adulterous behaviour violates the conjugal tie and the laws of the *polis*. Moreover, when we consider the seriousness with which the Athenians treated adultery, Elektra's accusation is less puzzling; it may in fact reflect the extent to which she is governed by masculine and democratic ideals of the *polis* than give any deep insight into her psyche. For the Athenians, adultery was not solely a concern to the *oikos*, but to the *polis* as well, as this often debated passage from Lysias' speech shows:

οὕτως, ὦ ἄνδρες, τοὺς βιαζομένους ἐλάττονος ζημίας ἀξίους ἡγήσατο εἶναι ἢ τοὺς πείθοντας· τῶν μὲν γὰρ θάνατον κατέγνω, τοῖς δὲ διπλῆν ἐποίησε

---

[35] Blundell 1989: 168–169. For Blundell, the implication is plain. If Klytaimnestra repays murder with adultery, what of repaying adultery with murder?

[36] Woodard 1964: 166.

[37] Segal 1981: 261. See also Winnington-Ingram 1980: 231 who claims that it would be "perverse to deny that there is a sexual component in the Sophoclean Electra's hatred of her mother, her hatred of Aigisthos"; and Ewans 1984: 145 who sees the strong sexual element of Strauss' opera (Elektra's sexual obsession with her father, her hostility at her mother for replacing him with Aigisthos; her "feeling that Klytemnestra was inadequate as a sexual partner to the true king") already "set out fairly explicitly in Sophokles' exposition."

[38] Cairns 1993: 241 & n. 93. Jones 1962: 149–53 has a much more balanced treatment of the sexual theme of the play pointing out that Sophokles designs the confrontation so that "it becomes inescapably relevant to enquire why Clytemnestra killed her husband." (p. 151).

τὴν βλάβην, ἡγούμενος τοὺς μὲν διαπραττομένους βία ὑπὸ τῶν βιασθέντων μισεῖσθαι, τοὺς δὲ πείσαντας οὕτως αὐτῶν τὰς ψυχὰς διαφθείρειν, ὥστ᾽ οἰκειοτέρας αὐτοῖς ποιεῖν τὰς ἀλλοτρίας γυναῖκας ἢ τοῖς ἀνδράσι, καὶ πᾶσαν ἐπ᾽ ἐκείνοις τὴν οἰκίαν γεγονέναι, καὶ τοὺς παῖδας ἀδήλους εἶναι ὁποτέρων τυγχάνουσιν ὄντες, τῶν ἀνδρῶν ἢ τῶν μοιχῶν. ἀνθ᾽ ὧν ὁ τὸν νόμον τιθεὶς θάνοτον αὐτοῖς ἐποίησε τὴν ζημιάν. (1.32–1.34)

> Thus the lawgiver, sirs, considered that those who use force deserve a less penalty than those who use persuasion; for the latter he condemned to death, whereas for the former he doubled the damages, considering that those who achieve their ends by force are hated by the persons forced; while those who use persuasion corrupted thereby their victims' souls, thus making the wives of others more closely attached to themselves than to their husbands, and got the whole house into their hands, and caused uncertainty as to whose the children really were, the husbands' or the adulterers'. In view of all this the author of the law made death their penalty.[39]

A woman's chastity is of a concern not just to her family but to the state as a whole, as a seduced woman is more likely to pass off the adulterer's children as her husband's, making claims to inheritance and to citizenship doubtful. Not only has a woman with a lover (μοιχός) taken control of her own sexuality, but she has placed the satisfaction of her sexual desires above the interests of her husband, children, and the future of the *oikos*. In this play, Klytaimnestra has been "persuaded" by Aigisthos, who, as a result, has gained custody of all Agamemnon's possessions, including his right to rule. Even worse, Klytaimnestra has not just cast doubt on claims of inheritance, she has deprived the legitimate children of their social and political functions. Elektra designates the *moicheia* of her mother as the αἴσχιστα πάντων ἔργα (586) because it is the *fons et origo* of all

---

[39] *On the Murder of Eratosthenes* 1.32–34 (trans. by W.R.M. Lamb) This passage has sparked debate over whether the Athenians considered adultery a worse crime than rape. See Harrison 1968: 34; Pomeroy 1975: 86–87; MacDowell 1978: 124; and Cole 1984: 97–113 who all argue that seduction was seen as worse than sexual assault. Harris 1990: 370–377 on the other hand argues that both were treated with equal severity. For other discussions of *moicheia* see Cohen 1984: 147–165 and 1991: 98–132, 133–70; the recent discussion between Cantarella 1991: 289–296 and Foxhall 1991: 297–304; Blundell 1995: 125–26; and Foxhall 1998: 132–33. The punishment for an adulterous woman was less severe. Her husband was legally bound to divorce her or risk losing citizen rights. The woman was barred from participating in any religious activities and any man who saw her attending one could tear off her clothes and beat her. Aischines (1.183) says "the lawgiver seeks to disgrace such a woman and make her life intolerable."

of Klytaimnestra's crimes: it drove her to kill Agamemnon; it caused the exile of her son; and it has resulted in the replacement of his children with those of Aigisthos. While Agamemnon's death deprived the *oikos* of its head and the *polis* of its ruler, Klytaimnestra's continued adultery threatens to destroy the *oikos* completely, for it destroys its future and has serious political consequences in that it leaves the *polis* enslaved to tyranny. It is this which makes it the αἴσχιστα πάντων ἔργα—not Elektra's difficulties with sexuality.

Each has made her charges of shamelessness against the other and Klytaimnestra, as we have seen, has defended herself on grounds that she is simply responding to her daughter's abuse. Elektra has her own defense of her shameless behaviour. To her mother's charge that she abuses her, Elektra responds:

> ἀλλ' οὐ γὰρ οὐδὲ νουθετεῖν ἔξεστί σε,
> ἢ πᾶσαν ἵης γλῶσσαν ὡς τὴν μητέρα
> κακοστομοῦμεν. καί σ' ἔγωγε δεσπότιν
> ἢ μητέρ' οὐκ ἔλασσον εἰς ἡμᾶς νέμω,
> ἢ ζῶ βίον μοχθηρόν, ἔκ τε σοῦ κακοῖς
> πολλοῖς ἀεὶ ξυνοῦσα τοῦ τε συννόμου. (595–600)

> But no, it is not possible to admonish you,
> who send forth every kind of voice that I
> slander my mother. And yet I consider
> you more a mistress than a mother to me.
> Indeed I live a laborious life, always living with
> many torments because of you and your consort.

Elektra's charge that her mother acts more like a δεσπότις than a μήτηρ has been interpreted as her rejection of blood-ties. Blundell, for instance, claims that Elektra's words reflect the problematic nature of her argument, as blood ties cannot be invalidated at the will of the speaker.[40] Elektra may argue, Blundell says, that Klytaimnestra has forfeited the rights of kinship based on her actions, but this does not give her the right to disown their natural relationship. Yet Elektra's description of her mother as a δεσπότις is not the outright rejection of blood ties that Blundell sees, for she does not disown their natural relationship as much as establish the contradictory aspects of her mother's claim to justice. Indeed Elektra speaks in terms of more and less: "for me, you are *more* a mistress than a mother" (598).

---

[40] Blundell 1989: 166.

More important, as we shall see, Elektra's expression of shame shows that she still recognizes the authority of blood-ties. Klytaimnestra's defence depends upon accepting that kinship ties are the highest bonds, a sound enough argument were it not coming from a woman whose present actions so plainly do not recognize the ties of blood, as Elektra points out. Obligations of kinship, for Klytaimnestra, are something to be recognized at her own convenience; that is, to demand respect from her daughter while refusing to show any regard for her own duties and obligations as a mother in her treatment of Elektra and Orestes.

Perhaps the most controversial aspect of this confrontation is the statement with which Elektra ends her speech to her mother. Not only does she seem to admit to sharing a *physis* with her mother, but her confession of shame even seems to indicate how much she has become like her enemies:

> τοῦδέ γ᾽ οὕνεκα
> κήρυσσέ μ᾽ εἰς ἅπαντας, εἴτε χρῇς κακήν
> εἴτε στόμαργον εἴτ᾽ ἀναιδείας πλέαν.
> εἰ γὰρ πέφυκα τῶνδε τῶν ἔργων ἴδρις,
> σχεδόν τι τὴν σὴν οὐ καταισχύνω φύσιν. (605–9)

> As far as that goes
> denounce me to all, whether you declare that
> I am worthless, loudmouthed, or full of *anaideia*
> if I am familiar by nature with such deeds,
> I hardly put your nature to shame.[41]

---

[41] The response of the Chorus (ὁρῶ μένος πνέουσαν· εἰ δὲ σὺν δίκῃ ξύνεστι, τοῦδε φροντίδ᾽ οὐκέτ᾽ εἰσορῶ. 610–11) to these words of Elektra has caused some debate. Some see the Chorus as referring to Elektra: Jebb *ad* 610; Booth 1977: 466–67; Burton 1980: 187; Gardiner 1986: 149f; Blundell 1989: 169–70. In support of this view, it is argued that nowhere else in the extant plays of Sophokles do we have an instance of a Chorus ignoring a speech and instead commenting upon an action which takes place during the speech. Blundell argues (citing Burton and Gardiner in support) that we should expect the Chorus to comment on the preceding speech. Others take them as referring to Klytaimnestra: Gregor 1950: 87–8; Campbell; Kells; Kamerbeek *ad loc*. Campbell argues that Klytaimnestra's reply suggests that she is responding to the Chorus. Kamerbeek thinks that it is unlikely the Chorus would be calling into question Elektra's concern for justice while Kells argues that Klytaimnestra has clearly lost her temper and the Chorus is commenting on that. The text itself does not offer any help here, but both Campbell and Kamerbeek's arguments seem to have more validity based as they are on internal evidence of the play, while the opposing side relies primarily on evidence external to the play. See also Lilley 1975: 309–311 who proposes that the lines be assigned to Klytaimnestra instead of the Chorus. Mastronarde 1979: 34

Cairns, rightly, sees the words as evidence of Elektra's lack of *aidos* for her mother but more significant for him is the similarity in their *physis*. There is, of course, a certain irony in Elektra's words, for in admitting that her behaviour makes her the daughter of her mother, she must concede a lack of *aidos*. This, however, is an affected irony, employed in order to entangle her mother in a charge of shamelessness. Cairns admits as much, but wants to see more in these words. For him, the real irony works behind Elektra's back in that what she thinks is ironic is actually true, namely that "the similarity in *phusis* between the two is genuine."[42] Yet this is to overwork the irony, which is simply a rhetorical concession granted in order to make an accusation against her mother.[43] It is similar to her earlier strategy against her mother at 577–79 when she had granted her mother's argument in order to defeat it on its own grounds. Here, she admits to shameful behaviour, but does so in order to score points against her mother. That the remark hits home is evident from Klytaimnestra's response: she is outraged and charges her daughter with *hybris* (613) and shamelessness (615). It is at this point that Elektra expresses her deep sense of shame at her behaviour:

> εὖ νῦν ἐπίστω τῶνδέ μ' αἰσχύνην ἔχειν,
> κεἰ μὴ δοκῶ σοι· μανθάνω δ' ὀθούνεκα
> ἔξωρα πράσσω κοὐκ ἐμοὶ προσεικότα.
> ἀλλ' ἡ γὰρ ἐκ σοῦ δυσμένεια καὶ τὰ σὰ
> ἔργ' ἐξαναγκάζει με ταῦτα δρᾶν βίᾳ·
> αἰσχροῖς γὰρ αἰσχρὰ πράγματ' ἐκδιδάσκεται. (616–21)

Know well that I am ashamed of these things even
if I do not seem so to you. I am aware that
my actions are wrong for my age and not seemly for me
But the hostility that comes from you and your
actions constrains me by force to do these things.
For shameful deeds are taught by shameful deeds.

---

makes the observation that choral couplets which appear between long *rhesis* "are often virtually ignored" by characters; he cites these two lines as an example.

[42] Cairns 1993: 246. See also Segal 1966: 499; Winnington-Ingram 1980: 245–246 and Blundell 1989: 169.

[43] Stinton 1986: 96 n. 78 makes this point as well in response to scholars such as Segal and Winnington-Ingram (see note 42 above) who make too much out of the irony of her reply to her mother, but it is equally applicable to Cairns and Blundell. Stinton argues that Elektra's discreditable behaviour "is not due to a faulty *physis*; it is imposed on her by her situation (307–9), and this is her tragedy."

And she goes on, as earlier, to justify her actions by pointing to Klytaimnestra's behaviour. Cairns draws a parallel between 609 (if she
is full of *anaideia*, it is due to the nature she inherited from her
mother) and 620 (her shameful actions result from the education she
received from her mother). From this, he concludes:

> on both sides of the great fifth-century antithesis between heredity and
> education, *phusis* (nature) and *nomos* (convention, law), Elektra's char-
> acter, from which springs her conduct, including her eventual partic-
> ipation in matricide, is the counterpart of her mother's.[44]

Cairns has half the antithesis correct since Elektra's admission at 621
quite clearly credits her mother's model as the source of her behaviour. However, he ignores that Elektra's acknowledgment of a lack
of *aidos* at 609 is a rhetorical concession. Here she claims that it is
not character which makes her act like this but circumstances, which
is precisely why she emphasizes the educative aspects (αἰσχροῖς γὰρ
αἰσχρὰ πράγματ' ἐκδιδάσκεται. 621). She may act shamefully and
this behaviour may have as its model Klytaimnestra's behaviour, but
it is not her nature (*physis*) or character, but her schooling which
makes her act that way. She has had to learn to be shameful and
her mother's shameful deeds have been her teacher.[45]

More important, however, is that these words are immediately followed by Elektra's confession of shame at her treatment of her
mother, an admission which explicitly refutes Klytaimnestra's charge
that she is without *aidos*. Elektra quite clearly has a strong sense of
aidos, as in the most bitter and acrimonious exchange with a woman
she plainly detests, she expresses her shame; it is Klytaimnestra who
loses her temper and resorts to name-calling. Moreover, the expression of shame towards her mother shows that Elektra does not ignore
ties of kinship (*pace* Blundell). Klytaimnestra in a very real sense has
lost her right to demand any form of *eusebeia* from her daughter and
thus Elektra is justified in charging that Klytaimnestra is more of a
mistress than a mother to her. This, however, is not an outright
denial of the biological bond she shares with her mother. In other
words, Elektra recognizes the validity of blood-ties; she may choose
to act according to the other obligations (i.e. the ethical ties of com-

---

[44] Cairns 1993: 247.
[45] Segal 1966: 500 points out that Klytaimnestra in schooling Elektra in *ta ais-
chra* has failed in her duty as a parent which was to teach one's children *ta kala*.

munal life), but the actions of her mother have forced this choice. This involves her in shameful behaviour, but Elektra is well aware of this. Of course, it is not good to feel shame, for it means that one has done something that is judged shameful; but to do wrong and not feel shame is the worst thing of all; as Aristotle states, being impervious to shame is indicative of a wicked character and thus, for him, *aidos* is a kind of quasi-virtue.[46] Whatever else this confrontation establishes, it makes one thing clear, Klytaimnestra has no shame. In seeing nothing wrong in the killing of her husband, the exiling of her son, and the mistreatment of her children, she is the perfect example of Aristotle's shameless person, the one whom shame would not prevent from doing or saying anything.[47] *Aidos* in this exchange ultimately distinguishes Elektra from her mother. It reveals the moral conflict in which she finds herself and her recognition that she is bound by both the claims of blood and civic ethics. Her expression of shame is a reflection of her awareness that her decision to choose one over the other makes her behaviour to some degree discreditable. Far from equating her morally with her mother, this establishes the moral superiority of Elektra's position.

The conclusion of the debate between mother and daughter confirms Elektra's triumph over her mother; her expression of shame and the justification of her behaviour enrages Klytaimnestra, who in her anger, resorts to verbal abuse, calling her daughter ὦ θρέμμ' ἀναιδές (622). Elektra on the other hand refrains from this sort of behaviour; she emerges victorious, while Klytaimnestra is reduced to pleading for silence for her prayer (631–32). Most commentators willingly concede that Elektra wins the debate, but for many this is a kind of Pyrrhic victory which leaves her occupying the same moral ground as her mother. Blundell and Cairn both adopt this position, arguing that, although Elektra has justice on her side, her personal motives undermine the legitimacy of her arguments. In this view, mother and daughter make the same accusations, defend themselves by the same questionable arguments, and betray the same character traits, all of which conspire to suggest that the daughter is no different

---

[46] Aristotle speaks about *aidos* in the *Nicomachean Ethics*, *Eudemian Ethics* and *Rhetoric*. In *NE* 1128b10–16 *aidos* is defined as a pathos, a fear of a bad reputation. It cannot be a virtue because a virtuous man should never do anything shameful. At 1108a31–5 *aidos* is described as a mean and thus for Aristotle is praiseworthy.

[47] Aristotle *NE* 1128b10–35.

from the mother. But this minimizes the disagreement between Elektra and Klytaimnestra; moreover, it is based upon the erroneous assumption that mother and daughter are equally in pursuit of justice; and finally, it ignores the substantial differences Sophokles brings out between the two women. Klytaimnestra consistently argues from a perspective based on entirely personal claims to Iphigenia and on her personal honour, a reflection of the subjective quality underlying all her actions. Elektra, on the other hand, argues on behalf of her father and his *oikos*, continually raising the debate above the level of personal suffering and individual retaliation in order to expose her mother's breach of the laws of the *polis*. They may make similar charges against the other, but they are not given similar defences; and while both may have personal motives, Klytaimnestra has *only* personal ones. Finally, Blundell and Cairns miss the extent to which Elektra's sense of *aidos* distinguishes her from her mother. Both may engage in shameful behaviour, but the one does so in a pursuit of *dike*, fully aware that she fails to uphold other standards, while the other does so to satisfy base desires, oblivious to her own criminality. That Elektra has personal motivations is hardly surprising given what she has suffered at her mother's hands; but she argues less from these than from ethical principles which transcend the domestic sphere of the *oikos*. She may not be the most objective witness to her mother's crimes, but we should also remember that the Chorus, in its capacity as representatives of the community, consistently confirms the validity of Elektra's charges. While her personal animosity towards her mother prevents her from being impartial, there is something which will serve as an objective touch-stone: the *dolos*. Elektra may expose the motives of her mother, but it is the *dolos*, sanctioned by Apollo, that will elicit a reaction from Klytaimnestra that will convict her by her own words rather than her daughter's accusations.

4.4 *Ritual Activity*

This confrontation ends, just as the previous one did, with a ritual action which looks ahead to the success of the vengeance and future prosperity of the offspring, while boding ill for Klytaimnestra. Like Chrysothemis, Klytaimnestra has come out of the palace to perform a ritual: a sacrifice and prayer to Apollo. Clearly this is a woman who takes no chances; since her dream she has undertaken a num-

ber of ritual activities, all designed to dissipate any evil omen it may
signify.[48] As Chrysothemis reports, she has recounted the dream to
the sun god, Helios, in order to avert any ominous significance it
might have.[49] Next, she has sent her daughter with ritual offerings
to Agamemnon's tomb in order to placate the dead man. Not content with these two actions, she has come out in order to perform
her own sacrifice and prayer to Apollo.

This is an apotropaic ritual, one performed in a time of crisis
often motivated by fear or sometimes hope for success. An appeal
is made to the gods, generally accompanied by some sort of sacrifice, as a way to avert disaster or bring about success. Here Klytaimnestra prays to Apollo to release her from the fear she suffers as a
result of her dream, making offerings of fruit (634–35). She addresses
Apollo first as προστατήριε, "protector" (637), and as Λύκει' ἄναξ
(645). These different forms of address invoke Apollo in his dual
capacity as "defender of the house" and "destroyer of foes".[50] While
she has been frightened by her dream initially, she now seems unsure
how to make out its significance. She accepts it as a portent, as do
Elektra and the Chorus; however, while they interpret it as an aus-
picious sign for them, Klytaimnestra thinks the dream δισσῶν, capable of different interpretations.[51] There are elements which could be
interpreted favourably, such as the flourishing of the tree, generally

---

[48] Bowra 1944: 223–227 is one of the few critics who discusses the dream in any
detail. Devereux 1976: 219–255 attempts to psychoanalyze Klytaimnestra based on
this dream but makes little reference to the play. More recently, Bowman 1997:
131–151 interprets the dream as a reflection of the exclusion and marginalization
of the females in this play. Klytaimnestra is an 'onlooker' in her own dream, analogous to her status in the drama. Understanding the play as the representation of
the transfer of power from father to son, Bowman argues that Klytaimnestra is for
the most part irrelevant to the dramatic action while Elektra is similarly excluded
and silenced at the end of the tragedy. We can now see why Bowman denies the
sexual meaning of ὁμιλία: it would weaken her argument considerably in that it
would make Klytaimnestra more than an 'onlooker' in her own dream. Given that
she is an adulteress and that Elektra continually refers to her illicit passion for
Aigisthos, and that ὁμιλία is used to refer to the sexual act itself, it seems likely
that sexual undertones are present. See Chapter 3 n. 10 above.

[49] There may be a subtle reference to Apollo here, as by the fifth century Apollo
was associated both with light and in particular the sun. See Horsley 1981: 22;
Woodard 1965: 230 n. 52.

[50] Jebb ad 637 notes that Klytaimnestra is particularly calling upon Apollo as the
'averter of evil'. See Appendix ad 6f for Jebb's discussion of the Lykeios epithet of
Apollo as well as the remarks of Segal 1966: 477 note 11.

[51] Bowra 1944: 223–226 makes a great deal out of this ambiguity. He argues
that Klytaimnestra forgets the negative aspects of the dream in favour of its favourable

a good sign pointing to fertility and success. Yet placed within the context of the dream and given that Agamemnon has appeared in it, Klytaimnestra is no doubt justified in her fear. Seeing a dead man in a dream is never a good sign.[52] Being the careful person she is, Klytaimnestra addresses both meanings, asking the god to accomplish the dream if it is favourable and, if not, to turn it against her enemies.

During the absence of Orestes and the *paidagogos* from the dramatic action, there has been no reference to Apollo, although the theme of *dolos* has been kept alive through its association with Klytaimnestra. Her prayer connects the *dolos* with Apollo anew, as she prays to the god to protect her from the *dolos* of her enemies in order to secure and protect the fruits of her crimes. To the audience, aware of the connection between Orestes and Apollo and the divine sanction of *dolos*, the irony of all this is readily apparent. She is praying to a god who has already been engaged by her enemies:

> καὶ μή με πλούτου τοῦ παρόντος εἴ τινες
> δόλοισι βουλεύουσιν ἐκβαλεῖν, ἐφῆς,
> ἀλλ᾽ ὧδέ μ᾽ αἰεὶ ζῶσαν ἀβλαβεῖ βίῳ
> δόμους Ἀτρειδῶν σκῆπτρά τ᾽ ἀμφέπειν τάδε,
> φίλοισί τε ξυνοῦσαν οἷς ξύνειμι νῦν
> εὐημεροῦσαν καὶ τέκνων ὅσων ἐμοὶ
> δύσνοια μὴ πρόσεστιν ἢ λύπη πικρά. (648–54)

> And if some are plotting to rob me of my
> present wealth by deceit, do not allow it,
> but grant that I may always live a life without harm
> ruling the house of Atreus and wielding the sceptre
> associating both with the friends with whom I now live
> happily and with all those of my children from whom
> there is no hostility for me or bitter grief.

She ends her prayer to Apollo in silence, since, as she says, the son of Zeus sees everything (659); her silence is generally understood as an unstated wish for the death of Orestes.

---

elements and thus "relapses in her old self-satisfaction." He thinks that the dream represents her "last chance to amend". Bowman argues that his argument contains two errors. First, he ignores the origin of the branch and second, prophecy never serves as a warning in Sophokles. For Bowman 1997: 140 n. 17 there is no hint that Klytaimnestra is anything but doomed. It is not a final warning, but simply tells the dreamer what is to happen.

[52] Bowra 1944: 225.

The confrontation with Elektra had delayed Klytaimnestra's actual performance of the prayer and sacrifice. In this way, Sophokles makes the appearance of the *paidagogos* with the report of Orestes' death seem to be the instantaneous fulfillment of her prayer, although not in the manner expected by Klytaimnestra. In response to the deceptive silence in which she cloaks her wish for her son's death, Apollo sends his own deception. Klytaimnestra is correct: Apollo knows well what her prayer signifies and in answer sends the *dolos* of Orestes' death. What Klytaimnestra does not realize is that Apollo will act in the capacity which she requests: he will defend the *oikos* and he will destroy its foes. The vision which Klytaimnestra has seen (*phasmata* 644) is thus answered with a fiction, that of Orestes' death. Klytaimnestra who hides a truth within silence will be deceived by a lie which hides a truth, her own impending doom.

Just as Klytaimnestra's earlier ritual action ends in failure when Chrysothemis tosses her offerings to the winds, her prayer for her continued success will similarly end in failure. In each case, Elektra plays a role, as it is she who convinces her sister not to make the offerings and it is again she who, by keeping silent as Klytaimnestra asks (630–31), enables her to carry out her ritual. There is a certain irony in that Elektra grants her request to make a prayer which signals her own impending doom. Though unaware of it, Elektra moves in a direction parallel to that of the gods.

CHAPTER FIVE

THE 'DEATH' OF ORESTES

5.1   *Preliminary Remarks*

The *paidagogos* returns to the dramatic action, entering in the guise of a messenger from a guest-friend of Klytaimnestra and Aigisthos. As planned, he has come to report the death of Orestes and he does so with a speech that is a set piece of rhetorical virtuosity.[1] Aischylos' *Choephoroi* and Euripides' *Elektra* similarly employ a lie, but neither gives it the prominence and central position that it has in this play. Not only does Sophokles have Apollo specifically sanction its use in the oracle (36–37), but the poet draws our attention to it again by having Orestes express in a rather long speech some hesitancy over being reported dead (56–66). The lie has enough significance in the overall dramatic action to warrant its own introduction.[2] Moreover, it takes the *paidagogos* a good eighty-four lines (680–763) to recount the tale of Orestes' death, and however thrilling this account is, it has struck many critics as conspicuously lengthy. As Winnington-Ingram pointedly reminds us, Sophokles is not a poet to waste lines.[3] Its length, elaborate detail, and pivotal position in the play all suggest that it serves some vital dramatic purpose.

---

[1] So much so that some have asserted that the speech does little more than provide Sophokles with the opportunity to display his skill as a poet. See Harsh 1944: 135. Reinhardt 1979: 151–152 remarks that the *rhesis* is "little more than a virtuoso display" but he does go on to see more in it. He suggests that "everything that a Greek would have called *peitho*—in all of these the deception obtrudes so obviously that only someone who was totally ignorant of style, tone and dramatic art could fail to perceive it." Others have similarly thought that the speech with its numerous rhetorical figures has an air of implausibility which attests to its falsity. Adams 1957: 71–72 thinks that the *paidagogos* comes close to overplaying his hand; Seale 1982: 65 thinks that the *paidagogos* gives the game away with his exaggerated assurance that he saw the event. Garner 1990: 119–120 thinks that the lack of any significance in its being based upon the chariot race in the *Iliad* only points to the fictional nature of the speech. Aristotle calls the speech improbable although it is not clear in what sense he means this (1460a27–32).

[2] Winnington-Ingram 1980: 236; Scodel: 1984: 80; Stinton 1986: 82 all note that this speech of Orestes functions as a kind of prologue to the lie itself.

[3] Winnington-Ingram 1980: 236.

Attempts to explain the significance of the speech have been many. Some, impressed by the length and sheer wealth of detail, have suggested that it is designed to create such a vivid account of Orestes' death that we forget it is false; consequently our sympathy for Elektra is not undermined by our knowledge that her sorrow is caused by a lie.[4] This has provoked the reply that we can hardly forget that it is false, having been told about the deception in advance.[5] Some have thought the details are necessary for credibility, but as Gellie points out, "in what way do eighty-four lines of lie convey more verisimilitude than, say, thirty?"[6] Others see the importance of the narrative lying in the contrast it draws between the heroic Orestes of the speech and what they perceive to be the unheroic Orestes of the play.[7] This has been primarily the approach of those who offer an ironic reading of the play. Blundell, for instance, sees the speech as a presentation of "Orestes as he might have been—the heroic and glorious son of the great Agamemnon."[8] There is indeed a discernible contrast between the splendid deeds of the fictional Orestes and the grim and unheroic nature of his task in the play, but this need not serve to cast the justice of his deed in doubt. That Apollo has commended the *dolos* in order to carry out a just killing, however, does oblige us to consider its relationship to *dike*.[9] Others have

---

[4] Wilamowitz-Moellendorff 1917: 188–91. Waldock 1966: 184 points out that this interpretation seems to have been put forth by Kaibel first, then adopted by Wilamowitz 1917: 190 and followed by Webster.

[5] Waldock 1966: 183–84.

[6] Gellie 1972: 116 in response to Whitman 1951: 168 who suggests "a detailed lie works better than a sketchy one".

[7] Seale 1982: 66 writes that "in the play Orestes is everything that he is not in the story. The explicit and brilliant expectations attached to his return in the prologue are to be measured against the progressively darker implications of the revenge. May the audience be meant to take from this mass of fabrication the truth that the 'heroic' Orestes has in fact died?" There indeed may be an allusion to the death of the 'heroic' Orestes, but it may be better to understand this as an allusion to the death or end of the heroic values which inform Orestes' perception of his deed.

[8] Blundell 1989: 173–74. Segal 1981: 281–82 too takes this approach, pointing to the contrast between the heroic language of the speech and the unheroic nature of its purpose. The problem with many of the ironic interpretations of this speech is that they cast their nets too far. Orestes' deed in the play is certainly not a heroic deed worthy of glory and fame, but this does not necessarily mean that it casts the justice of the act in a dubious light as many argue. The whole point is to show this task not as heroic, but as just, the counterpart to Elektra's action, which is right, but shameful.

[9] Linforth 1963: 99 makes the rather lame suggestion that the speech may allude to some part of the Orestes legend now lost which mentions his great athletic suc-

focused on certain details of the speech, in particular the chariot race, connecting it with the reference to the race of Pelops, mentioned in the previous choral ode (504–15).[10] That Sophokles, alone of the tragedians, places an allusion to the family curse in the chariot race is taken by some to mean that the fictitious death is the report that ends the curse; for others, it is a reminder that the curse is still active.[11] There may be some subtle reference here, but it is hardly enough to warrant a speech of this sort.[12] Others again have seen its importance lying not in any of the details of the speech itself, but in the impact it has upon the two women.[13] In this context, Elektra's emotional response is generally regarded as the more important one, not only for what it reveals about her character, but also for the role it plays in later developments.[14] Klytaimnestra's reaction, on the other hand, has been given widely differing interpretations, ranging from that of the response of a grief-stricken mother to a sign of blatant hypocrisy.[15] Most concede that her immediate

---

cess. That Sophokles inserts it only because he liked it and knew that it would appeal to "sport-loving Greeks" as well is perhaps one of the least likely reasons for its inclusion.

[10] A number of commentators have pointed to the parallel between the race of Pelops in the choral ode (515ff) and the chariot race: Musurillo 1967: 99; Webster 1969: 105–6; Gellie 1972: 113; Kamerbeek *ad* 504–515; McDevitt 1983: 9–10. Thompson 1941: 357 thinks the reference to the race is enough to make us "realise that [Orestes] is doomed." I would argue on the other hand that as we listen, we realize that Klytaimnestra is doomed.

[11] Musurillo 1967: 99 thinks the curse is ended while others such as McDevitt 1983: 9–10 see it very much alive. See Chapter 2 n. 28 above regarding McDevitt's reading.

[12] See Stinton 1986: 79 for critical remarks on seeing an allusion to a curse in the choral ode (504–515). If the curse is so important, he asks, why does Sophokles not mention it? As for it anticipating the chariot race of Orestes with the reference to the horsemanship of Pelops, Stinton comments that "an unconsciously ironic reference to a non-event is a little far-fetched."

[13] Adams 1957: 72 argues that the dramatic relevance of the speech must be located here; its length is necessary so that the audience has sufficient time to grasp the full consequences to each of them. Yet it seems unlikely that the audience needs a speech of this length to recognize that it will be devastating news to the one and a welcome relief to the other. Kamerbeek seems closer to the mark with his point that this scene allows us to see what the circumstances would be if Orestes were dead.

[14] Schadewaldt 1926: 59 n. 1 argued that the speech was designed to create such a believable account that we understand Elektra's refusal to believe the evidence Chrysothemis brings in the next scene. Both Gellie 1972: 290 n. 12 and Whitman 1951: 158 find this suggestion convincing to some extent.

[15] Sheppard 1918: 86 thought that Klytaimnestra's reaction whereby she becomes "a mother instead of a fiend . . . is enough to justify the old man's story."

response is a genuine and sincere display of emotion, however fleeting it may be; few, however, have considered why the *paidagogos* should wish to give an account of Orestes' death which would awaken Klytaimnestra's pity.[16]

This brief overview of the various responses to the messenger speech reveals that for the most part critics have seen its main function lying either in providing a convincing account of Orestes' death or in the dramatic impact it has upon Elektra. Those with an affirmative reading have the least to say about the speech itself and it has been left to the 'ironists' to draw attention to the discrepancy between the heroic Orestes and his unheroic task.[17] That the whole speech is "a complete and utter lie from start to finish"[18] told solely

---

Kells (p. 7) is one of the few critics to see Klytaimnestra's reaction as the most important, writing that her reaction signals an "enormous reversal in the stage action" which has "far-reaching significance for the play's total meaning." His attempt at white-washing Klytaimnestra has him elevate her pain, which is really only momentary, above her more extended show of relief a few lines later. At the other end of the spectrum stands Waldock 1966: 183 with his rather biting comment on Klytaimnestra's reaction: she "drops a tear and notes her emotion with surprise. It is only a passing pang, a reaction to some nerve of motherhood, not quite atrophied even in her. She smothers it with no trouble. The feeling that floods her being is one of vast relief." March 1996: 70 endorses this view with her remark that Klytaimnestra overcomes her "first slight pang of sorrow and gloats over Electra's genuine grief." See note 33 below for discussions of Klytaimnestra's reaction.

[16] There have been other approaches to the messenger speech in recent years. Scodel 1984: 82 sees the speech as a "fable of common Greek morality. No analogy for human life is as popular as a race, and no tenet is as trite, especially in tragedy, as the warning to judge nothing and no one before the end." For other occurrences of this "look to the end" theme in tragedy, see Scodel 1984: 142 n. 9. Scodel's metaphorical interpretation which understands the speech as a warning directed at Klytaimnestra and Aigisthos comes close to my view of it as a kind of test. Kitzinger 1991: 302 on the other hand calls the *paidagogos'* lie a "speech act that changes the way the audience hears and views the characters and what they do" because it possesses knowledge that the actors do not. Batchelder 1995: 87–110 sees the messenger speech as the beginning of a play directed by Orestes so that he becomes producer and director of his own drama.

[17] Waldock's 1966: 183 comment that this *"tour de force* of the Paedagogus calls merely for our tribute in passing" is indicative of the tendency of many critics of the affirmative persuasion to disregard this speech. Bowra 1944: 248, for instance, has little to say about the speech itself, although he does concede its devastating impact on Elektra; others, such as Alexanderson 1966: 79–98; Stevens 1978: 11–20; March 1996: 65–81 make no mention of the speech at all. Gardiner 1986: 169 thinks that the emphasis on the glorious presentation of Orestes only makes Klytaimnestra's evident relief all that more despicable. Burnett 1998: 123–124, the most recent affirmative advocate, calls it a "glorious" lie which serves to keep the "disengaged and hypothetical nature of Elektra's project uppermost in our minds".

[18] Ewans 1984: 146.

to further matricide is for many enough to cast a shadow over the enterprise and call into question the justice of the vengeance.

The alliance between *dolos* and *dike* is disturbing; that justice should be so rooted in guile seems to weaken the foundation upon which it rests. Yet its sanction by Apollo should warn against any quick condemnation of it. *Dolos* has been a persistent theme from the very beginning; and to understand its significance, we should first examine it within the broader context of the play. We have observed its first occurrence in the oracle, which advocates its use in order to carry out "just slaughters". While no reason is given for the use of deception, there is the suggestion that in some fashion the *dolos* serves *dike*. The second reference to *dolos* in Orestes' speech (59–66) is often said to serve as an introduction to the lie itself. There we saw that the *dolos* posed a conflict for Orestes between what he perceived to be the heroic nature of his undertaking and the unheroic means by which he must carry it out. In this scene, we see that the *dolos* presents Klytaimnestra with a conflict as well: whether to rejoice at her good fortune or feel pity for the suffering of another. The second element to consider is that the speech, with its theme of the 'fall from high' and its exaggerated and ornate language, seems devised specifically to appeal to the emotions of the audience. Yet if the purpose of the report is simply to further the vengeance by convincing Klytaimnestra that her son is dead, awakening her maternal emotions seems a rather odd strategy. But if we accept the words of the oracle, that is, that the use of *dolos* will bring about just killings, we may see the purpose of the deception in a different light. The *dolos* is delivered in the manner it is, not in order to deceive Klytaimnestra, but in order to make her deliberate. The *paidagogos* creates a set of fictional circumstances which are meant to arouse her fear and pity, two emotions considered necessary for the proper functioning of a person's moral being. In this way he forces her to consider the relationship between herself and Orestes. In this respect, we may see the ultimate purpose of the speech as the demonstration of a truth which will secure the justice of the vengeance. This makes her reaction crucial, but, as we shall see, the *dolos* forces every person in this play to make a decision, which will have consequences equally significant for both Orestes and Klytaimnestra. Finally, although most critics simply see it as a lie from start to finish, we shall see that it does contain a truth, one which hints at the impending downfall of Klytaimnestra.

5.2 *The Messenger Speech*

Klytaimnestra has just finished her prayer to Apollo with its unstated
wish for Orestes' death when the *paidagogos* shows up in the guise of
a messenger. His words throughout this exchange are double-edged,
having one meaning for the audience and quite another for Klytaimnestra. For the audience, his appearance brings to mind the connection established between Apollo and Orestes at the beginning of
the play and is a reminder that the *dolos* comes with divine sanction.[19] To Klytaimnestra, however, he seems to be the immediate
answer to her prayers. The *paidagogos* begins with the announcement
that he has good news for her and Aigisthos: ὦ χαῖρ', ἄνασσα. σοὶ
φέρων ἥκω λόγους ἡδεῖς φίλου παρ' ἀνδρὸς Αἰγίσθῳ θ' ὁμοῦ. (666–67).
The abrupt enjambement places the emphasis on ἡδεῖς: his words
will be "sweet" for her. Klytaimnestra receives his "omen" (τὸ ῥηθέν)
and, after ascertaining that he is "from a friend" (παρὰ φίλου), accepts
that his words will also be "friendly" (προσφιλεῖς λέξεις λόγους 672).
The audience, who has just heard the blasphemous prayer of Klytaimnestra to Apollo, will not miss the hidden assumption in the *paidagogos'* remark: she will be overjoyed at the death of her son.[20] For
Klytaimnestra, however, his presumption that she will greet the death
of her son with joy only confirms his trustworthiness, for being from
a guest-friend, he would be aware of Orestes' status as an exile and
thus the threat he poses to their power.[21]

Without further ado, the 'messenger' announces that Orestes is
dead. Given what we have seen of both mother and daughter thus

---

[19] The connection between the *paidagogos* and Apollo has been noted by many.
Adams 1957: 71 writes that the god "all but steps upon the stage himself." See
also Kitto 1966: 133; Minadeo 1967: 124 and 1994: 117; Horsley 1980: 22.

[20] The irony in this exchange is what Hester 1995: 115–16 calls "deceptive irony":
the speaker and audience are both aware of the significance of the words, but the
listener is not. "In effect", Hester says, "the author, the speaker, and the audience
are in conspiracy against the interlocutor." There is, as well, the obvious irony in
the circumstances of Orestes' death, for according to the report of the *paidagogos*,
the man who is in fact the avenger of Apollo, is brought down at the Pythian
games held in honour of the god. For Klytaimnestra, this will appear as a rather
fitting fulfillment of her prayer to Apollo; for the audience, it is another reminder
of Apollo's role in her downfall. Sophokles achieves this at the cost of a small
anachronism for the Pythiads were not instituted until 582 BC.

[21] *Contra* Kitzinger 1991: 319 who thinks that the *paidagogos* is playing a risky
game here since "the stranger he is pretending to be should not expect her to be
elated by her son's death". But he is not pretending to be a stranger; rather he is
from Phanoteus, a guest friend of Aigisthos and an enemy of Agamemnon.

far, their immediate reactions come as no surprise. Elektra is at once devastated by the report while Klytaimnestra is barely able to control her excitement: her repeated τί φής, τί φής betrays an unnatural eagerness for having the death of her son confirmed.[22] She immediately presses the *paidagogos* for details, telling him to pay no attention to her daughter; she wants to hear how Orestes died. In response to her request, the *paidagogos* recounts an elaborate tale about Orestes' performance at the Pythian games. On the first day, Orestes enters all the events, emerging as victor in every one. The *paidagogos* describes the brilliant figure he struck and how he won the admiration of all. At the end of the day, he is announced as Orestes, the son of the famed Agamemnon (694–95). At this point, the *paidagogos* breaks off from his narrative to insert a *gnome* of his own to the effect that not even the most powerful can escape the gods (696–97). He then returns to his story and recounts the events of the day of the chariot race, describing each entrant and his team in careful detail. When the race begins, Orestes stays behind at first, putting his trust in the finish. He successfully avoids a disastrous crash which destroys every other competitor except an Athenian. The race between the two is neck and neck until the last circuit when Orestes, striking a turning post, is thrown to his death. Tangled up in the reins, he is dragged by his horses until his body is so mangled that no one of his friends is able to recognize him. His body is burned on a pyre and his ashes placed in a small urn. Such was the event, the *paidagogos* concludes, terrible to tell and terrible for those who saw it (761–63).

As pointed out, this is a speech whose length and wealth of details seem out of all proportion to its apparent purpose. Puzzling as well is why the *paidagogos* ignores Orestes' explicit instructions to state that he died in a chariot race and add a false oath.[23] If he is the immoral sophist some make him out to be, adding a false oath should not cause a problem. Nor is it clear why he should wish to give a speech specifically designed to awaken Klytaimnestra's maternal feeling if his purpose is simply to provide a credible account of Orestes' death

---

[22] Campbell and Kamerbeek *ad* 675; Kells writes that "[Klytaimnestra] can scarcely believe it; it is too good to be true."

[23] Orestes' instructions to add a false oath are most often taken as evidence of his sophistic nature. See Chapter 1 n. 33 above.

in order to further the vengeance.[24] The last thing the *paidagogos* should want is a grief-stricken mother on his hands. As a sophistic speech designed to further the vengeance, it makes no sense; but as an artful piece of rhetoric designed to arouse fear and pity, it does.

Aristotle's *Rhetoric* is useful here as it includes one of the few detailed discussions of the emotions of fear and pity as well as offering specific advice on how an orator may arouse them in his audience. Fear and pity, Aristotle states, are painful emotions; the former is aroused by a "mental picture (*phantasia*) of some destructive or painful evil" that we think could happen to us (1382a21–22); while the latter is "caused by the sight of some evil, destructive or painful" which befalls another. Fear, then, is primarily a self-regarding emotion while the most fundamental aspect of pity is that it is felt for another. There is, however, an interdependent and causal relationship between these two emotions which Aristotle points to when he writes that "anything causes us to feel fear that when it happens to, or threatens, others causes us to feel pity" (1382b26–27) or as he puts it later, "what we fear for ourselves excites our pity when it happens to others" (1386a28–29). For Aristotle, since fear is caused by the prospect of one's own suffering, the people who do not feel fear are those who believe that they could not suffer anything from anyone (1382b31–33), i.e., the *hybristai*, those whose great prosperity makes them "insolent, contemptuous, and reckless" (1383a1–2). Pity, on the other hand, because it requires the identification of oneself with another, and because it rests upon the recognition of a sense of commonality between people, is, as Nussbaum puts it, "the bridge between

---

[24] Kells *ad* 680–763 is one of the few who sees the speech specifically devised to arouse Klytaimnestra's maternal feelings, although he interprets this in an entirely different way: "The detailed persuasive account was intended to involve Clytaemnestra so deeply in an impression of the death of Orestes, that she will be convinced of its reality, and so thrown off her guard when the living Orestes comes to attack her." The narrative presents Orestes then "behaving as a son *of whom she might be proud*." For Kells, the result of this is a complete reversal in her emotions and Klytaimnestra now becomes a grief-stricken mother. Thus when it comes time for the matricide, Orestes' killing of her becomes all the more worthy of moral condemnation. It does not seem to bother Kells that there is little need for the *paidagogos* to go to such lengths to convince Klytaimnestra that her son is dead. Nothing in the play suggests that the news itself is so unbelievable as to necessitate a speech of this sort. Nor again does Kells ever explain why he would want his charge to face a grief-stricken mother. However, given his view of the *paidagogos* and Orestes as immoral and depraved sophists willing to do anything to achieve their goal, killing a mother overcome with grief would not appear to pose a problem.

individual and community."[25] Without this awareness of our vulnerability to suffering, we have only "arrogant harshness."[26] For Aristotle, it seems the ability to experience the emotions of pity and fear is an important factor for the moral being of man.

Since fear is awakened by the realization that we are vulnerable to misfortune, Aristotle suggests that the best way for the orator to arouse this emotion is to make his audience think that they are in danger of suffering something. Thus he advises the speaker to make the following points: others greater than they have suffered; others like themselves have suffered; others have suffered from those they least expected to suffer something in an unexpected way and at a time when they did not expect to suffer (1383a9–12).[27] The sufferings of powerful and successful people are particularly effective in this regard, for these are the people who are thought least likely to suffer anything. The audience thus reasons that if these people suffer, then they might too or as Aristotle puts it, if the least likely has occurred, then what is more likely to occur will also occur (1392b15–16). Fear thus causes one to deliberate; the unexpected nature and form of suffering help in creating a sense of imminent danger and making the audience aware of its own vulnerability to misfortune. When fear is aroused in this fashion, then another emotion is similarly awakened, pity. We pity others, Aristotle says, when we remember that similar misfortunes have happened to us or we expect them to happen (1386a1–2). Aristotle's *Rhetoric* allows us to see the reasoning process by which people are led to feel first fear for themselves and then pity for others, but there are numerous examples in literature and oratory which show the arousal of fear and pity being accomplished in a similar manner.[28]

---

²⁵ Nussbaum 1996: 28.

²⁶ Nussbaum 1996: 34.

[27] The method laid out by Aristotle in the *Rhetoric* is similar to the way the poet is said to arouse pity and fear in the *Poetics*. See Belfiore 1992: 246–253 on this aspect of Aristotle's *Rhetoric* and its relationship to the *Poetics* and the tragic emotions of fear and pity.

[28] One of the best examples of fear and pity being aroused in a manner similar to that offered by Aristotle occurs in the *Iliad* 24.507–516. See Belfiore 1992: 250–253; 351–353 on this scene and Chapters 6 and 7 *passim* on the emotions of fear and pity in the *Rhetoric* and *Poetics*. See also the discussions of MacLeod 1983: 26–27 and Crotty 1994 on pity in Homer; for discussions of appeals to pity in drama and the Attic orators, see Kolakis 1986: 170–178 and Stevens 1944: 1–25. Dover 1974: 197 points out that misfortune when contrasted with previous good fortune was thought to evoke the strongest feelings of pity.

If we examine the speech of the *paidagogos* from this perspective, that is, as an attempt to awaken the emotions of fear and pity, the emphasis on Orestes' heroic deeds and the necessity for the lengthy chariot race are more readily understood. The first part of the speech portrays Orestes in a manner befitting the most glorious of heroes and his accomplishments as the greatest of heroic deeds. Indeed, claims the *paidagogos*, he knows of no other man who has accomplished such feats (689). In other words, he presents Orestes as a man greater than those listening, but also like them, being an Argive and a *philos* (694–95). With his pre-eminent performance at the games, Orestes appears as a man at the height of great success. The next logical step in the story is obvious: to show the downfall of this man who seems most unlikely to suffer anything, and to show it happening in an unexpected fashion, and from those it seems least likely to suffer something, for all these elements make danger seem close; moreover, to present his downfall in such precise detail and with such vividness that the audience will feel as if they are actual spectators at the event.[29] In this way, the chariot race becomes for its audience a *phantasia kakou*, an image of painful destruction which makes misfortune seem close and danger imminent. When disaster strikes all the charioteers except an Athenian and Orestes, the stage is set for the thrilling neck and neck race between two opponents. There appears only one final obstacle to Orestes' victory, and defeat, if it comes, is expected from this quarter. Instead at the last minute, with success in sight, Orestes relaxes his grip and unawares, strikes the pillar (744–45). Forgetting his earlier method of keeping a tight rein on his inner trace horse (721), his misfortune comes as a result of his own mistake and he suffers death from those least expected, his own horses. At an unexpected moment, from those whom it is least likely to suffer something, his death is a complete and utter reversal in fortune, a veritable *peripety*. The *paidagogos* even gives some indication of the proper response to this occurrence with his description of the crowd which reacts with a wail at seeing such a terrible misfortune after such splendid achievements.

---

[29] At 1382a21–22 Aristotle says that fear is aroused by the "*phantasia* of some destructive or painful evil" and that "those who heighten the effect of their words with suitable gestures, tones, dress and dramatic action generally, are especially successful in exciting pity: they thus put the disasters before our eyes and make them seem close to us" (1386a31–34).

The *paidagogos* thus presents the 'death' of Orestes as the downfall of a glorious hero. Reduced to its simplest form, the story comes remarkably close to the pattern of tragedy: the downfall of a great hero who suffers a complete reversal in fortune (*peripety*) through some *hamartia* (1453a12–17). Here, however, it is empty of any tragic force or significance, and Orestes' *hamartia* is no great intellectual or moral error, but simply an oversight. As pitiful as the downfall is, there is nothing *tragic* in this story, but this is the difference between tragedy and rhetoric. Tragedy arouses fear and pity in a manner similar to rhetoric but is far more effective in this because the best tragic plot shows the suffering not just contrary to expectation (1452a3–4) but also as probable or necessary (1451a38). Moreover, tragedy is most effective at arousing pity and fear when the suffering comes from a *philos* (1453b19–22). Orestes does not suffer disaster from a *philos* but his own horses; nor is there anything which makes his downfall seem probable or necessary, but there is something which suggests the probability of Klytaimnestra's. While recounting the events of the two days, the *paidagogos* inserts the mention of another hero who also suffers a terrible misfortune after great success, Agamemnon:

> . . . Ἀργεῖος μὲν ἀνακαλούμενος,
> ὄνομα δ' Ὀρέστης, τοῦ τὸ κλεινὸν Ἑλλάδος
> Ἀγαμέμνονος στράτευμ' ἀγείραντός ποτε.
> καὶ ταῦτα μὲν τοιαῦθ'· ὅταν δέ τις θεῶν
> βλάπτῃ, δύναιτ' ἂν οὐδ' ἂν ἰσχύων φυγεῖν. (693–97)

> He was announced as an Argive, by the
> name of Orestes, son of Agamemnon who once
> gathered the famed armament of Greece.
> And so far, thus; but when one of the gods
> does harm, not even a mighty man can escape.

Orestes is identified by his city and name, but the most detailed and elaborate description is his identification through his father. The *hyperbaton* of the line with the irregular placement of Ἀγαμέμνονος makes the reference all the more conspicuous. The mention of Agamemnon's heroic exploits which seems at first glance gratuitous and unnecessarily lengthy in this context, as it momentarily deflects attention from son to father, draws a parallel between their fates.[30]

---

[30] Kells *ad* 692ff points out that at the games, an official proclamation was made

Both perform glorious deeds followed directly by terrible misfortunes. Orestes' death is a fiction, but Agamemnon's is not. The *paidagogos* leaves Agamemnon's fate unstated but no one, least of all Klytaimnestra, would need reminding of the terrible fate he suffered after his triumph at Troy. It is at this point that the 'messenger' breaks off from his narrative and speaks ἔξω τοῦ πράγματος, interjecting a warning: no one, he tells her, not even the powerful, can escape, when one of the gods does harm.[31] Ostensibly the moral is made in reference to Orestes' fate, but it is just as easily applicable to that of Klytaimnestra. She is the powerful and successful one, the one whose victory and success seem assured; and she is the one who called for the intervention of a god with her blasphemous prayer to Apollo for her son's death. Given the reference to Agamemnon, the history of the House of Atreus, and more important, given Klytaimnestra's own defence of *talio* justice (and Elektra's explicit reminder of what this means at 582–83) what seems probable, indeed even necessary, is not the downfall of Orestes, but the death of Klytaimnestra. Lurking at the heart of this deceptive tale is a truth which serves both as a warning and an omen of things to come for Klytaimnestra. Like the dream, the *dolos* contains a truth, one which points to her impending doom. The queen should be afraid or at the very least consider her response carefully, which she does, but this only makes it all the more damning.[32]

---

after each event, which gave the name of the winner, the name of his father, and his nationality. Thus, as Jebb *ad* 693ff notes, the official proclamation would be Ὀρέστης Ἀγαμέμνονος Ἀργεῖος. See also the remarks of Batchelder 1995: 99–100 in this regard.

[31] Bremer 1969: 168–69 argues that the *paidagogos*' words strike a false note. Comparing this line to a similar one in *Aias* (εἰ δέ τις θεῶν βλάπτοι, φύγοι τἄν χὠ κακὸς τὸν κρείσσονα 456–57), he argues that here "the tone of tragic suffering is authentic because the hero feels outraged by the gods. In the mouth of the Paedagogus, however, the same words sound hollow, because they are part of his effort to make his story as pathetic as possible." These two situations are so different that these two lines cannot properly be compared.

[32] There are a number of parallels between the speech itself and the rest of the play that suggest it may be read as a narrative of the return and revenge of Orestes. The *paidagogos* structures his speech so that it falls into two clear parts, which are separated by the insertion of his moralizing comment. This parallels the structure of the play, which is divided into two parts separated by the *paidagogos*' tale. Moreover, within the speech itself there are clear parallels to other parts of the play. The *paidagogos* begins his tale by describing how Orestes went to the games at Delphi (κεῖνος γὰρ ἐλθὼν ἐς τὸ κλεινὸν Ἑλλάδος πρόσχημ' ἀγῶνος, Δελφικῶν ἄθλων χάριν 681–82), which corresponds to Orestes' description of his visit to Apollo's oracle at Delphi

5.2.1 *The reaction of Klytaimnestra*

The *dolos* has obviously had an impact on Klytaimnestra. Her earlier excitement has vanished and she now appears apprehensive and unsure of her response:

> ΚΛ. ὦ Ζεῦ, τί ταῦτα, πότερον εὐτυχῆ λέγω,
> ἢ δεινὰ μέν, κέρδη δέ; λυπηρῶς δ' ἔχει,
> εἰ τοῖς ἐμαυτῆς τὸν βίον σῴζω κακοῖς. (766–68)

> ΚL. O Zeus, what should I say of these things? Should
> I say they are fortunate or terrible yet profitable. It is
> painful if I should save my life by misfortunes.

This is not the instantaneous celebration that we expect from a woman who in the past reacted with rage at the mere mention of her son's name (293–98) and who, just moments earlier, was praying for his death. Yet it is not quite the grief-stricken mother either. Instead, Klytaimnestra wavers, torn between seeing his death as "fortunate" or "terrible but a gain" (766–67).[33] Either way it is a *kerdos* and thus the choice she is faced with is simply between celebrating

(ἐγὼ γὰρ ἡνίχ' ἱκόμην τὸ Πυθικὸν μαντεῖον ὡς μάθοιμ' ὅτῳ τρόπῳ πατρὶ δίκας ἀροίμην τῶν φονευσάντων πάρα 32–33). The second day foretells Klytaimnestra's own fortunes, for like Agamemnon, she will be brought down by one of her own. Batchelder 1995: 100–102 as well notes some similarities between the speech and the rest of the tragedy, although she veers off in another direction with her argument that the speech is the beginning of a play directed by Orestes, while Klytaimnestra is "audience, participant, and sacrificial victim."

[33] These words have been taken in a variety of ways from a genuine maternal grief that redeems her to a blatant display of hypocrisy. That her response is simply hypocritical seems unlikely, however; not only would this deprive the scene of all emotion and power, but it deprives Klytaimnestra of all complexity. As Gellie 1972: 117 rightly notes, this scene would be "grotesque" without at least a gesture toward some maternal feeling. See also the comments of Kamerbeek *ad* 766. Segal 1966: 498 offers perhaps the most typical view, seeing Klytaimnestra's words as evidence of genuine feeling which passes quickly. So too Linforth 1963: 100 and Adams 1957: 72. Seale 1982: 65 notes that Klytaimnestra has been affected by the speech but her apprehension soon turns into relief. Kells attaches the most significance to these words allowing them to overshadow everything else, even her obvious relief. Having redeemed Klytaimnestra, Kells is able to indict the offspring, for what could be more heinous than a child killing a parent grief-stricken at his death? Obviously, nothing, but this is not what happens. His interpretation of this scene (and the whole play) forces us to accept that the *paidagogos'* speech goes dreadfully awry in its purpose, for now Orestes must kill a mother who is "grief-stricken" at his death. Not even Euripides goes this far in his rehabilitation of Klytaimnestra or his condemnation of Orestes. Of course, by Kells' reading, everything in this play from Orestes' perspective goes dreadfully awry from the moment he asked the wrong question of the oracle.

this good fortune or recognizing that her gain has come at a terrible price (767). She appears to move in the direction of grief with her acknowledgement that saving her life comes at the cost of suffering maternal pain. The *paidagogos*, noting this response, questions her apparent despondency; in response, Klytaimnestra reflects upon the strange power which the maternal bond possesses; even when a mother is treated badly by her children, she does not hate them (δεινὸν τὸ τίκτειν ἐστίν· οὐδὲ γὰρ κακῶς πάσχοντι μῖσος ὧν τέκῃ προσγίγνεται 770–71). The report has affected Klytaimnestra, forcing her to consider her own fortunes and the nature of her bond with Orestes.

The *paidagogos*, observing her hesitation and the ambivalent nature of her response, remarks "we have come in vain it seems" (772). Most commentators have assumed that he simply remains in his role as a messenger who, upon discovering his words were not as welcome as he originally supposed, expresses his disappointment that he will receive no reward.[34] However, he also speaks as the agent of Apollo, testing her one more time to ascertain the depth of her maternal feelings, thus forcing her to make a choice, and Klytaimnestra does:

> οὔτοι μάτην γε. πῶς γὰρ ἂν μάτην λέγοις;
> εἴ μοι θανόντος πίστ᾽ ἔχων τεκμήρια
> προσῆλθες, ὅστις τῆς ἐμῆς ψυχῆς γεγώς,
> μαστῶν ἀποστὰς καὶ τροφῆς ἐμῆς, φυγὰς
> ἀπεξενοῦτο· (773–77)

> Not in vain indeed, how could you say 'in vain'?—
> if you have come with trusting proof of his death,
> who, although born from my life, turned away from
> the nurture of my breasts and became an exile.

Klytaimnestra thus overcomes the conflict presented to her by the *dolos* and makes her decision: Orestes is a *phugas*, an exile rather than a son. In using the word *phugas* Klytaimnestra reveals that she sees him more as a political rival and a threat to her power than she does as a son.[35] Segal aptly captures the relationship apparent between mother and son here when he writes:

---

[34] Campbell, Jebb, Kamerbeek, and Kells (*ad* 772) are all in agreement on this point.

[35] See Chapter 1 n. 25 above.

> [Klytaimnestra] describes his absence not as a parent speaking of a child, but as a ruler speaking of a dissident subject: he has *'revolted from her breasts and nurture'* (ἀποστάς, the regular word for civic dissension and political rebellion) and has become an 'exile' (φυγάς, 776). Here speaks the woman whom her daughter characterizes as 'tyrant (*despotis*) rather than mother' (597–98).[36]

Klytaimnestra, who is initially troubled enough by the story to reflect upon her relationship with Orestes, decides in the end that he is more of an adversary than anything else. Choosing to understand his exile as a rejection of her as a mother, Klytaimnestra feels free to reject him as a son; his death becomes proper recompense for what he has done to her.[37]

The tie of *philia* which Klytaimnestra has rejected, however, is a blood relationship. The Greek concept expressed by *philia* covers, as often pointed out, a much broader range of relationships than our word 'friendship', including civic, political, and social friendships as well as family relationships.[38] As Cooper observes, family ties such as those between parents and children, siblings, and husband and wife "are in fact the original and, in some ways, the central cases of φιλία."[39] Aristotle, in the prelude to his discussion of the three forms of friendship in the *Nicomachean Ethics* says that friendship exists where one wishes what is good for another for his own sake and this feeling is returned (1156a3–5). Common to all forms of friendship for Aristotle is the reciprocity of good will.[40] He does, however,

---

[36] Segal 1966: 498.

[37] It is made clear throughout the play that Orestes' exile was out of a desire to protect him from suffering the same fate as his father. See lines 296–297; 637–638; 780–782.

[38] Most scholars take the terms *philos* and *philia* to denote the same wide variety of relationships subsumed under the idea of friendship, including that of kin (Fisher 1976: 21; Strauss 1986: 21; Humphreys 1986: 85 n. 3; Blundell 1989: 40–43; Pakaluk 1991: xiv all use *philos* to mean friend as well as kin). See, however, the recent article of Konstan 1996: 71–94, which is critical of the indiscriminate use of these terms. He argues, using Aristotle and the Attic orators, that the noun *philos* would not apply to family relationships and that it comes closest to our use of 'friend' while *philia* covers a broad range of relationships including that of kin. I have followed the standard practice of the majority of commentators in using *philos* and *philia* to refer to a kinship relationship. For treatments of *philia* in individual tragedies, see Konstan 1985: 176–185; Schein 1988: 179–206; Stanton 1990: 42–54. For an overview of *philia* prior to Aristotle, see Fitzgerald 1997: 1–34 (it does not, however, treat *philia* in Greek drama).

[39] Cooper 1999: 313.

[40] See Cooper 1999: 316–317 on this point and Chapter 14 for a discussion of Aristotle on the types of friendship. In the *Rhetoric* Aristotle defines friendship in

cite certain forms of *philia* which are exceptions to this mutuality, such as the bond between mother and child. This relationship may be entirely one-sided, since a mother loves a child regardless whether the feeling is returned.[41] For the Greeks, some relationships endured despite the absence of good-will, and while family *philia* was considered to be a relationship in which reciprocal feelings of good will should exist, "their absence did not destroy the φιλία itself."[42] Klytaimnestra recognizes this when, in response to the *dolos*, she claims that a mother does not hate her children, even if they treat her badly. In other words, the *dolos* has made Klytaimnestra reflect on the maternal bond between parent and offspring, and she clearly recognizes that a blood relationship should properly transcend feelings of friendship or hostility. Yet having identified the fundamental nature of this tie, she goes on to reject it for one based upon friendship and enmity. What is more important to her than anything else is the insult she considers herself to have suffered from Orestes' exile and thus the need to reciprocate in kind. That is, a regard for her own honour is more important than the tie of blood; indeed it is so important that she extends the relationship of enmity beyond life so that even in his death, her son is still an enemy.

The brief exchange between mother and daughter serves to underscore the nature of Klytaimnestra's choice; not only does she have no pity for her son, but she treats her daughter with contempt bordering on cruelty that highlights her utter lack of regard for others. Exulting in her triumph over her offspring, she now claims that she will live free from the fear posed by them (786–87). Joy at her apparent success and good fortune supplants any pain she might have initially felt at the death of her son. Klytaimnestra's final words on stage are an outright rejection of the blood-ties between mother and offspring. When the *paidagogos* suggests that he should depart now, Klytaimnestra refuses to let him go, declaring that such treatment

---

similar terms as mutual wishing well out of a concern for another (ἔστω δὴ τὸ φιλεῖν τὸ βούλεσθαί τινι ἅ οἴεται ἀγαθά, ἐκείνου ἕνεκα ἀλλὰ μὴ αὐτοῦ 1379b35–36).

[41] Aristotle writes, "for some mothers hand over their children to be brought up, and so long as they know their fate they love them and do not seek to be loved in return (if they cannot have both), but seem to be satisfied if they see them prospering; and they themselves love their children even if those owing to their ignorance give them nothing of a mother's due" (1159a29–34).

[42] Cooper 1999: 313 n. 3; he also cites in support of this a quotation from Euripides' *Phoenissae*: φίλος γὰρ ἐχθρὸς ἐγένετ᾽, ἀλλ᾽ ὅμως φίλος (1446).

would be unworthy of him and the one who sent him (800–1). She invites the 'messenger' inside the palace while leaving her own daughter outside to cry forth her sorrows, thus sealing her negation of the most fundamental human relationship, the tie between mother and offspring.

5.2.2 *Sophistry versus rhetoric*

Those who consider the *paidagogos* an immoral sophist willing to employ any means to further the vengeance overlook the extent to which this speech is far more than some sophistic trick to convince Klytaimnestra that her son is dead. Here Aristotle's distinction between the sophist and the true rhetorician is helpful. Concerned with showing that rhetoric is a rational art, necessary for advancing the true and just, he draws a distinction between the type of argumentation practiced by the rhetorician and the base practices of sophists. He defines rhetoric as the ability (*dynamis*) to see and find in each particular case the available means of persuasion (*ethos, logos, pathos*); the function of the rhetorician is to distinguish between the truly persuasive and the apparently persuasive.[43] Like all arts, then, rhetoric has two ends: an internal end (finding the available means of persuasion) and an external end (persuasion). The true practitioner of the rhetorical art lets his practice be guided by the internal ends of his art, while the sophist, having no such internal end, is guided solely by his external end, persuasion pure and simple; thus he can choose any means he wishes to achieve it. In this way Aristotle separates genuine persuasion achieved by legitimate means (valid arguments achieved by syllogism/enthymeme and *pisteis*) from manipulation achieved by specious argumentation through apparent syllogism. Thus when Aristotle writes that "what makes a man a sophist is his preference" (*prohairesis*) (1355b17–18), he is referring to the sophist's deliberate choice of fallacious or apparently persuasive arguments.[44] In distinguishing the rhetorician and the sophist on the basis of their

---

[43] These means of persuasion (1355b26–28) are the *pisteis* of which some are nonartistic (oaths, contracts) in that they are at hand while the artistic proofs (*ethos, logos, pathos*) have to be discovered.

[44] The full passage is as follows: "It is the function of one and the same art to see the persuasive and [to see] the apparently persuasive, just as [it is] in dialective [to recognize] a syllogism and [to recognize] an apparent syllogism; for sophistry is not a matter of ability [*dynamis*] but of deliberate choice [*prohairesis*] [of specious

choice of argumentation, Aristotle makes an ethical distinction between the two; and sophistry, without the internal constraints of rational persuasion, is rhetoric cut loose from its ethical moorings.[45]

As a sophist, the aim of the *paidagogos* should simply be to convince Klytaimnestra that her son is dead in order to further the vengeance. He has the perfect means for accomplishing this purpose, one which Orestes himself had suggested (47), a false oath, that is, a sophistic "apparent means of persuasion". Yet he scorns this device in favour of lengthy speech which comes close to awakening Klytaimnestra's maternal feelings. Not only would the speech be entirely gratuitous for a sophistic *paidagogos* but also counterproductive; for having Orestes face a mother overcome with grief would seem to be unnecessary risk if his plan is simply to carry out a successful vengeance. In short, there seems to be no good reason for the *paidagogos* as a sophist to want to deliver a speech of this nature. On the other hand, if we apply Aristotle's distinctions, we see that the *paidagogos* is far closer to the true rhetorician than he is to the immoral sophist. He chooses not to rely upon a sophistic trick of swearing a false oath (illegitimate means of persuasion), but a carefully crafted account which appeals to her emotions by means of a rational argument (legitimate means of persuasion). That is, he has not made her the passive victim of a deception, but, by engaging her in a reasoning process, has turned her into an active participant in an argument which allows her to make her own reasoned determination. His speech has the same effect as a false oath would have in that he has convinced Klytaimnestra that Orestes is dead; but in being guided by genuine persuasion achieved by legitimate means, the *paidagogos* makes an ethical choice, and in doing so he reveals his own moral character.

Most commentators have never seen the *dolos* as anything but a mere lie from start to finish; that justice should be grounded in such a duplicitous device is often thought to call in question the legiti-

---

arguments]. In the case of rhetoric, however, there is the difference that one person will be [called] *rhetor* on the basis of his knowledge and another on the basis of his deliberative choice, while in dialectic *sophist* refers to deliberative choice [of specious arguments], *dialectician* not to deliberate choice, but to ability [at argument generally]" (1355b15–21). Translation by Garver 1994: 164. For discussions of Aristotle's distinction between the sophist and rhetorician, see Garver 1994: 206–231 and Arnhart 1981: 33–34.

[45] Garver 1994: 164.

macy of the vengeance. Telling a lie with the sole intention of deceiving someone may be immoral and corrupt, but the *paidagogos* tells a lie, the ultimate purpose of which is to expose a truth. In other words, the *dolos* has an ethical basis in that it advances the cause of justice. For with his deceptive speech the *paidagogos* has created a set of fictional circumstances which have the greatest possibility of revealing Klytaimnestra's capacity for pity as well as allowing her the opportunity to determine herself the nature of the relationship she has to Orestes. In choosing to exult in her own good fortune Klytaimnestra has revealed her incapability for pity and thus her hybristic nature. The capacity to feel this emotion reflects an awareness of the ties which should exist between people who are members of any *koinonia*. It may be understood as the emotional substratum necessary for and constitutive of ζῷα πολιτικά, beings who live in the *polis*. In exposing her refusal to recognize any of the ties of the community, the *dolos* serves to demonstrate her unworthiness of the claim to have this emotion felt for her. In this way, the *dolos* has the important function in establishing the justice of the matricide. Klytaimnestra cannot later claim the status of mother, having forfeited it by her own repudiation of it; nor, more significantly, does she have the right to ask for pity, for devoid of it herself, she has lost the right to demand that it be shown to her. The *dolos* stratagem then functions in revealing the grounds upon which she may be killed with justice. What we discern from the messenger *rhesis* is not a *dike* rooted in deception, but a deception rooted in *dike*.

There is yet another way in which the speech works as less a lie than as a deceptive form of truth-finding, for the *dolos* of Orestes' death contains in disguise the truth of Klytaimnestra's fate: she is vulnerable to misfortune and she, like Agamemnon, is going to fall. Klytaimnestra, who sends a deceptive prayer to the god and asks the *paidagogos* for the truth (ἐμοὶ δὲ σύ, ξένε, τἀληθὲς εἰπέ 678–79), is answered with the truth in the disguise of a lie. Yet just as she was blind to the message of her dream, so too is she blind to the hidden truth in the words of the *paidagogos*. Our last glimpse of Klytaimnestra as she departs inside the palace gives us not Kells' "horror-stricken mother", but a woman overjoyed and full of relief at the death of an enemy: her son. Elektra's words, after her mother has left the stage (804–7), confirms Klytaimnestra's rejection of her maternal role and her utter lack of pity: she who should be mourning the death of a son instead when out of sight is gloating (ἐγγελῶσα φροῦδος

807). Given the chance to show herself worthy of pity, Klytaimnestra has failed and has condemned herself by her own words.

5.2.3 *The reaction of Elektra*

Most commentators have pointed to the devastating effect Orestes' 'death' has on Elektra, who, in stark contrast to her mother, appears destroyed by the news. Bowra calls the effect on Elektra "appalling" while others speak of the callous cruelty of the *paidagogos* and Orestes in not taking Elektra's feelings into account.[46] One critic goes so far as to suggest that the fictitious death of Orestes causes the psychological 'death' of Elektra.[47] There is a certain validity in some of these charges, for neither the *paidagogos* nor Orestes informs Elektra of the deception beforehand; but to suggest that Sophokles means us to understand this as evidence of their cruelty misunderstands the function of the *dolos*. It ignores that although initially devastated, Elektra does not remain in this state; instead, showing remarkable strength in adversity, she gathers her resolve and decides to kill Aigisthos. Like Klytaimnestra, Elektra has two responses: her grief over the news of Orestes' death and her anger at her mother's reaction. Given how utterly dependent Elektra is upon Orestes' return, her grief comes as no surprise; more significant is her response to her mother's treatment of her son.

Elektra's immediate reaction to the announcement that her brother is dead is the realization that her cause is lost (οἲ 'γὼ τάλαιν', ὄλωλα τῇδ' ἐν ἡμέρᾳ. 674). Her fortunes have always been bound up with Orestes' return; with his death Electra sees all her hopes die as well. Yet after the *paidagogos* has finished recounting his deceptive tale and Elektra observes the reaction of her mother, her grief becomes suffused with anger. Klytaimnestra's evident pleasure at his death, Elektra claims, is an act of *hybris*:

> ΗΛ. οἴμοι τάλαινα· νῦν γὰρ οἰμῶξαι πάρα,
> Ὀρέστα, τὴν σὴν ξυμφοράν, ὅθ' ὧδ' ἔχων
> πρὸς τῆσδ' ὑβρίζῃ μητρός. ἆρ' ἔχω καλῶς;
> ΚΛ. οὔτοι σύ· κεῖνος δ' ὡς ἔχει καλῶς ἔχει. (788–91)

---

[46] Bowra 1944: 248; Seale 1981: 65 and Schein 1982: 76–77 all speak of the callousness of Orestes and the *paidagogos*.
[47] Horsley 1980: 25.

EL. Ah, wretched me. For now I may lament your
misfortune Orestes, when in this way you are
insulted by this mother of yours. Am I not well?

KL. Not you; but as he is, he is well off.

Klytaimnestra's pitiless reply confirms Elektra's charge and prompts her invocation of *Nemesis*, the goddess of Retribution (ἄκουε, Νέμεσι τοῦ θανόντος ἀρτίως 792), the "spirit of just allotment".[48] Most have supposed that the reference to *Nemesis* here is primarily to the *nemesis* of the dead.[49] Fisher points out that it may refer to either the "general personified power of *nemesis* . . . which shows particular outrage at insults to the dead, or, as often taken, 'the specific *nemesis*' of the dead, a sort of chthonic power".[50] No doubt there is an association between *nemesis* and the dead, but whether it is to the dead in general or Orestes in particular seems less important than the point that Klytaimnestra's behaviour is a form of *hybris*, which rightly provokes *nemesis*. More significant is the intimate association between *aidos* and *nemesis*; given that this occurs in the context of a tragedy in which *aidos* has such a prominent role, it seems likely that this invocation of *Nemesis* has a greater significance than is usually acknowledged.

5.3 *Hybris, Aidos, and Nemesis*

There is a close association amongst these three terms and to understand the significance of Elektra's actions and the later matricide, it is necessary to clarify their relationship to one another within the context of the dramatic action. *Hybris* is a term which appears frequently in this play, most often, as has been seen, in reference to Klytaimnestra's behaviour.[51] Like most Greek ethical terms, *hybris* does not translate easily into English, as we have no precise equivalent

---

[48] Campbell *ad* 792; Fisher 1992: 300 points out that this appeal to *nemesis* in connection with *hybris* is "one of the only two unambiguous associations" of the two terms in Attic tragedy (the other is Euripides' *Phoenissae* 183). In Herodotos, it is used in connection with Croesus' *hybris* in thinking himself to be the most prosperous of men. As a result a "great *nemesis* from god took Croesus" (1.34).

[49] Fisher 1992: 298–302; Kamerbeek *ad* 792.

[50] Fisher 1992: 301.

[51] *Hybris* or a form of it occurs at 271, 522, 523, 613, 790, 794, and 881. The occurrence at 881 is by Chrysothemis with reference to her report about the presence of Orestes.

to this concept.[52] Fisher, in his recent treatment of it, defines *hybris* as "the committing of acts of intentional insult, of acts which deliberately inflict shame and dishonour on others."[53] His definition is inspired largely by Aristotle, but as Cairns points out, it is one which emphasizes intention over the disposition which produces it. Aristotle may speak about *hybris* as "doing or saying things that cause shame" but he begins by defining *hybris* as a kind of attitude, namely as *oligoria* that manifests itself in the words and actions of a person (1378b14; 1378b23–25). For Cairns, the most important aspect of *hybris* is not the intention or the act, but the subjective attitude of the hybristic actor. Accordingly, he would prefer to define *hybris* as the "excessive self-assertion in the face of others' claims."[54] *Hybris* may be used with reference to either the act or disposition and thus the difference between Cairns and Fisher is to some degree on which aspect each one focuses. Fisher stresses the act and intention while Cairns emphasizes its dispositional sense. Yet the *intention* to inflict harm on someone is not fundamental to the concept of *hybris*, for an act can be hybristic without it deriving from some specific intention to dishonour someone, as Cairns rightly points out.[55] As he observes, the source of *hybris* stems from the agent's subjective view of his superiority over others or his excessive valuation of self.[56] Hybristic acts then are "those which the possessor of a particular *hexis* would perform", and the *hexis* from which *hybris* springs is, for Aristotle, that of injustice.[57] Quite clearly, *hybris* and *aidos* occupy opposite ends of the moral spectrum; one entails the utter disregard for the claims of others, while the other requires the recognition and respect not just of the honour and claims of others, but the claims of society as a

---

[52] *Hybris* has been defined by MacDowell 1976: 30 as "having energy or power and misusing it self-indulgently"; and by Dickie 1984: 101 as "an arrogant and over-confident state of mind, brought on by good fortune and showing no awareness of the limits of the human condition." Dickie holds the orthodox view that tends to see *hybris* in dispositional terms while Fisher challenges this view with a more behaviourist or legalist definition of *hybris*. Aristotle defines it as "doing or saying things that cause shame to the victim, not in order that anything may happen to you, nor because anything has happened to you, but merely for your own gratification" (1378b23–25).

[53] Fisher 1994: 148.

[54] Cairns 1996: 32 n. 149.

[55] Cairns 1996: 9–10.

[56] Cairns 1996: 7.

[57] Cairns 1996: 5.

whole. Both, however, involve ways of treating others; thus both reveal much about the attitude and character of the agent.

Nemesis, on the other hand, has its most intimate ties with *aidos* and in Homer at least, they often appear together or in close proximity to one another.[58] *Nemesis* is usually translated as 'righteous' or 'moral indignation' and is the most powerful expression of disapproval. Redfield calls the two terms a "reflexive pair" observing that while "*aidos* shrinks away and draws back, *nemesis* is an invasive passion that drives one to intervene in the affairs of others."[59] While *aidos* often operates in a prohibitory manner that prevents shameful action, *nemesis* drives one to attack those who are themselves lacking a proper *aidos*. *Aidos*, as Redfield puts it, is "a kind of hypothetical anticipation of *nemesis*."[60] Cairns, in agreement with Redfield on this point, argues similarly that "*aidos* foresees and seeks to forestall *nemesis*."[61] *Nemesis*, he writes, "connotes anger in which the subject feels himself justified, anger which is directed at some transgression or deficiency on the part of another."[62] The relationship between *aidos* and *nemesis* is so close that, in some cases, as Cairns points out, they involve virtually the same reaction: the rejection and avoidance of something shameful.[63] The distinction between the two was pointed out by Murray who wrote: "*Aidos* is what you feel about an act of your own: *Nemesis* is what you feel for the act of another."[64] *Nemesis* then is the counterpart and companion of *aidos*, the angry resentful aspect of *aidos* which comes into operation at the lack of it in another.

---

[58] *Aidos* often appears with *nemesis* in the epics. See Cairns 1993: 51–54 for a list of occurrences.

[59] Redfield 1975: 116 and 115.

[60] Redfield 1994: 116.

[61] Cairns 1993: 52. Erffa 1937: 30 also makes this point.

[62] Cairns 1993: 52–53; 83–84; For other discussions of *nemesis*, see Erffa 1937: 30–5; Scott 1980: 26–30; Redfield 1994: 115–119. Aristotle classifies indignation as an emotion, characterized by turmoil. It is an intrusive feeling that occupies the mind and because it is an emotion, it may affect our judgement. We are roused to indignation at the undeserved good fortune of another (1386b10).

[63] Cairns 1993: 84 and n. 120; Erffa 1937: 33. Cairns expresses the relationship between the two as follows: "There are two sides to the reaction of shame at the prospect of disgrace: the inhibitor, when the agent suppresses the action which might lead to ignominy; and the angry, resentful aspect which comes into play when the reprehensible action is abandoned and positive steps are taken to wipe out any suggestion of an insult."

[64] Murray 1924: 83.

Unlike *aidos* and *hybris, nemesis* is not a term common in tragedy and Elektra's use of it in connection with *hybris* is striking, for it is only one of two such associations in extant Greek drama.[65] Given the close relationship which exists among these terms together with their appearance in a play that is so concerned with the ethics of *aidos* and *eusebeia* and breaches thereof, Elektra's invoking of *Nemesis* has some significance beyond calling upon the power of the dead. First, it shows that she responds to the truth that the messenger speech has exposed: Klytaimnestra's lack of pity and her hybristic nature. Up to this point, mother and daughter each has accused the other of *hybris* and each has defended herself: Elektra, by citing the behaviour of her mother, and Klytaimnestra by claiming the need to retaliate for the abuse she suffers at the hand of Elektra. For the mother, it is a question of personal honour; for the daughter it is a question of the honour of her *oikos* and the maintenance of communal standards. Yet Elektra's expression of shame invalidates her mother's charges, while Klytaimnestra's lack of *aidos* confirms Elektra's accusations. At this point, however, Klytaimnestra no longer feels the need to defend her behaviour, but flushed with what she takes for victory, she proceeds to make the even more outrageous remark that Orestes is well-off dead (791). Not only has she demonstrated an appalling lack of pity for her son, but she takes his death as cause to celebrate her freedom from fear (νῦν δ'—ἡμέρᾳ γὰρ τῇδ' ἀπηλλάγμην φόβου πρὸς τῆσδ' ἐκείνου θ'· 783–84). It is to these two remarks that Elektra reacts: to the first (783–84) with a charge of *hybris*, and to the second (791), by calling upon *Nemesis* (792). Nothing could distinguish mother and daughter more clearly than their radically different responses to the *dolos*: Klytaimnestra exults in her own good fortune while Elektra responds with grief at the misfortune of her brother and outrage at the lack of *aidos* in her mother.

These responses are entirely characteristic and consistent with what we have seen of mother and daughter thus far. The gratuitous inso-

---

[65] See note 48 above. It is far less frequent in tragedy (*Seven against Thebes* 235; *Oidipous at Kolonos* 1753; *Philoktetes* 518, 602). For occurrences in Hesiod and the lyric poets, see Cairns 1993: 133 n. 262. It is also discussed in Plato's *Laws* 717d in connection with the importance of not offending one's parents in speech: "for there is a very heavy penalty for light and fleeting words, since appointed as overseer for all such things is *Nemesis*, messenger of Justice". Cairns in his discussion of the play does not mention Elektra's use of the term.

lence involved in Klytaimnestra's action is a quality which has always informed her behaviour; not content with simply killing Agamemnon, she continues to renew the insult month after month with the institution of a ghastly ritual sacrifice in celebration of the murder. Elektra and the Chorus identified the original crime of Klytaimnestra from which her other crimes flowed, her passion for Aigisthos. Now we see that behind this passion for Aigisthos lies the true origin of all Klytaimnestra's crimes, her *hexis*, a disposition that consistently places her own success and pleasure above all else. Without fear or pity, she displays the over-confidence and inflated sense of self so characteristic of a *hybristes* and in the end she reveals herself as *adikos*, *asebes*, and *anaides*. Elektra's charge of *hybris* pronounces the truth about Klytaimnestra which the *dolos* of the *paidagogos* has revealed. Elektra may think her mother has won, but her words ὕβριζε· νῦν γὰρ εὐτυχοῦσα τυγχάνεις. (794) carry an underlying significance for the audience. Klytaimnestra should enjoy her good fortune, for it will be short-lived.

As to Elektra's response of moral outrage and anger at her mother's *hybris*, Aristotle is enlightening: anger is a painful emotion and, as he notes in the *Nicomachean Ethics*, "no one commits *hybris* while feeling pain, but anyone who acts in anger feels pain, whereas the man committing *hybris* acts with pleasure" (1149b20–3).[66] For Aristotle, no matter how deeply felt anger is, it cannot be called *hybris*; indeed even acts of revenge, performed out of anger at a previous outrage, cannot be called *hybris*. Anger is more of an emotional response to

---

[66] This discussion of anger occurs in Aristotle's treatment of the distinction between incontinence with respect to anger (*akrasia thumou*) and incontinence with respect to the desires (*akrasia epithymion*) in *NE* Book 7.6. As Fisher 1992: 15 points out, for Aristotle *akrasia* of anger is less shameful than *akrasia* of desire because anger involves reason (reason tells a person that he has been insulted and it is right to resist such a thing 1149a31–33), while this is absent in desire. Desire also involves plotting and deceit and is therefore more unjust than an open display of anger (1149b14–15). In the *Rhetoric*, Aristotle defines anger as a desire for revenge accompanied by pain on account of slight to oneself or to one's own, the slight being unjustified (1378a30–32). Anger then is caused by *thought* of outrage just as fear is caused by the *thought* of imminent danger and shame, by the *thought* of disgrace. Outrage then is the efficient cause of anger; by positing thought as the cause of emotions, Aristotle is able to show that an emotional response is reasoned rather than irrational behaviour and is thus open to reasoned persuasion. See Fisher 1992: 15–17 for a discussion of Aristotle's distinction between anger and *hybris*. For a discussion of the cognitive basis of emotion in Aristotle, see Fortenbaugh 1975: 11–18; Nehamas 1994: 262–268.

what we regard as an unwarranted assault, and thus it expresses a
sense of justice. Elektra's response then is justified anger at the *hybris*
and lack of *aidos* of her mother, signalled by her call upon *Nemesis*
and it, like her earlier lamentation, has its source in *aidos*. Thus the
dolos has revealed the moral character of both by displaying their
reactions to the death of Orestes: one responds with an act of *hybris*;
the other with an act of *aidos*.

Elektra's call upon *Nemesis* identifies Klytaimnestra's true crime,
but it also has some significance for her. As we saw in the earlier
exchanges, Elektra's strong sense of *aidos* drives her to defy her mother
with her continual lamentation in order to uphold a broader form
of *eusebeia* towards the gods and the community. As much as Elektra
may act disrespectfully towards her mother, her expressions of shame
showed, as we have seen, that she still recognizes the authority of
the blood-tie between her and her mother. Elektra never moves
beyond this open show of resistance, for her belief that Orestes would
return as well as her own recognition that her behaviour was, in
some respects, discreditable prevents her from acting any further. In
the first half of the play, then, she only seeks to maintain the legitimate *oikos* until such time Orestes sees fit to return and restore order
in the *polis*. Now with Orestes presumed dead and confronted with
her mother's outrageous behaviour, Elektra's invoking of *nemesis* signals her determination to move from an open show of resistance to
an aggressive form of action. From this point on, Elektra ceases to
express that retrospective sense of shame at her behaviour; instead
her *aidos* will now operate as a force which drives her to plan a
physical action to avoid the prospect of a shameful life. We should
remember, however, that this comes only after Klytaimnestra repudiates her own maternal role and shows herself devoid of all pity.
The scene of lamentation which follows this provides the necessary
impetus for Elektra to translate the anger she expresses here into a
form of physical action.

5.4 *Elektra and the Chorus: The Kommos*

The *kommos* (823–70) has caused a slight unease among some commentators who find this scene of lamentation between the Chorus
and Elektra awkward given the fact that we know it is based on a

misapprehension of the situation.[67] Yet its purpose is less to make
us sympathize with Elektra's grief than to have us recognize the legitimacy of the despair and outrage she feels, and thus the necessity
of vengeance. This scene reflects in a ritual form what has happened
in the previous exchange and thus acts as a transition from the anger
and despair of Elektra to the new resolve she expresses to Chrysothemis.
Her grief, however, is misguided, and although her lamentation provides her with the impetus to undertake a physical action, it is indeed
a false step, based upon a misunderstanding of the circumstances.
In her rejection of the Chorus' consolation and its mythological parallel, we see a foreshadowing of the following scene with her sister
in which Chrysothemis is right and Elektra wrong. The *kommos* marks
the movement of Elektra into a world in which she undertakes a
decision based upon the false apprehension of her circumstances.

The Chorus begins with words which express its sense of outrage:

ποῦ ποτε κεραυνοὶ Διός, ἢ ποῦ
φαέθων Ἅλιος, εἰ ταῦτ᾽ ἐφορῶντες
κρύπτουσιν ἕκηλοι; (823–25)

Where are the thunderbolts of Zeus, where is
the blazing sun, if seeing these things,
they peacefully conceal them?

This is not an expression of despair at the gods' failure to show concern for the affairs of humans, as it is sometimes thought, but of
outrage at the undeserved death of Orestes and apparent victory of
Klytaimnestra.[68] That it seems to be intended as belief in the rightness of vengeance rather than hopeless despair is confirmed by Elektra

---

[67] Vickers 1973: 569–70, for instance, writes "Sophocles has in fact undercut the
central situation of his play, Electra's solitude, her suffering, her doubts, her power-
lessness to take revenge. We know that in fact she is no longer alone, her doubts
are illusory, her revenge already under way . . . for this reason it is impossible for
us to be really moved by her sorrow at the news of Orestes' death, for the news
is false, and her sorrow comes to seem false, worked up." Burton 1980: 206 sees
this scene important for understanding the following exchange between Elektra and
Chrysothemis: "[her lamentation] makes explicit the psychological barrier against
the merest hint that Orestes may be alive, so that when Chrysothemis enters immediately afterwards and states that he is indeed alive, we are prepared for Electra's
reception of the news."

[68] Kamerbeek *ad* 823–5 points out that this sentiment of the Chorus could be
interpreted as a kind of consolation: "if the gods see this and do not punish, they
are nowhere, but since they exist, they will punish."

who responds by rejecting any suggestion of false hope from the
Chorus. The Chorus tries again to offer some hope by citing as a
mythological parallel the story of Amphiaraos. But, Electra points
out, Amphiaraos had his son Alkmeon as his μελέτωρ; she has no
one, as Orestes is dead (ἐμοὶ δ' οὔτις ἔτ' ἔσθ'· ὃς γὰρ ἔτ' ἦν, φροῦδος
ἀναρπασθείς 847–48). The example which the Chorus sees as proof
of its belief in justice is taken by Elektra as evidence of the hopeless-
ness of her situation. The story of Amphiaraos is sometimes thought
to be a poor example, but it is not as inadequate as it seems, for
it reflects the true reality of the situation: Orestes is present and will
avenge Agamemnon. Thus the parallel the Chorus makes between
Agamemnon/Klytaimnestra/Orestes and Amphiaraos/Eriphyle/Alk-
meon holds. The Chorus is right, and it is Elektra who is wrong, a
theme which will be fully exploited for all its dramatic irony in the
following scene between her and Chrysothemis. The Chorus attempts
again by reminding her that all mortals must die. In response, Elektra
points out that no one should die as Orestes did, in a foreign land,
without his family. The Chorus finally gives up all attempt to console Elektra and in the end simply join her in her sorrow and grief.

Elektra's grief and sense of despair are objectively groundless,
caused as they are by the *dolos* of the *paidagogos*. Too often, however,
critics have focused exclusively on the deceptive nature of the speech,
seeing it as either evidence for the brutal indifference of Orestes and
the *paidagogos* to the suffering of Elektra or a way to cast the vengeance
in doubt by grounding it in treachery and deceit. Yet we have seen
that this deceitful fiction does reveal a truth—the immoral character
of Klytaimnestra. Elektra's reaction is, in part, a response to this
truth, but as she too believes the *dolos*, she fails to see that it hides
an inner reality, which, like Klytaimnestra's dream, points to the
downfall of the tyrants. Elektra only holds a partial truth and thus,
while the *kommos* may provide her with the emotional stimulus necessary to make the movement from passive resistance to action, it
shows her lack of awareness of the nature of her circumstances. In
the following scene we see that Elektra in all her determination and
resolve shows only a partial understanding of her undertaking as well.

CHAPTER SIX

ELEKTRA AND CHRYSOTHEMIS II: CIVIC ANDREIA AND FEMALE SOPHROSYNE

6.1 *Preliminary Remarks*

Chrysothemis returns from her visit to Agamemnon's tomb, filled with joy at what she has discovered there. She is certain that Orestes is present and that their troubles will soon be over. Elektra thinks she is deluded but listens to her story nonetheless. With great excitement, Chrysothemis describes the ritual offerings and lock of hair she found at the tomb, but her mood rapidly changes when her sister informs her that their brother is dead. Elektra then appeals to Chrysothemis for assistance, presenting her with a glorious vision of the fame and honour they will win, if she joins her in the killing of Aigisthos. Not unexpectedly, Chrysothemis does not share this vision; rebuffed, Elektra declares her intention to act alone. A rather lengthy exchange follows, taking the form of a *stichomythia* which hearkens back to many of their arguments in the first half of the play, but this time the sisters are irrevocably alienated and Chrysothemis departs to return to the palace, not to be heard from again.

This confrontation shows a number of parallels with their earlier exchange, but the movement of the first is reversed in the second. While the first one began in hostility, it ended with a tenuous alliance when Elektra convinced Chrysothemis to replace her mother's ritual offerings with her own; this confrontation begins with the alliance still in force, but it soon dissolves when Chrysothemis rejects her sister's plan. In both exchanges, a sign appears: Klytaimnestra's dream in the first and the ritual offerings left on Agamemnon's tomb in the second. The first one is properly interpreted by Elektra and unites the two sisters; the second is interpreted properly by Chrysothemis and leads to their estrangement. Many commentators, but in particular those with a 'darker' reading, focus upon the irony of the situation: Elektra, who always faced up to the grim truth of their circumstances and was able to interpret the meaning of her mother's dream, is now wrong, while Chrysothemis, who seems to live in a world cushioned from the harsh reality of their situation, is right. Those adhering to an ironic interpretation have variously understood Elektra's failure to recognize the significance of the ritual offerings as the fallibility of all humans to acquire knowledge; a sign of her increasing marginalization and loss of power; and one critic has even detected evidence of her growing madness.[1] While they willingly concede the heroic nature of her decision, it is often interpreted as an empty gesture which amounts to naught, as Orestes is present and the plan for vengeance already underway. Many as well take a rather dim view of Elektra's failure to mention Klytaimnestra as part of her revenge plan, seeing it as an attempt to deceive her sister as to the true nature of her plans.[2] The more positive reading usually downplays Elektra's inability to see the truth which the ritual offerings signify and concentrates instead on the decision to undertake the killing of Aigisthos. For these critics, it is evidence of her heroic determination and resolve and, while unnecessary, the decision is thought to be as important as the act itself.[3] They see nothing sinister in her failure to mention her mother for the simple reason that she has no plans to kill Klytaimnestra at the moment.

---

[1] Blundell 1989: 181 argues that "coming as it does so soon after the 'messenger' speech, with its powerful assault on our rational beliefs, this scene demonstrates the fallibility of human means of acquiring knowledge." Seale 1982: 68 takes a similar approach arguing that Elektra's acceptance of the *paidagogos'* lie and her rejection of Chrysothemis' evidence show the "delusion inherent in the human condition." Kitzinger 1991: 319–20 takes a more feminist approach arguing that her belief in the *paidagogos'* lie as well as her evident grief make Elektra an object of pity rather than the "persuasive interpreter" she had been earlier. Orestes' 'death' thus signals the loss of her presence and begins the movement away from her dominance on stage. Kells (p. 10) on the other hand imagines an Elektra who, overcome by grief at the 'cruel' deceit of Orestes, will show increasing "signs of madness". Bremer 1969: 167–69 in his study on *hamartia* says that Elektra's error is to believe the report of Orestes' death at the games and to reject her sister's good news. This error, however, does not bring about her ruin, rather it has the dramatic function of showing a contrast with her earlier scenes of lamentation. Aristotle's *hamartia* does not strictly apply to Elektra unless one interprets in a rather limited way as "a mistake concerning someone's identity" or pinpoints it precisely to that moment (955) when she decides to go ahead with her suicidal plan for revenge. Bremer concludes that *hamartia* in Sophokles' *Elektra* is deprived of its force.

[2] The absence of Klytaimnestra's name has been taken in a variety of ways. See note 7 below for references.

[3] Bowra 1944: 212–60. Whitman 1951: 149–74; Lesky 1965: 119; Segal 1981: 254 and 1986: 125 while recognizing that anything heroic in the play lies with Elektra, sees the heroic aspects of her action as "yet another inversion of normal values, the exchange of male and female roles."

We should remember that first, no matter how "deluded" Elektra appears here, the *dolos* is ultimately revealed to her; that is, the irony will be resolved. Second, regardless of what Elektra or Chrysothemis believe, the offerings left on the grave are one in a series of signs which all point to the same thing, the downfall of the tyrants. Third, in some ways, given how the *dolos* has operated thus far, it is necessary that Chrysothemis be convinced of Orestes' death in order that we see her response. The significance of this exchange then does not lie solely in the irony of the situation, i.e., that one sister is right and the other wrong, but how each responds once convinced of the death of their brother. In other words, the theme of *dolos* continues to function as it did in the previous exchange. Just as it exposed Klytaimnestra for what she is, it discloses the character and motivations of the two sisters. Once Chrysothemis has been convinced of the 'lie', we see how her response confirms her basic weakness and lack of moral core. Given the chance to redeem herself, Chrysothemis again thinks only of her personal safety and thus casts her lot in with the tyrants. Elektra, on the other hand, responds by appealing to *eusebeia* and *eleutheria*, principles of the civic ethics which have always guided her behaviour. Yet for all her heroic determination, there is something faintly disturbing in her vision of glory and the absence of any mention of her mother's name. Like her brother, Elektra, in seeing their undertaking as an act worthy of fame and glory, fails to recognize anything shameful in it. Both siblings remain partially blind to the nature of their deed and the operation of *dike*.

6.2 *Elektra and the Persuasion of Chrysothemis*

Chrysothemis returns from her errand and, knowing nothing of the news the messenger has brought, is elated by what she has discovered at Agamemnon's tomb: signs of Orestes' return. When Elektra asks her where she heard this story, Chrysothemis makes it clear that she herself saw the evidence (885–86). Perhaps still sensitive to her sister's accusation that everything she says comes from Klytaimnestra, and nothing from herself (343–44), Chrysothemis now emphasizes that she saw σαφῆ σημεῖα. When Elektra asks for proof, she describes in detail what she saw on the grave of Agamemnon: flowing streams of milk; their father's urn crowned with every type of flower;

and at the edge of the tomb, a newly cut lock of hair, which she assumes to be from Orestes. She goes on to reason by a process of elimination that it must be their brother who left these things: she did not leave them; Elektra could not have left them; and Klytaimnestra would never do such a thing. No, she confidently concludes, they must have been left by Orestes. She ends her speech on the hopeful note that their fortunes have now taken a turn for the better. Of course, Chrysothemis' reasoning is correct. To Elektra, however, who has heard the speech of the messenger, she seems hopelessly misguided and she proceeds to inform Chrysothemis of what she has learned in her absence: a messenger has come with news of Orestes' death. She concludes that these offerings must have been from someone who left them in memory of Orestes. Chrysothemis is easily persuaded of her error in judgement and her joy is replaced by despair when she realizes things are even worse than before.

Each sister has good reason to believe what she does. Chrysothemis has seen convincing evidence on her father's tomb and Elektra has heard a convincing eyewitness account of Orestes' death. Both are described in a lengthy and detailed fashion. Chrysothemis initially is as persuaded by what she has seen as Elektra is by what she has heard; and the joy of one sister is matched by the despair of the other. There is a symmetry and parity in the way the evidence has presented itself to each sister that reflects a common origin. Both the *dolos* and ritual offerings have their source in Apollo and both are done in order to further the same end: the successful overthrow of the tyrants. In this respect, it makes little difference what the two sisters believe, as Orestes is present and the vengeance underway.

There is, however, some sense in which the easy persuasion of Chrysothemis and the outright refusal of Elektra to believe the evidence of her sister reflect something particular about each sibling. We saw in the first confrontation between the two sisters a weakness in Chrysothemis which left her open to persuasion. Governed by a concern for personal safety and comfort, she conceives of all correct conduct in terms of obedience, and is thus easily enslaved to the will of her mother. Yet because Chrysothemis recognizes that her sister has justice on her side, she is vulnerable to persuasion; the act with which the first confrontation ends reflects the moral confusion in her position. Bound to obey her mother, she takes the latter's sacrilegious offerings to the grave; recognizing that Elektra is right, she is persuaded to throw them to the winds. Ultimately, however, this is an act which can be performed at no cost to her personal safety; and while it provides important confirmation of the rightness of Elektra's arguments, it exposes the weakness of Chrysothemis. She will only act in the absence of danger and thus, as susceptible as she is to the words of another, her secret defiance of her mother is as far as she will go. In this second confrontation, Chrysothemis is soon swayed by the words of Elektra to doubt evidence she has seen with her own eyes, and the ease with which she is convinced by her contains the inherent weakness in her stance. Elektra's refusal to accept the evidence her sister brings is, in one way, less troublesome than Chrysothemis' easy surrender of her belief; since she has an ethical basis for her arguments, her essential position never changes. Regardless whether Orestes is dead or alive, Elektra continues to move towards the same end, the just punishment of her father's murderers. Chrysothemis, however, in acting according to personal motivations, must continually shift ground in order to adapt to the present circumstances. Both sisters may be persuaded to believe something which is false: Elektra by the *dolos* of the *paidagogos*, and Chrysothemis by the words of her sister, but the persuasion of one results in a decision which works to the same end as that of Orestes and Apollo; while the conversion of the other results in a decision which is nothing more than an endorsement of tyranny.

We cannot, however, simply ignore the fact that Elektra does reject the truth for a lie. Some have suggested that Elektra's refusal to believe Chrysothemis is understandable given the persuasive speech of the *paidagogos*; deliberate deception is at work here, and we should not expect Elektra on the basis of anything Chrysothemis says to reject what she has heard from the messenger.[4] Yet Elektra has been portrayed up to this point as a faithful upholder of ritual; that she who is the most knowledgeable of ritual norms should now fail to recognize the significance of her brother's offerings is something more than an 'understandable' response to the *dolos* of the *paidagogos*, no matter how convincing the messenger speech was. Elektra may be said to suffer from a kind of intellectual blindness and a blurring of her moral vision which comes as a result of her outrage at her

---

[4] Harder 1995: 28 argues that Sophokles is careful to show that the only time Elektra is wrong is when she is "more or less forced" to reject Chrysothemis' words because of the messenger speech. Seale 1982: 68 suggests this, but does go on to see far more in her rejection of the truth.

mother's *hybris*.[5] Her *aidos*, which previously was the source of her self-awareness and sensitivity, is now what blinds her to the truth which the ritual offerings signify. Chrysothemis may recognize them as σαφῆ σημεῖα but because of her general weakness gives up a truth for a lie; while Elektra's failure to see them as σαφῆ σημεῖα is not so much the rejection of a truth for a lie, but the embrace of one truth which blinds her to another. Elektra still has a limited understanding, which will become even more evident in her plan. She deludes herself into thinking that she can kill Aigisthos alone, revealing not only a lack of self-awareness, but a failure to recognize an essential truth about the deed: that it will involve the shedding of kindred blood.

6.3   *Elektra's Plan*

Having instructed Chrysothemis about her 'error', Elektra now attempts to enlist her assistance. Before she launches into her appeal, there is a brief exchange between them in which Elektra prepares her sister for what is to follow (938–46): if Chrysothemis obeys her, they can lighten the burden of their present troubles, but she warns, it will involve hard work. There is a suggestion here that Elektra's plan will involve physical action, and as compliant as Chrysothemis is in assenting to her sister, she only agrees to help to the limit of her powers (ὅσονπερ ἂν σθένω 946). From the earlier confrontation, we know how limited her powers are; thus as we listen, we realize that Elektra's bid for assistance is bound to fail.

Elektra begins by emphasizing their isolation. They are without *philoi* (948–49); Hades has taken their relations and they alone are left (949–50). With Orestes alive, she always had hope that he would return to avenge their father; now that he is dead, his duty has fallen to them, and Elektra looks to her sister for support. She must not shirk from her duty: to kill Aigisthos. How far must things go, Elektra asks her sister, before you do something (958). From here, she moves on to an examination of their situation: how things will be if they

---

⁵ This failure comes close to what North 1966: 51 calls a "second-species of failure in *sophrosyne* (and this is clearly a failure in self-knowledge)—namely, delusion." As she points out, this theme of delusion is intellectual rather than moral and is often associated with a failure to understand properly an oracle or prophecy.

do nothing. They have no hope for any kind of life as long as Aigisthos rules. They will be cheated of their father's wealth (960) and Chrysothemis will grow old without marriage (962). Aigisthos is not so foolish, Elektra tells her sister, to allow them to wed, as their offspring would pose a threat to his power. On the other hand, if Chrysothemis joins her, they will win praise for their piety from their father and their brother (εὐσέβειαν 968); they will regain their freedom (ἐλευθέρα καλῇ 970–71) and Chrysothemis will make a worthy marriage (γάμων ἐπαξίων τεύξῃ 971–72). Finally, in the most rousing section of her speech, Elektra presents a vision of the glory and fame they will win (κλέος 985) if they kill Aigisthos. She concludes her speech with the assertion that "it is shameful to live shamefully for those who are nobly-born" (989).

Elektra's plan has been called many things: "self-destructive", "suicidal", "rash", and even "pathetic".[6] For some it is evidence of her heroic nature, for others, her delusion. Many commentators, while acknowledging the obvious heroic nature of her decision, are troubled by the failure to mention Klytaimnestra's name, and some have taken this as evidence of Elektra's cunning nature and her attempt to hide her true motives from her sister.[7] Yet this is a speech ill suited for rallying Chrysothemis to arms. All the motivations and reasons for action have been the concern of Elektra rather than of her sister. For Chrysothemis, being *eusebes* means obeying her mother

---

[6] Woodard 1964: 188; Knox 1995: 17; Linforth 1962: 103; Gellie 1972: 120 respectively.

[7] There have been various responses to the absence of Klytaimnestra's name: Kirkwood 1942: 90 suggests that Elektra unconsciously leaves out Klytaimnestra and thus deceives herself as well as Chrysothemis as to the nature of the action. Others have interpreted it as an underhanded attempt to deceive her sister that casts her character in a rather unpleasant and morally questionable light. Johansen 1964: 21–22 takes this approach, and his reading is embraced by Kamerbeek. Others who have argued similarly include Kells *ad* 957; Segal 1981: 284 and 465 n. 56. Kitzinger 1991: 321 endorses this view but adds the suggestion that there may be a hidden assumption that they will only have the chance to kill one before they are stopped. On the other side are Adams 1957: 73 and Linforth 1963: 102–3. Gellie 1972: 119–120 and those who point out that Aigisthos is the main enemy; thus there would be no point in killing Klytaimnestra without Aigisthos. For these scholars, the main purpose of the scene is to emphasize her courage and determination to attack the enemy. Waldock 1966: 185 points out that the reaction of Chrysothemis is significant here, for she does not mention Klytaimnestra either. He sees the scene as further evidence of how all mention of the matricide is suppressed. Alexanderson 1966: 88, while conceding that it may be possible to see the craftiness of Elektra, stresses her heroic determination.

even if this involves her in an action that is *asebes* towards her father, the community and the gods. Freedom is simply being free to live in safety and comfort and move about the palace unhindered while honour means simply looking out for one's interests. Elektra is not very optimistic that Chrysothemis will agree to her plan as her later words indicate (1017–18), but she makes the attempt nonetheless because she sees her sister bound by the same obligations as she is. If Elektra only wished to secure the assistance of Chrysothemis, rather than the much more difficult task of attempting to persuade her sister of her duty, then she would have been better off hiding her plan altogether. Aigisthos is an opponent far more likely to frighten Chrysothemis than her mother. It seems unlikely then that we are to image that Elektra is plotting to kill Klytaimnestra and cunningly keeps this knowledge from her sister, as Johansen and Kamerbeek have argued.[8] If we examine her speech for what it reveals about her motives, we may better understand the reasons for the singling out of Aigisthos and the significance of the absence of Klytaimnestra's name.

Elektra appeals first to two principles that formed the basis of her earlier confrontation with the Chorus and her sister, *eusebeia* (968) and *eleutheria* (970). Her claim that they will win praise for their piety from their father and brother embraces not simply a form of familial piety, but involves care for the dead and their claim to justice, principles basic to the foundation of any community. To be *eusebes* means above all to uphold traditional beliefs (*patrios nomos*). Aigisthos' position as ruler of the *polis* and head of the *oikos* constitutes a breach of every form of *eusebeia*. His continued prosperity is an affront to the gods, the community, the family, and the dead, and thus his overthrow is necessary to restore *eusebeia* to the *polis*. Elektra's second claim is that they will win their freedom. As the earlier debate with her sister has established, for Elektra, *eleutheria* is the freedom to uphold the traditional beliefs of the community and the freedom to fulfil their social and biological roles within the *oikos* and *polis*. Chrysothemis' way of life is a negation of both, for she has enslaved herself to the will of another and is willing to endure the negation of her role within the community in order to maintain a restricted form of freedom. Aigisthos' denial of their freedom in order to protect his rule is a contravention of the fundamental norms of society;

---

[8] See note 7 above.

and his overthrow is the only way in which they may attain the freedom which is in accordance with their *physis*. Unlike her sister's, Elektra's motives here are ethical and this aspect of her speech is entirely consistent with her earlier reasoning in her exchange with the Chorus and Chrysothemis. In this respect, the mention or failure to mention Klytaimnestra seems irrelevant. Aigisthos is the one who has usurped Agamemnon's position and holds all the political power; and he is the one who prevents their marriages and deprives them of their patrimony. Equally significant, that Elektra makes him their opponent rather than Klytaimnestra is clear evidence that she is not driven by a personal desire to retaliate for the wrongs she has suffered at the hands of her mother.

It is Elektra's final appeal which strikes a decidedly different note; not only is it one least likely to convince her sister, but given that it is an appeal to the desire for honour and glory, it is also the one which is least appropriate for their situation:

> τίς γάρ ποτ᾽ ἀστῶν ἢ ξένων ἡμᾶς ἰδὼν
> τοιοῖσδ᾽ ἐπαίνοις οὐχὶ δεξιώσεται,
> "ἴδεσθε τώδε τὼ κασιγνήτω, φίλοι,
> ὣ τὸν πατρῷον οἶκον ἐξεσωσάτην,
> ὣ τοῖσιν ἐχθροῖς εὖ βεβηκόσιν ποτὲ
> ψυχῆς ἀφειδήσαντε προὐστήτην φόνου.
> τούτω φιλεῖν χρή, τώδε χρὴ πάντας σέβειν·
> τώδ᾽ ἔν θ᾽ ἑορταῖς ἔν τε πανδήμῳ πόλει
> τιμᾶν ἅπαντας οὕνεκ᾽ ἀνδρείας χρεών."
> τοιαῦτά τοι νὼ πᾶς τις ἐξερεῖ βροτῶν,
> ζώσαιν θανούσαιν θ᾽ ὥστε μὴ 'κλιπεῖν κλέος. (975–85)

> Who of citizens or strangers, when seeing us
> will not hail us with such commendation,
> "Look at these two sisters, friends,
> who saved their father's paternal household,
> who risking their lives, once took
> murderous action against their powerful
> enemies who were safely placed.
> It is necessary to love them and for all to respect them;
> in feasts and in gatherings of the whole citizen body
> everyone must honour these two on account of their courage."
> Every single person will say such things of us
> so that our fame will never stop, living or dead.

Elektra's vision of glory takes the form of an imaginary speech of praise, a type of speech which projects the imagined future opinion of others and is often introduced by the *topos* "someone will see you and say".[9] Sometimes called *tis* speeches, they are given in order to persuade a person to action by imagining the future praise which will be won; or sometimes they take the form of a speech of blame in which negative public reaction is projected in order to discourage cowardly or discreditable conduct. Like *aidos*, then, a *tis* speech may either function in a prohibitive manner to restrain behaviour of a certain type or conversely, work as a powerful incentive to action. Indeed, perhaps nothing is more characteristic of the concept of *aidos* than this type of speech which imagines "what people will say", for it has its source in the same thing: the awareness of and the respect for the perceived ideal norms of society.

Elektra attempts to move Chrysothemis to action by imagining the future praise which they will win for their bravery if they kill Aigisthos, not from any anonymous *tis*, however, but from the whole *polis*, both citizens and visitors. Like her earlier lamentation, which was an attempt to uphold communal standards, here too, Elektra defines her action with reference to the *polis*. Citizens and strangers alike will hail them, praising them as the sisters who saved their father's *oikos*, avenging the murder of their father (975–80). For their *andreia*, they are bound to be rewarded by the community with *philia*, *sebas*, and *time* and gain undying *kleos* (981–85).[10] While Elektra's

---

[9] Wilson 1979: 1. See Wilson's article and de Jong 1987: 69–84 on imaginary speeches on praise in Homer. This aspect of Elektra's speech has inspired a number of arguments: Kamerbeek *ad* 976 thinks that her words resemble a "laudatory epitaph" that suggests the praise she sees them as winning may come after their death. Juffras 1991: 101–102 on the other hand argues more specifically that this speech is designed to evoke the image of a statue commemorating the two sisters as tyrannicides, comparable to the tyrant slayers, Harmodios and Aristogeiton. As Juffras notes, these types of speeches usually take one of two forms: (1) a speech delivered at a tomb (e.g. Hektor's speech at 7.87–91 where he imagines men one day speaking at the tomb of a man; Agamemnon's speech at 4.176–82 where he imagines how the Trojans will react with scorn if Menelaos dies at Troy) (2) the imagined response to the behaviour of the speaker himself (e.g., *Il.* 8.68–150). Unlike Kamerbeek, Juffras suggests that the speech is designed in such a way so that it can suggest honours to the sisters while living as well as later. Kitzinger 1991: 321 follows Kamerbeek here suggesting that while Elektra holds out marriage to Chrysothemis when she speaks of the rewards she will gain, it is only the honour that is paid to their tombs.

[10] The type of courage expressed by Elektra is a kind of political or civic *andreia* distinguished by Aristotle in the *Nicomachean Ethics* as a variant of true courage (1116a15–32). True courage is an *arete* because it is done for the sake of τὸ καλόν (1116a12), while political courage (πολιτικὴ ἀνδρεία) is exercised because of customs (διὰ τὰ ἐκ τῶν νόμων), honour (διὰ τὰς τιμάς), and *aidos* (δι' αἰδῶ) (1116a18–19). Political courage is most like true courage, but because it is associated with hon-

motives thus have their basis in the beliefs and customs of the *polis*, *eusebeia* and the desire to restore their freedom, she is also driven by the desire for fame and glory. For her, the killing of Aigisthos is a heroic deed which will bring them everlasting glory and which will be celebrated by the *polis*. With its explicit mention of everlasting *kleos* and *time*, as well as the male virtue of *andreia*, this speech is the most masculine and heroic sounding one of the play.

What is so disturbing about this speech is that it betrays a perception of the vengeance as a heroic deed worthy of honour and glory strikingly similar to Orestes. As we have seen, he overcame his hesitation at the use of deception by the thought of the great *kleos* he would win through defeating his enemies. He too failed to mention his mother and instead spoke only in the vaguest terms of falling upon his enemies. Elektra, who was always so aware of the shameful means by which she maintained her belief in *dike* has now overcome this conflict by the same dubious rationale which informed her brother's reasoning, that is, by reference to the winning of *kleos* and *time*. With Orestes 'dead' and Klytaimnestra's blatant act of *hybris*, we saw the other side of Elektra's *aidos* becoming operative: the angry resentful aspect of *aidos* which acts to avoid ignominy and disgrace. Now, driven entirely by the desire to avoid a shameful and discreditable life, she is blind to everything else. Both Orestes and Elektra conceive of the deed in terms of honour and glory and both fail to acknowledge that in their case their enemies are also related to them by blood. In terms of the heroic code, the defeat of one's enemies is an action which brings honour and glory to the hero. Yet this is a code that is ill-suited for their circumstances, which include a royal *oikos* corrupted by adultery and murder, and a *polis* oppressed by tyranny. As necessary as it may be to kill their enemies in order to restore order, it should not be conceived as a heroic action worthy of *kleos* and *time*, as this ignores the terrible breach of blood-ties involved. Sophokles in placing Elektra's perception of the vengeance

---

our, it is not a true excellence; at the same time it is superior to the courage which comes from fear. One might be tempted, Aristotle notes, to place in this category those who are compelled to act by their rulers; but these men are inferior, inasmuch as they act not because of *aidos*, but because of fear and a desire to avoid not the shameful, but the painful. Of course, for Aristotle, courage was primarily a male virtue (the word itself is etymologically derived from ἀνήρ). Women were thought capable of achieving the virtues of self-control, justice and even courage, but only with reference to their capacity for subordination (*Politics* 1260a and 1277b).

as a heroic deed which will win them *kleos* within a set of fictional circumstances alludes to the falsity inherent in this understanding.[11]

Moreover, for all her determination Elektra has no real plan to speak of, other than "kill Aigisthos". She makes no mention of how they are to accomplish this, but speaks to why they should kill him, what their lives will be like if they do not, and what they will gain if they do. The absence of any mention of 'how' alludes to the impossible nature of it, reminding us of the need for the masculine strength of Orestes. On one level, then, the *dolos* establishes that Elektra moves to the right end, the restoration of order; on another, it shows her as much lacking full understanding as Orestes regarding the true nature of their deed. Each offspring has only a partial understanding of the act: Elektra who understands its necessity for the restoration of freedom and *eusebeia*, and Orestes who understands how it is to be accomplished. Ultimately, however, it is the *dolos* commanded by Apollo which contains the potential for the deed to be carried out with justice. The test of their capacity for pity is what will bring them to an understanding of the nature of *philia* and allow them to conceive the deed in terms of *dike* rather than honour and glory.

6.3.1   *The reaction of Chrysothemis*

Compliant though Chrysothemis appears, she only agrees to help to the limit of her strength; as Elektra's plan involves physical action, her response is predictable. In words that recall their earlier opposition, Chrysothemis accuses her sister of acting without sense or caution:

---

[11] It could be argued that the mention of Aigisthos' name together with Elektra's vague reference to enemies (979) is meant to refer to the order of the killings. As Kamerbeek points out, the "killing of one involves the killing of the other and Electra would act out of character if indeed she planned the death of Aegisthus while sparing Clytaemestra." For him, this means that Elektra is attempting to deceive Chrysothemis but it is not necessary to understand deliberate guile at work here (that would be just as much as acting out of character for Elektra as well). It could be that the audience would assume the killing of Klytaimnestra and that the mention of Aigisthos' name means that he would be killed first and then Klytaimnestra, i.e. the order of the killings in the *Oresteia*. In other words, we could see a subtle allusion to the *Choephoroi*. Yet this is not what happens in the play as Klytaimnestra is killed first and then Aigisthos. Placed in the false circumstances of Orestes' death, the allusion to the *Oresteia* could be taken as a rejection of the *lex talionis* and the pursuit of the Furies.

καὶ πρίν γε φωνεῖν, ὦ γυναῖκες, εἰ φρενῶν
ἐτύγχαν᾽ αὕτη μὴ κακῶν, ἐσῴζετ᾽ ἂν
τὴν εὐλάβειαν, ὥσπερ οὐχὶ σῴζεται.
ποῖ γάρ ποτε βλέψασα τοιοῦτον θράσος
αὐτή θ᾽ ὁπλίζῃ κἄμ᾽ ὑπηρετεῖν καλεῖς; (992–96)

Before speaking, women, if she had
good sense, she would be observing
due caution, as she does not.
Where have you looked arming yourself with
such boldness and calling upon me to second you?

She then proceeds to remind Elektra of her female *physis*: "You are
a woman, not a man, and your strength is less than that of your
adversaries" (997–98). Chrysothemis may appear morally weak and
her concern for physical safety less than admirable, but she does see
things realistically. Elektra does not have the masculine *sthenos* of her
enemies and her plan is certain to end in their defeat. Chrysothemis
ends her speech to her sister with the same plea she made earlier:
be sensible and give in to those in power.

Rejected by her sister, Elektra declares her intention to act alone:
"But I must do this deed single-handed and alone; for I will not
leave it unattempted" (1019–20). The determination with which she
expresses herself surprises her sister: "Ah! Would that you had shown
such a mind when our father died; for you would have accomplished
anything" (1021–22). Elektra's answer (ἀλλ᾽ ἦ φύσιν γε, τὸν δὲ νοῦν
ἥσσων τότε. 1023) with its contrast between *physis* and *nous* is generally taken to mean that she now has a maturity and intelligence
which she lacked earlier.[12] Yet the response that her *physis* was the
same but her mind weaker points to the difference in her behaviour
now that she has assumed the role of Orestes. Previously, Elektra's
aidos never drove her to do anything more than lament, an effective
form of action in that it brings discomfort to the usurpers, but it is
done in line with a typically female role, that of mourning. With
Orestes dead, Elektra sees herself as not only obliged to act but also

---

[12] Jebb *ad* 1023 takes it to mean that she did not have the "ripe intelligence to
grasp the whole situation", while Kells *ad* 1023 translates it as "I was inferior in
my intelligence on that day." Kamerbeek comes closest to the sense in which I take
it with his suggestion that it means of 'mental energy', that is mind in relation to
a person's ability to decide on his course of conduct.

having the authority to do so as the sole representative of her father's *oikos*. Her use of the word *nous* here is to signify not only greater mental maturity, but also a reflection of the authority she feels she has to decide her own course of action.

At this point, the opposition between the two sisters is most pronounced, and it is clear that Elektra will never convince Chrysothemis. Yet Sophokles extends their discussion in the form of a *stichomythia*, and this part of the debate strongly recalls their earlier controversy over what constitutes *sophron* behaviour in their circumstances. The rapid cut-and-thrust of the *stichomythia* highlights and intensifies the complete antithesis in attitude and behaviour between the two sisters. Chrysothemis' first priority is looking out for herself and avoiding harm, and because the plan is bound to come to grief, she sees no reason for undertaking it. For Elektra, such thoughts of physical safety are a form of cowardice (*deilia* 1027) and lead to dishonour (*atimia* 1035). Elektra may have justice on her side, but the recognition that the pursuit of justice brings harm (1042) is enough to stop Chrysothemis from acting. For one sister, physical safety takes precedence over honour and for the other, honour demands that she have no concern for her own safety. They stand at opposite ends of the moral spectrum and may as well be speaking different languages; neither can reconcile the other's actions to her own ethical code. The departure of Chrysothemis into the palace seals the irrevocable separation that now exists between the two sisters.

6.3.2 τὸ μὴ καλόν

The choral ode coming directly after this has caused some debate among critics, partly because of the elusive language, but primarily because many suspect corruption in the text. The general meaning, however, seems clear. The Chorus sings the praise of the wisest race of birds, those which repay the debt to their parents in contrast to the negligence of humans. It calls upon φάμα to bring this news of the conflict between the sisters to the Atreidai below. After Elektra's determination to go ahead with her plan despite Chrysothemis' refusal to help, the Chorus is clearly rebuking Chrysothemis for her betrayal and abandonment (1074), and praising Elektra for her loyalty to her father (εὔπατρις 1081). As Burton points out, Orestes was called εὔπατρις by the Chorus (162) and by Elektra (858). Now that he is thought dead, she receives her brother's epithet when she assumes his duty.[13]

There is, however, an important hint about the nature of the deed which Elektra resolves to embrace:

> οὐδεὶς τῶν ἀγαθῶν ζῶν
> κακῶς εὔκλειαν αἰσχῦναι θέλει
> νώνυμος, ὦ παῖ παῖ,
> ὡς καὶ σὺ πάγκλαυτον αἰ-
> ῶνα κοινὸν εἵλου,
> τὸ μὴ καλὸν καθοπλίσα-
> σα δύο φέρειν <ἐν> ἑνὶ λόγῳ,
> σοφά τ' ἀρίστα τε παῖς κεκλῆσθαι.[14] (1082–89)

No one of those who are noble wishes to shame
a good repute by living basely, so as to
become inglorious, my child,
as you chose an all-lamentable
shared life so as
to win, having made ready the shameful,
two names in one: to be called wise
and a most loyal daughter.

Elektra is commended for undertaking a deed which will win her praise, but is at the same time called μὴ καλόν. This line has always caused problems for critics, as the Chorus, having first praised Elektra for her plan, then proceeds to call it μὴ καλόν, 'not *kalos*' or 'shameful', a blatant contradiction which has led many to suspect some sort of corruption.[15] Many solutions have been proposed over the years

---

[13] Burton 1980: 210; Winnington-Ingram 1980: 245 n. 91.

[14] I have followed the text of Pearson here rather than that of L-J & W for reasons made clear in the following discussion.

[15] The MSS all have τὸ μὴ καλὸν καθοπλίσασα and many editors simply translate καθοπλίσασα as 'having vanquished', a translation which has its source in the Scholiast (who glosses it as καταπολεμήσασα "having warred down' and supports it by the analogies of κατακοντίζειν, κατατοξεύειν, καταταιχμάζειν). But this, as often pointed out, gives a sense to the word not found elsewhere. καθοπλίσασα generally means 'equip', 'arm' or 'prepare' and thus many suspect corruption. A number of solutions have been proposed to this problem. Some replace καθοπλίσασα with some other word: Hermann 1864: 156 (καθιππάσασα); Gleditsch (δ' ἀποπρύσασα) 1867: 15; Gräber (ἀπολακτίσασα) 1870: 15. See Most 1994: 132–133 and n. 24 for bibliography on these citations as well as others below. Benardete 1961: 96 suggests ὑπεροπλίσασα 'spurning', 'rejecting' and this has been followed by Kamerbeek and Burton 1980: 213–214 n. 41. Others have focused their attention on τὸ μὴ καλόν. Lloyd-Jones 1954: 95 proposes ἄκος suggesting that τὸ μὴ = τομή, a gloss

with some emending the participle καθοπλίσασα and others τὸ μὴ καλόν.[16] If we accept the text as transmitted (as I do) and place the words within the moral framework established by the play, their contradictory nature may be seen as a reflection of the moral dilemma

---

on ἄκος and this reading has been followed in the OCT 1990. The sense now would be 'arming a (cutting) remedy'. But this is a radical solution to the problem of καθοπλίσασα. Bremer and van Taalman Kip 1994: 242 criticize this reading for its obscurity while Kirkwood 1991: 22–31 calls it "ingenious, but not very probable"; he goes on to suggest that it is not altogether certain that τὸ μὴ καλὸν καθοπλίσασα is wrong, as there are many ways in which the revenge can be viewed as something other than *kalon*. Kopff 1993: 155, however, thinks Lloyd-Jones' reading is to be preferred over other attempts to preserve the manuscript reading. Kells on the other hand proposes τὰ μὴ καλ' οὐ so that the line now has the sense "not having armed (or equipped) ignobility (so as) to win two prizes at once" (see Appendix 2). Lloyd-Jones 1975: 11 criticizes the insertion of οὐ before καθοπλίσασα as "flat". Most 1994: 135 suggests τομῇ so that the line now means "having armed a noble cutter". There have been a few attempts to retain the original reading. Whitelaw and Hermann argue that the Chorus is referring to her plan to kill her enemies and they have been followed most recently by Stokes 1979: 134–143 who suggests that the Chorus recognizes what is praiseworthy in her actions but still express its disapproval at her plan to kill her enemies and Stinton 1986: n. 80. L-J & W² criticize Stokes for translating τὸ μὴ καλόν as "evil" and Stinton for translating καθοπλίσασα as "having made ready". The objection has also been made that μή is too general and abstract to refer to a particular event such as the killing of Aigisthos and Klytaimnestra. Other discussions of these lines include Booth 1976: 127–33 and 1986: 103–6; West 1979: 104–5. Most 1994: 129–134 provides a comprehensive overview of the debate as well as offering his own solution (see note 16 below).

[16] Scholars have often suspected corruption in ὡς καὶ σὺ πάγκλαυτον αἰῶνα κοινὸν εἵλου as well. Here the problem is twofold: first, to what decision does εἵλου refer? Her loyalty to her dead father or her recent decision to avenge Agamemnon? Many think that the more logical choice is the latter (Winnington-Ingram 1979: 9–10; Stinton 1986: 100; Most 1994: 135–137). More irksome, however, is κοινόν, which seems to make no sense, for in what way could Elektra be thought to be choosing a "shared" life. Some have proposed that this common fate refers to death (Erfundt and Hermann); others take the adjective to mean that Elektra will share a life with the dead (Jebb and Kells). Winnington-Ingram 1979: 9 criticizes this reading but goes no further than suggesting simply that the text be obelized. Kamerbeek *ad* 1085, 1086 suggests that κοινόν is being used in the sense of κοινωνόν, and he translates it as "you chose a lifetime of sorrow as your partner." Most 1994: 136 objects that "the meaning is strained, the personification of αἰῶνα implausible, and the adjective on this account otiose." Given these problems, many simply declare the text corrupt and numerous emendations have been proposed: κεῖνον (Fröhlich, Blumenthal, Schuppe); κλεινὸν (Sirks, followed by L-J & W); ἀμείνον (Giesing, West). L-J &W² argue that the Chorus calls Electra's life κλεινόν since "the life of a matricide, however glorious, is a life of many tears." Bremer and Erp Taalman Kip 1994: 241–242 point out that this reading makes little sense within the tragedy as a whole, as the Chorus never suggests the revenge will result in a life of tears. See Most 1994: 137 for a full list of the emendations. For Most 1994: 158 the problem is not κοινὸν at all but εἵλου. His solution is to obelize εἵλου and read τομῇ for τὸ μὴ. If we retain the text, there is some sense in which *koinon* could be

which lies at the heart of Elektra's tragedy.[17] Her conflict has always been that she must act shamefully in some respect in order to uphold the principles of *eusebeia* and *aidos*. We saw this in the first confrontation with the Chorus in which Elektra claimed that her behaviour upholds *eusebeia*, but at the same time recognized its shameful nature (307–9); we saw this again in the confrontation with her mother in which she claimed that Klytaimnestra's actions, even if they were just, were shameful (558–60). She then proceeded to show that the killing of Agamemnon was not just, but the implication remained that an act can be shameful even if just. With Orestes still alive, Elektra's shameful actions involved a lack of respect for her mother and behaviour unsuitable for a woman. Confronted with Orestes' 'death' and her mother's outrageous behaviour, the overriding desire to avoid a shameful life takes precedence. As she says, it is αἰσχρόν to keep living αἰσχρῶς for those who are born καλῶς (989). The Chorus recognizes the validity of this assertion by calling her an ἀγαθή who would never damage her fame by living κακῶς, but then also proceeds to call her plan μὴ καλόν. Before we regard this with most critics as an intolerable contradiction, we should consider that what the Chorus sings about here, perhaps unconsciously, is a truth which Elektra has failed to grasp: her undertaking will involve her in a just yet shameful action. The Chorus praises Elektra for her willingness to undertake this, calling her a wise and a most loyal daughter (σοφά τ' ἀρίστα τε παῖς κεκλῆσθαι 1089), but in designating it as μὴ καλόν it reminds us what her deed will involve: the spilling of kindred blood. Just as in the *kommos*, where the words of the Chorus speak to the truth of the situation, here too, the Chorus' reference to the deed as μὴ καλόν reveals a truth to which

---

read as the principle involved in Elektra's decision, that is, Elektra chooses a life shared with the community rather than family. In other words, in choosing to kill the tyrants, Elektra must reject blood-ties for communal ties. This comes close to Heiden's suggestion (mentioned in a footnote by Most 1994: 136 n. 52) that *koinon* refers to the οἱ ἀγαθοί mentioned at 1082. She chooses a life shared with them rather than her family.

[17] Others who have similarly wished to retain the text include Whitelaw 1883 and, more recently, Stinton 1986: 84 & 100. Whitelaw thinks that "Electra has resolved to do a deed which, till it is done, looks to all eyes as to those of Chrysothemis, unlovely and a crime; but, having done it, she knows that the universal voice will approve alike her wisdom and her piety." Stinton departs slightly from this reading with his suggestion that there is a "double irony: the act Elektra intends is indeed unlovely, not καλόν".

Elektra is blind: the matricide. The objection that μή is too general to refer to a particular act such as the killing of Aigisthos and Klytaimnestra misses the point. The Chorus is not referring to the killing of the tyrants at all (Elektra's plan only mentions Aigisthos), but reminding us of the terrible violation of blood-ties involved in the coming deed. A breach of *philia*, especially between blood relatives, is a breach of *aidos* and is an act that arouses the greatest feelings of horror. We shall see that for the remainder of the play the Chorus will consistently recognize the dual nature of this deed, as something terrible but not blameworthy. Here too, while the Chorus may sing about the horror of the deed, it affirms its justice and its final words are a wish that her piety may be rewarded by the triumph over her enemies, for in upholding the highest laws of Zeus (μέγιστ' . . . νόμιμα 1095–96), she has suffered an unhappy fate.

CHAPTER SEVEN

ELEKTRA AND ORESTES: REUNION AND VENGEANCE

7.1 Preliminary Remarks

The last section of the play consists of the reunion of sister and brother (fourth *epeisodion* 1098–1383) and the vengeance (*exodos* 1398–1510). The recognition scene between Orestes and Elektra is a crucial theme in all three Elektra tragedies, but in Aischylos and Euripides, the reunion occurs early in the play and Elektra is fully informed of the planned vengeance.[1] Sophokles, however, has delayed it until almost the end of the play, and Elektra, unaware of Orestes' plan, has fallen victim to the deception. Orestes and Pylades enter in the disguise of Phocians, accompanied by attendants carrying the urn of ashes. Orestes fails to recognize the wretched girl before him as his sister, but her lamentation over the urn easily identifies her. After gently divesting her of the urn, Orestes reveals his identity, showing her the signet ring of their father. Brother and sister are reunited, and Elektra's grief turns to joy. There is a touching μέλος ἀπὸ σκηνῆς or 'recognition duo' between the siblings; then Orestes' thoughts turn to those inside. The *paidagogos* returns, berating them for their foolishness in such dangerous circumstances, and another recognition takes place between Elektra and the *paidagogos*. He gives his report on the situation within the palace and plans are made. Elektra makes a prayer to Apollo, and the Chorus, in a very brief third *stasimon* (1384–97) imagines the human avengers as the twin Erinyes carrying out the killings.[2] The last part of the play focuses on the vengeance itself: Klytaimnestra is killed first; instead of presenting it as a confrontation between mother and son, Sophokles has us witness the matricide through the reaction of Elektra. Although a powerful scene, the killing of Klytaimnestra is over quickly and the poet turns our

---

[1] For a good comparison of the three recognition scenes see Solmsen 1967: 31–67.

[2] The Chorus here may be referring to either Orestes and Elektra or Orestes and Pylades.

attention away from the matricide to the confrontation between Orestes and Aigisthos. Three times Aigisthos attempts to delay his entrance into the palace but his tactics are to no avail, and finally he is ushered inside to be killed by Orestes. The Chorus ends the play with a brief summation: the offspring of Atreus have won their way to freedom. Critics have debated aspects of the recognition scene, but it is, not unexpectedly, the killings themselves that have sparked the greatest controversy. The vengeance, however, cannot be properly understood without first understanding the full significance of what takes place in the recognition between brother and sister.

7.2 *The Reunion*

Critics have often reacted uneasily to the recognition scene, as Sophokles' seems to prolong Elektra's lamentation needlessly by delaying Orestes' revelation of his identity. Some, finding it difficult to sympathize with Elektra's grief given the presence of her brother, think that the play falters at this point. For these critics the misplaced grief diminishes the tragic stature of Elektra and the whole scene strikes a false note.[3] Others think that the lengthy display of grief over the urn points to Orestes' apparent indifference to the plight of her sister.[4] Whether he recognizes her immediately, as some suppose, or only after the lamentation, he is often thought heartless, and even those who acknowledge a genuine pity or "new warmth" in Orestes, are dismayed by its brevity.[5]

---

[3] Vickers 1973: 570 for instance, thinks that "since we know that Elektra's grief is entirely misplaced, the irony of Orestes being present at his own elegies backfires, makes the scene ring even more false." Stevens 1978: 118 thinks that the superior knowledge of the audience diminishes the tragic stature of Elektra to some extent. Others think that the audience's inability to sympathize with Elektra is evidence of her increasing loss of power in the play. Kitzinger 1991: 322 takes this approach, arguing that "the listener cannot wholly enter into her feeling, or be informed by her emotion, or allow it to dominate his point of view."

[4] Others have gone as far as to accuse Orestes of cruelty for recognizing Elektra, but then allowing her to continue lamenting in ignorance of his identity. Such is the view of Schein 1982: 77 who speaks of the "callous cruelty of Orestes in forcing Elektra to endure such grief" and the delay which reflects "his indifference to her feelings." Seale 1982: 70 as well speaks of the "cold indifference" of Orestes.

[5] As Blundell 1989: 174 does. She discusses the pity Orestes feels for his sister, remarking that this emotion which has been little in evidence now seems to introduce a "new warmth". She suggests that it functions to provide emotional confirmation

We should remember, however, how the 'lie' of the *paidagogos* has functioned thus far. It has served to expose Klytaimnestra as a woman with no respect for any law, moral or otherwise; to confirm that Chrysothemis will always choose the path of least resistance, forfeiting justice or anything else that might infringe upon her personal safety; and to reveal the determined heroism of Elektra's moral will. In the recognition scene, as we shall see, the *dolos* of Orestes serves to show us the terrible price in suffering Elektra has paid to maintain her moral beliefs; but it will also be revealed that nothing, neither hatred nor desire for vengeance, is as great as the bond of *philia* which exists between her and her brother; for Orestes, the witnessing of his sister's grief for him awakens his compassion and brings him to a greater understanding of the nature of the deed he is about to undertake. The killings coming afterwards must be largely understood in the light of this scene.

As often pointed out, the appearance of Orestes immediately after the final words of the *stasimon* makes him seem the answer to the Chorus' wish just as the *paidagogos* appeared to be the answer to Klytaimnestra's prayer.[6] Orestes and Pylades, disguised as Phocians, come upon Elektra and the Chorus, and although he does not recognize his sister, he has the attendants give her the urn. We have already seen something of Elektra's reaction to her brother's death in an earlier speech (804–22), but that was more a response to the *hybris* of her mother than to the death of her brother. Now confronted with the tangible evidence of his death in the form of his ashes, Elektra faces the terrible reality of his death. With this realization, the masculine *arete* of the previous scene, her heroic determination and resolve to kill Aigisthos, vanish. Holding the urn in her arms and addressing it as Orestes, Elektra breaks down and mourns his death. There have been many scenes of lamentation in this play, but none had the pathos and intensity of this one. While she still had some hope of Orestes returning, Elektra always directed her lamentation to the living as a means of bringing about that day

---

of their alliance. Ultimately, however, what Blundell sees as its most striking aspect is its brevity, for Orestes displays little warmth after this; moreover, for her, the matricide dispels any lingering feelings of pity. Winnington-Ingram 1980: 229 too notes Orestes' pity, but makes little of it. See n. 9 below for discussions of Orestes' response to his sister.

[6] Gardiner 1986: 154; Burton 1980: 214.

when vengeance could be taken and justice restored. For the first time, her lamentation turns entirely on her sorrow and grief; all thoughts of revenge disappear. Instead, she sees only the futility of all her actions: her care, her labour, and the rescue of her brother have come to nothing. With both her father and brother dead, and her mother inside celebrating her victory, Elektra finally gives up, wishing nothing more than to join her brother in death. Those who suppose that the presence of Orestes reduces the stature of Elektra or diminishes the impact of her grief fail to recognize its purpose. The grief may be misplaced, but what it reveals about Elektra is not; for the *dolos*, in creating this false set of circumstances, lays open the terrible reality of her life. We are not meant to sympathize with her grief so much as feel pity for this woman who for years refused to acquiesce in the crimes of the tyrants; who was able to endure all the physical hardships they had imposed upon her; who, in the end, is brought down not by anything they have done to her, but by the assumed death of her brother. Not only do we see the cost of maintaining her beliefs, but we see that her desire for vengeance, her hatred of the rulers, is not as great as her *philia* for her brother. Grief and pity for her brother prevail over the desire for fame, glory, and vengeance. Yet in the fact of the *dolos* lies Elektra's *soteria*; for Sophokles, in having her destruction predicated on Orestes' death, secures her salvation, for the fictionality of his death and the reality of being alive restore her; his victory ensures hers.

Orestes, who initially fails to recognize this woman before him, realizes during her lament who she is and his first words reflect how deeply he has been moved by the intensity of her grief:[7]

φεῦ φεῦ, τί λέξω; ποῖ λόγων ἀμηχανῶν
ἔλθω; κρατεῖν γὰρ οὐκέτι γλώσσης σθένω. (1174–75)

---

[7] Despite all attempts by scholars to pinpoint that moment when Orestes recognizes Elektra, there seems no hard evidence to suggest anything more certain than that at some point during her lament he realizes who she is. Some, however, suppose that Orestes recognizes Elektra immediately: Jebb 1907: 151 thinks that the recognition occurs as early as 1106, but Orestes keeps silent about this until the Chorus mentions her name at 1171. On the other side are those who think that the lamentation identifies Elektra to Orestes: Bowra 1944: 249; Linforth 1963: 105–6: Solmsen 1967: 26 and n. 2; Kells *ad* 1123ff. Adams 1957: 75 wishes to wait until line 1171 when the Chorus actually says Elektra's name. Kamerbeek *ad* 1117, 8 strikes a kind of compromise between these two views with his claim of Orestes' "certain inner probability" that is confirmed by the lament.

> Alas, alas, what should I say? Which words, helpless that I am,
> am I to use? For I no longer have the strength to control my tongue.

His immediate reaction to the grief of his sister is a feeling of pain
at her wretched condition. Orestes' distress is apparent from his
repeated φεῦ φεῦ (1174) as well as from Elektra's question: τί δ'
ἔσχες ἄλγος; (1176). Lacking the strength to control his tongue to
sustain the *dolos*, Orestes virtually puts an end to it with his own
lament for her: οἴμοι ταλαίνης ἆρα τῆσδε συμφορᾶς. (1179).[8] He sees
before him a body dishonoured and ruined (ὦ σῶμ' ἀτίμως κἀθέως
ἐφθαρμένον. 1181); unwed and alone, she has been reduced to a
wretched condition (φεῦ τῆς ἀνύμφου δυσμόρου τε σῆς τροφῆς. 1183).
Orestes' reaction is not simply an expression of pain at her grief but
becomes an insight into his own condition, for in her sufferings he
recognizes his own fortunes (ὅσ' οὐκ ἄρ' ἤδη τῶν ἐμῶν ἐγὼ κακῶν.
1185).[9] In other words, Orestes recognizes that he too could suffer
and this awareness arouses his pity. In this way, he is brought to
understand his own life through the experience of hers and he realizes
that his well-being is deeply involved with that of his sister. Elektra,
surprised at the kindness of this stranger, reveals how much more

---

[8] *Sthenos* occurs at 333, 348, 604, 946, 998, 1014, 1175, and 1425. *Sthenos* means
strength, especially bodily strength in the Homeric epics, but by fifth century had
acquired a moral sense as well. Both meanings are used in this play. For Chrysothemis,
action requires physical strength (*sthenos*) which neither she nor Elektra possesses, so
she sees little reason for action. Elektra admits that she does not have *sthenos*, but
for her resistance only requires moral strength. Her plan, however, does require
sthenos which is one of the reasons Chrysothemis refuses to help. Orestes on the
other hand lacks the strength (*sthenos*) to carry through with the deception. The final
use of it is during the matricide in which Elektra tells Orestes, if he has the strength,
strike a second blow.

[9] Adams 1933: 210 and 1957: 74–76 (and Kirkwood 1958: 142–43 n. 33 who
supports him) states that Orestes shows a "deep personal concern for Elektra" which
shows his recognition of the terrible suffering she has endured. Both Adams 1957:
75–76 and Bowra 1944: 249 suggest that Orestes has a new motive for killing the
tyrants. For Adams, this is Apollo's doing as he recognizes the need for Orestes to
have such a new motive; for Bowra, Orestes' relationship was partial and abstract
and now it gains strength and form. Linforth 1963: 107 n. 4 rightly criticizes the
arguments of Adams and Bowra for their lack of evidence. Reinhardt 1979: 160–61
too sees a change in Orestes, but he interprets this as a shift from the "eager hero
bent on victory" to the brother whose contact with his sister has stirred his feelings. Gellie 1972: 123 and 290 n. 21 on the other hand thinks that this scene is
extended to reveal to us something about Orestes' character whom he calls apa-
thetic and blockish. Segal 1966: 513–516 and 528 has some sensitive and perceptive remarks about the reunion which he thinks has "deepened" Orestes' understanding.
See also Woodard 1964: 191.

she has suffered than this: she must live with the murderers of her
father (1190); she has been enslaved by force (1193) by a mother
who abuses and torments her (1197). In response to this revelation
of the circumstances of her existence, Orestes expresses his pity:

Ορ.   ὦ δύσποτμ᾽, ὡς ὁρῶν σ᾽ ἐποικτίρω πάλαι.
Ηλ.   μόνος βροτῶν νυν ἴσθ᾽ ἐποικτίρας ποτέ.
Ορ.   μόνος γὰρ ἥκω τοῖσι σοῖς ἀλγῶν κακοῖς. (1199–1201)

Or.   Unlucky one, I have long looked on you with pity.
El.   Know that you alone of mortals pity me.
Or.   Yes, for I alone have come feeling pain at your troubles.

Touched by this man's words, Elektra thinks he must be a kinsman
(ξυγγενής 1202) and Orestes, after ascertaining the trustworthiness of
the Chorus of women watching, slowly leads her to the realization
that he is her brother. Orestes then has been profoundly affected by
seeing the condition of his sister and unable to deceive her, chooses
to reveal himself to her.

Orestes' disclosure of his identity to Elektra is often criticized for
being unnecessarily extended, and some have seen this as cruelty on
his part. Yet the slow and gentle manner in which he leads his sister to the knowledge of his identity attests more to his compassion
than anything else. The lengthy *stichomythia* between the two is not
some misstep on Sophokles' part, but a crucial component in the
dramatic action, necessary in order that we recognize Orestes' willingness to call off the *dolos*-strategy of the vengeance out of pity for
his sister. He has witnessed the devastating effect his reported death
has had upon her and understands the need to divest his sister of
the urn which she assumes to contain his ashes before identifying
himself.[10] Thus he does not abruptly confront her with the truth,

---

[10] See Segal 1966: 514–15 and Solmsen 1967: 56–67 on how "gently Orestes
reveals his identity." Segal is surely right to emphasize how important it is that
Orestes first divests her of the symbol of his death before he reveals his identity.
In recent criticism, this urn has been made to bear the burden of some bizarre if
not fatuous theorizing. Rehm 1996: 55, for instance, calls the scene a "decon-
structionist's dream, for the urn embodies the tangible presence of absence, serv-
ing as the locus for conflicting meanings and a concrete expression of the gap
between sign and signified." Ringer 1996: 97 writes that "seldom has an empty
container carried so much significance. The urn is the central metaphor of this
play. As an empty vessel it also symbolizes the phenomenon of metaphor itself: it
serves as a metaphor of metaphor." For Ringer, the urn creates a "sense of metathe-
atricality". Burnett 1998: 128 on the other hand asserts that the urn "contains the

but allows Elektra to come to the realization herself that he is alive. The recognition between them is sealed first by the sign of his father's ring (1222–23) and then by the embrace of the two siblings (1226).

Pity is the impulse which has moved Orestes to reveal himself to her. In giving up the *dolos* strategy and leading Elektra to the knowledge that he is her brother, he acts solely for her benefit. This is most significant, as he places a *philia*-relationship above everything else, even risking the failure of the vengeance, and in his abandonment of the *dolos*, he makes a decision that would seem to work against his best interests, as it places him at some risk and jeopardizes the success of his enterprise. Thus the revelation of his identity is the act of someone who understands what constitutes the basis of *philia*; we only have to remember Klytaimnestra's lack of pity for her son's death and the explicit rejection of the *philia* relationship to see how fundamentally different Orestes shows himself to be from his mother. Orestes' act of *philia*, although it delays the vengeance and potentially threatens its success, is a decision which will work to his advantage in that it deepens his understanding of the nature of a *philos* relationship and prepares him for carrying out his deed as an act of justice.

7.2.1 *Dolos and dike*

Revealing the *dolos* to Elektra was not part of the original plan and to understand how this fits in with the vengeance, we need to review what we have discovered so far about the function of *dolos*, and then come to a final assessment of its function in the broader context of the whole drama and the working of *dike* in it. The oracle of Apollo brought together two apparently contrary elements: justice and deception. The use of deception was initially troubling to Orestes, but instead of overcoming his doubt by reference to *dike* he does so with the thought of winning *kleos*. The instruction to use *dolos* should have reminded Orestes of the unheroic nature of his enterprise; not yet understanding the nature of justice or what kind of action his undertaking would involve him in, he was able to resolve his conflict by

---

matricide since it contains the means to that deed." Others have seen an allusion to Aischylos here: Garner 1990: 221 suggests that this "Aeschylean image which never makes an actual stage appearance has been developed into a vivid focus of attention in Sophocles' play".

the thought of fame and glory. It was the interruption of Elektra's voice which indicated what the true conflict would be for him, and although Orestes hesitated, urged on by the words of the *paidagogos*, he left his sister to lament her sorrows inside the palace. Whether the *paidagogos* understood the necessity for the *dolos* or not, his obedience to divine command and loyalty to the *oikos* of Agamemnon prevented any meeting from taking place between brother and sister before the *dolos* came into operation. Orestes, who did not initially perceive the problematic nature of his undertaking, was nevertheless equipped by Apollo with something which would make him perceive it: the deception. Sophokles has radically realigned events so that Orestes is forced to face the questionable nature of his deed, not as in the *Oresteia*, through a confrontation with his mother but through an encounter with his sister. In effect, the *dolos* strategy brings Orestes to the recognition of the moral paradox of the vengeance first hinted at in the oracle through the alliance of *dolos* and *dike*: it is a deed that for all its justice is shameful, an awareness which Orestes will display in his handling of the vengeance.

For Klytaimnestra, the *dolos* of her son's death presented her with a choice: treating a blood relative as a *philos* or an *echthros*, i.e. responding with pity at the suffering of another or expressing joy at her good fortune. She chose the latter and her hybristic exultation in her victory revealed her complete disregard for the ties of kinship. To the warning signs of the dream and messenger *rhesis* of the *paidagogos*, Klytaimnestra remained impervious. Just as with Orestes, the *dolos* strategy functioned as a moral test; and when Klytaimnestra showed herself incapable of pitying her dead son, she forfeited all claim to being pitied by her son. The *dolos* strategy in exposing Klytaimnestra's true moral character by giving her the chance to decide herself the nature of the relationship between her and Orestes revealed its grounding in the working of *dike*. Chrysothemis on the other hand was only indirectly exposed to the deception through Elektra, yet at the same time, this still revealed her essential moral weakness and served to break the tenuous alliance formed between the sisters.

The effect of the *dolos* strategy on Elektra is more complex, for while it showed her *aidos* and distinguished her moral character from that of her mother, it was also the cause of her movement into a world in which she acted in ignorance of the reality of her situation. Admirable though her decision was to assume Orestes' role and undertake the killing herself, we saw that Elektra, like her brother, was similarly motivated by a desire for glory and honour and thus, like him, betrayed an ignorance of the *aischron* nature of the vengeance. The one who previously had been so aware of her breaches of *aidos*, who accused her mother of a lack of *aidos* in not acknowledging the shameful nature of Agamemnon's killing, failed to perceive how applicable these words were to her own circumstances. Both brother and sister, in conceiving of their deed in heroic terms, revealed only a partial understanding of *dike* and the true nature of the enterprise. The reunion of the two, however, is the recognition of one another as *philoi* brought about by their reciprocal feelings of pity. For Orestes, the recognition of his sister brings him an understanding of *philia* and thus is an important preparation for carrying out the vengeance; for Elektra, it has secured her *soteria*.

That *dike* is associated with deception has always been thought to cast more than a shadow of doubt over the legitimacy of the vengeance. While few would doubt that Klytaimnestra should be punished, many have questioned the means and the moral character of those who carry it out. What kind of justice sanctions deceit? Many have answered this in the same fashion as Winnington-Ingram has: the *lex talionis*.[11] The use of *dolos* for these critics only confirmed this assumption as it has been associated with the actions of both mother and son; we seem to have a case in which murder is repaid by murder; *dolos* by *dolos*. Yet from our examination of the *dolos* stratagem, we see that *dolos* has not simply served vengeance but rather is what will bring about the "just slaughters", as Apollo's oracle decreed. Unlike the law of *talio* justice which operates without regard to character or motive, *dike* in this play is based on the moral character and intention, and it has been the *dolos* stratagem which has revealed this. This is not to say that there is no moral ambivalence to the use of deception; no doubt, there is. It is the same moral ambivalence we see in Elektra's conduct, which is by some standards right and by others wrong. Her breach of *aidos* has its source in the pursuit of justice and is necessitated by the circumstances. There is no way in which she can overcome this dilemma: for all its justness, her behaviour is still touched by τὸ αἰσχρόν. So too with the deception: it has its roots in the pursuit of justice and is necessitated by

---

[11] Winnington-Ingram 1980: 221.

the circumstances but there remains something inherently unsavory in the act of deception. The oracle with its alliance of *dolos* and *dike* sets forth the moral framework of the vengeance as an act *dikaion* but *aischron*.

7.3 *The Alliance*

Immediately after the reunion, Elektra introduces her brother to the women of Argos (ὦ φίλταται γυναῖκες, ὦ πολίτιδες, ὁρᾶτ' Ὀρέστην τόνδε 1227–28). She addresses the Chorus expressly with the word πολίτιδες, a rare occurrence of the feminine form of πολίτης.[12] Its pronounced use draws attention to the role of the Chorus as the representatives of the city and thus the important role it will have in voicing the sentiments of the *polis* during the killings. This is the second of three recognitions structuring the last part of the play which unites those who form the opposition to the tyrants inside.[13]

The following μέλος ἀπὸ σκηνῆς (1232–87) which takes place between Orestes and Elektra is sometimes thought to signal a separation between brother and sister with her highly emotional sung lyrics in contrast to his spoken and restrained iambic trimeters. Gardiner rightly cautions against such an interpretation, noting that any polarity between the two is diminished by the presence of the Chorus. She suggests that "the rejoicing is more that of a group than of a pair".[14] Moreover, if we are to use metre as a reflection of their emotional character, we should note that Elektra's lyrics have a touch of iambic trimeters (1235, 1256) and Orestes' a touch of lyrics (1276, 1280).[15] Critics have also made too much of Orestes' attempts to restrain his sister (1236, 1238, 1257, 1259), interpreting this as his "callous indifference" or even as evidence of Elektra's increasing marginalization in the play.[16] Orestes' cautious behaviour

---

[12] This is not a common word in Greek tragedy; other occurrences include Euripides' *Elektra* 1335; it also appears in Aristotle at 1275b32 and 1278a25; Demosthenes 57.30 and 59.112; Diodoros 12.11.1; Isocrates 14.51; Plato *Laws* 7.814c.

[13] There is an additional recognition which takes place between Orestes and Aigisthos.

[14] Gardiner 1986: 156.

[15] Campbell 1969: 216 and Kamerbeek 1974: 162 point out that Orestes becomes lyrical at 1276 and 1280.

[16] Schein 1982: 77 and Kitzinger 1991: 323 respectively.

is better understood as a reflection of the grave danger they are in.
He has been diverted from his original plan and now, standing outside the palace of those whom he is planning to kill, he is at great
risk. That Elektra is overcome with joy and singing in excited lyrics
naturally makes him nervous and fearful that they may be discovered. While the 'duet' begins with his cautionary words to keep silent
(1236), followed by a number of unsuccessful attempts to restrain
Elektra's exuberance, it ends with a gesture of *philia* as Orestes gives
in to the love expressed by sister for him:

Ηλ.   μή μ᾽ ἀποστερήσῃς
       τῶν σῶν προσώπων ἡδονὰν μεθέσθαι.
Ορ.   ἦ κάρτα κἂν ἄλλοισι θυμοίμην ἰδών.
Ηλ.   ξυναινεῖς;
Ορ.   τί μὴν οὔ; (1276–80)

El.   Don't deprive me of the pleasure
      of your face so as to lose it.
Or.   Indeed I would be angry with others seeing this.
El.   Do you consent?
Or.   Of course I do.

The emotional alliance formed between these two is translated into
cooperation and planning of the deed. From Elektra, who throughout the play has espoused the moral and ethical reasons for vengeance,
Orestes has learned of the necessity for vengeance, and now he proceeds to instruct his sister in the 'how' of the vengeance. She need
explain no further that their mother is *kake* (1289) or that Aigisthos
dissipates the family's wealth (1290–91) as he has seen enough from
Elektra's condition. Silence is more important than anything else;
talk, as he says, will only deprive them of the 'right time' (*kairos*
1292). Orestes explicitly makes Elektra a part of the planning asking
her what action will be best to take (1293–94), and instructing her
on how to behave by telling her to hide her joy behind lamentation (1296–99). She becomes part of the *dolos*-strategy which will now
be exclusively used against their enemies in accordance with *dike*.

The *paidagogos*' return to the stage and his harsh criticisms of their
behaviour are a reminder of the dangerous situation they are in and
the grim task which lies ahead of them:

ὦ πλεῖστα μῶροι καὶ φρενῶν τητώμενοι,
πότερα παρ᾽ οὐδὲν τοῦ βίου κήδεσθ᾽ ἔτι,
ἢ νοῦς ἔνεστιν οὔτις ὑμῖν ἐγγενής,
ὅτ᾽ οὐ παρ᾽ αὐτοῖς ἀλλ᾽ ἐν αὐτοῖσιν κακοῖς

τοῖσιν μεγίστοις ὄντες οὐ γιγνώσκετε;
ἀλλ᾿ εἰ σταθμοῖσι τοῖσδε μὴ ᾿κύρουν ἐγὼ
πάλαι φυλάσσων, ἦν ἂν ἡμὶν ἐν δόμοις
τὰ δρώμεν᾿ ὑμῶν πρόσθεν ἢ τὰ σώματα· (1326–33)

You complete fools, deprived of wits
don't you have any concern for your lives,
or have you no innate sense,
as you do not realize that you are not close to,
but in the midst of the greatest dangers?
But if I didn't happen to be on guard
at these doorposts, your intended deeds
would be in the house before your persons.

His outburst makes Orestes' cautionary words seem softhearted in comparison, but his anger only highlights the great risk Orestes took in revealing his identity to his sister as well as confirming that it was not part of the original plan. The harshness of the rebuke of the *paidagogos* also provides important confirmation that brother and sister placed their *philia* for one another over the *tisis* upon her enemies.[17] The entrance of the *paidagogos* at this point also allows the final recognition to take place between the legitimate members of the *oikos*.[18] When Elektra finds out who the *paidagogos* is, she imagines that she sees her father in him. For Kells, she is hallucinating, evidence of her growing madness but this is simply the recognition of the *paidagogos*' important role as Orestes' *kurios*.[19] His loyalty has always been to the *oikos* of Agamemnon and, as Elektra says, he was the one man she found loyal to her father at the time of the murder (1351–52). He is the link between Agamemnon and his offspring and his primary concern now is to ensure that the vengeance is carried out. Thus after his introduction to Elektra, he again warns them of the dangers of delay. They will have to fight others more numerous and skilled (1370–71).

---

[17] Scodel 1984: 87 makes a similar point (although with reference only to Elektra).

[18] Schein 1982: 77 speaks of the "maximum efficiency in executing his plans", calling him a "creature of opportunity"; the joy of Elektra is balanced by our realization that the "cruelty of her brother's deceit" has come at a great cost to her. Kitzinger 1991: 324 taking a slightly different approach sees this scene as the reflection of "Elektra's loss of control over the action".

[19] Kells has a distinctly odd reading of this whole scene: Elektra is now mad, and hallucinating, thinks she sees Agamemnon. In a rather grotesque rendering of lines 1357–63, Kells has Elektra get down on her knees and fondle the *paidagogos*' feet.

Elektra's cooperation in the *dolos* strategy is signalled by her prayer to Apollo, the god who has sanctioned its use. She calls upon Apollo to be a helper in the plan and to show mortals how the gods punish impiety. As has often been pointed out, this prayer parallels Klytaimnestra's earlier prayer to Apollo (634–59), and both are answered in the same fashion: with the death of Klytaimnestra.[20] Elektra's participation in the deed of vengeance is further indicated by her entrance into the palace after the men.[21] She will come out again to report on events; her entrance, seemingly superfluous, is necessary to reflect her full partnership in the deed. The Chorus sings an ode after all have entered the palace, which expresses its own approval of the rightness and justice of the vengeance. This is no euphemistic ode, for the Chorus, as Gardiner rightly remarks, is not a group of "starry-eyed idealists or frenzied partisans".[22] Instead the lyrics conjure up images rife with blood and battle: "See how the deadly god of war advances, breathing the blood born of strife. They are gone just now, under the roof of the house, the inescapable hounds pursuing the evil deeds" (1384–88).

More grim than this is the Chorus' image of Orestes being guided by the god, Hermes: "the stealthy-footed champion of the dead is led into the house to the seat of his father, rich from ancient time, having the newly sharpened [tool of] blood" (1391–94). Gardiner argues that there is nothing in the words of the Chorus that suggest that this is an act of vengeance:

> The women speak only in general societal terms: this is an act of war, to punish those who have committed all manner of crimes (1378: κακῶν πανουργημάτων) and to restore the rightful heir to his patrimony. The potential objection that deceit must be used to accomplish these worthy ends is answered by the sanction of the god Hermes.[23]

---

[20] Horsley 1980: 18–29 interprets the link between the prayers in an entirely different fashion. Both prayers are answered by Apollo and bring about their deaths: one physically and the other psychologically.

[21] Mantziou 1995: 194 interprets her entrance into the palace as the symbolic end to Elektra's status as an outsider in her *oikos* and the conditions that enforced her exclusion (Klytaimnestra). For her, the ending of the play reverses the circumstances of Elektra's life; she is no longer excluded from the palace. Interestingly enough Mantziou interprets her silence as the reversal of her earlier public lamentation; now that Elektra's *telos* has been achieved, she can finally fall silent. Thus Elektra's silence at the end is not a mark of her marginalization, but her "emotional satisfaction."

[22] Gardiner 1986: 145.

[23] Gardiner 1986: 156–157.

Gardiner may be correct to point out there is no mention of vengeance, but she downplays the horror of the deed which is contained within the imagery of this ode. They may not specifically mention the deed of matricide, but the repetition of the word 'blood' in each stanza and the explicit association of justice with darkness and stealth is enough to remind us of the grim nature of the task being carried out inside the palace. The view of the Chorus, as representatives of those outside the palace, is extremely important, as from the very beginning it has always represented a more objective stance and consequently, its view of the deed will have some significance for how we are to view the killings.

7.4 *The Vengeance*

The two main opposing viewpoints on this play diverge most sharply at this point, and we are left with two diametrically opposed readings of the play. Those with a dark reading of the tragedy see the last part of the tragedy thick with dramatic irony and full of dark and sinister possibilities, all of which are meant to bring out the dubious nature of the killings and are thought to suggest dire consequences in the future for Orestes and Elektra.[24] For some, Elektra has suffered irreparable damage to her "personality" or "soul", something which cannot be alleviated by the return of Orestes, who is himself blind to the dubious nature of his deed. Her behaviour during the matricide and the exchange with Aigisthos is generally thought to be that of a woman who has become consumed by her suffering and hatred and driven solely by the desire for revenge. Orestes, on the other hand, has shown himself from the beginning incapable of understanding the heinous nature of his deed. Without a second thought he kills his mother and leads Aigisthos off to the same fate. The utter lack of remorse of the two siblings is not a sign of their success but only of their "moral bankruptcy".[25] For these critics, Sophokles' *Elektra* is a grim and dark play, and the ending, full of foreboding, suggests a bleak and unhappy future. On the other side

---

[24] Winnington-Ingram 1980: 217–247; Kamerbeek 1974: 17–20; Seale 1982: 56–83; Blundell 1989: 149–183.
[25] Seale 1982: 82 n. 43.

are those who think that Orestes and Elektra successfully complete a divinely ordained task.[26] There are no ominous clouds on the horizon; no Furies waiting in the wings to pursue them; no hint of future retribution or trouble. The morality of the matricide is not questioned and its justness and necessity is everywhere self-evident. Any ominous hints in Aigisthos' words are the empty bluster of a doomed man. For these scholars, the final act of the play at long last brings to an end the chain of violence that has haunted the House of Atreus. The final words of the Chorus effectively sum up the action: Orestes and Elektra have won their freedom. These are two radically different, and mutually exclusive lines of interpretations: one sees the killings as legitimate and just; the other takes them as a grim and destructive form of justice.

To understand the nature of the killings, we should see them strictly within the moral framework laid down by the play itself. Mother and daughter have each claimed to have justice on her side while each accusing the other of committing shameful deeds. Klytaimnestra's claim to justice was exposed as vacuous and her killing of Agamemnon as shameful and criminal, while Elektra's behaviour is living proof that an act can be both just and shameful in a situation such as obtains after the murder of Agamemnon. The strategy of *dolos* creates a set of circumstances that allows us to make an impartial judgement of character and guilt independent of the claims of either mother or daughter. Klytaimnestra is given the opportunity to respond to the death of her son, and in this fashion, her response establishes her guilt based not solely on the performance of any past crime, but on the grounds of the moral character of one who would commit such a deed. The exposure of Klytaimnestra's lack of pity legitimates the refusal of Elektra and Orestes to respond with pity to her. While we have been made to understand the justice of the killing, what we witness during the matricide is the shamefulness or ugliness of the deed through the focus on Elektra's response; her killing for all its justice and necessity is μὴ καλόν, shameful. The killing of Aigisthos hearkens back to the oracle and again what we see is the suggestion that this too is a deed of necessary and lawful punishment rather than a heroic action worthy of fame and glory.

---

[26] Jebb; Alexanderson 1966; Erbse 1978: 284–300; Stevens 1978: 111–120; Szlezak 1981: 1–21; March 1996: 65–81.

7.4.1 *The killing of Klytaimnestra*

The *paidagogos* and Orestes are now inside the palace and Elektra, who has followed them in, comes back out again to watch for Aigisthos and to report to the Chorus what is going on inside. This sets the stage for the matricide to be seen through the reaction of Elektra. With the focus on her response to the killing, the whole scene is as much a deadly collision of mother and daughter as of mother and son:

> ΚΛ. ὦ τέκνον τέκνον,
> οἴκτιρε τὴν τεκοῦσαν.
> ΗΛ. ἀλλ᾽ οὐκ ἐκ σέθεν
> ᾠκτίρεθ᾽ οὗτος οὐδ᾽ ὁ γεννήσας πατήρ.
> ΧΟ. ὦ πόλις, ὦ γενεὰ τάλαινα, νῦν σοι
> μοῖρα καθημερία φθίνει φθίνει.
> ΚΛ. ὤμοι πέπληγμαι.
> ΗΛ. παῖσον, εἰ σθένεις, διπλῆν.
> ΚΛ. ὤμοι μάλ᾽ αὖθις.
> ΗΛ. εἰ γὰρ Αἰγίσθῳ γ᾽ ὁμοῦ. (1410–16)

> ΚL. Child, child, have pity on your mother!
> EL. But you had no pity on him, nor on the
> father who begot him!
> CH. City, unhappy race, now the day-by-day
> (mis)fortune is waning for you.
> ΚL. Ah, I am struck!
> EL. Strike a second blow, if you have the strength!
> ΚL. Ah, again!
> EL. I wish it were Aigisthos as well.

Klytaimnestra makes an appeal to Orestes based upon the ties of kinship, to which Elektra responds that she had no regard for these ties herself. Her plea for pity is thus rejected on the grounds that she had none for Orestes or Agamemnon. Klytaimnestra had her opportunity to show herself worthy of pity in her response to the reported death of Orestes; Elektra's words here are not so much a reminder of her crimes, but of the character of the person who committed them. Essentially all Klytaimnestra's crimes have the same *fons et origo*: the rejection and violation of the two closest ties of the *philia* relationship, spousal and blood-kin, the basic ties upon which any human community rests. She cannot rightly claim what she herself has rejected.

Although Elektra may be justified in denying her mother's claim for pity, her words, παῖσον, εἰ σθένεις, διπλῆν (1415) have almost always filled commentators with horror; repelled by their brutality, many see in them the sign of Elektra's moral or psychological destruction.[27] Even those who do not necessarily advocate an ironic reading are disturbed by what they see as the sheer vindictiveness of her words.[28] "Twisted by years of pure, unrelenting hatred", as one critic describes her, Elektra succumbs to her deep-seated feelings of revenge.[29] Gardiner is one of the few who attempt to strip these words of their offensive nature and free Elektra from moral condemnation.[30] She suggests that their force is mitigated by Klytaimnestra's threats of violence; that is, kill or be killed.[31] She further argues that the presence of a group of motherly women forces a comparison between their mutual respect and concern for Elektra as opposed to Klytaimnestra's appalling lack of the same. For Gardiner, the words are consistent with Elektra's conduct in the play in that "she approves the deed even when confronted by its reality and simultaneously uses her words to exhibit the figure of Orestes raising his arm for the second, killing blow."[32] Gardiner is right to be critical of the psychological interpretation, as there has never been any suggestion that we are to question the psychological health of Elektra. The play always presents the problematic aspects of her behaviour in moral

---

[27] See Stevens 1978: 119 and Hester 1981: 23–5 for pertinent comments in this regard. March 1996: 71 n. 20 suggests that one reason these words are spoken by Elektra is "to call forth Clytaemnestra's second cry, thus making the parallel with Agamemnon's death in Aeschylus complete."

[28] Minadeo 1967: 139 calls Elektra "bloodthirsty"; Kells *ad* 1415f speaks of the "sheer malice" in these words; Winnington-Ingram 1980: 234 calls them "horrifying"; Schein 1982: 78 "grisly" while Seale 1982: 74 speaks of the "gloating pleasure of Electra". Vickers 1973: 51 on the other hand, while noting that it sounds "savage" and perhaps is meant to, adds that it may also be "that Sophocles merely endorses it: he, like Electra, hates Clytemnestra." Segal 1966: 501 sees signs of Klytaimnestra's "sinister nature" in her words. He, like others (Bowra 1944: 232; Johansen 1964: 26) sees echos of the double blow which killed the Aeschylean Agamemnon. Bowra argues that the reference to Aischylos' play is intentional and is meant to recall the horror and justice with which Aischylos presents the matricide.

[29] Schein 1982: 71.

[30] Gardiner 1986: 171. Linforth 1963: 109 is another who attempts to downplay the force of these words to a certain extent when he suggests διπλῆν means a matching blow. The words then are addressed to Klytaimnestra rather than Orestes.

[31] Gardiner 1986: 171 misrepresents things somewhat, for the action of the play never presents the conflict between Elektra and her mother in such blatant terms. Moreover, at this stage of the action, we can hardly suggest that for Elektra, it is "destroy or be destroyed". Gardiner's reading of this scene ignores the tragic dimensions of Elektra's behaviour and thus undercuts the central conflict of the play.

[32] Gardiner 1986: 171–72.

terms. There is some sense in which we can see these words as Elektra's support for her brother, that is, she acts in full concert with him, but we should be careful not to deprive these words of their tragic significance, as I think Gardiner does.

To understand the significance of these words, we should recognize that the conflict between right and wrong has always resided within the character of Elektra and her struggle to uphold the principles of *eusebeia* and *aidos*. She has always presented herself as choosing between acting nobly or basely, and we see from all the confrontations in this play what constitutes being noble for Elektra: acting in accordance with the principles of *aidos* and *eusebeia*. Circumstances are such, however, that it is impossible to maintain these principles in all their particular aspects. In other words, upholding these principles necessitates a partial breach of them. I have argued that the conflict has its source in the blood-based ties of the *oikos* set against the civic oriented ties of the *polis*. Elektra breaches a narrower and familial form of *eusebeia* and *aidos* in order to maintain a broader and more communal form of these virtues. Indeed, her transgression of them is to a large degree what constitutes her conformity with their larger communal form. In circumstances such as these, Elektra tells the Chorus, it is impossible to be *eusebes* or *sophron* (307–9) in every respect. Her behaviour, however shameful, is necessitated by the circumstances. This is how she defends her behaviour to the Chorus, how she presents the choice to her sister, and, significantly, it forms the basis of her accusation against her mother. "You say that you killed Agamemnon", she says to her mother, "what statement could be more shameful than this, even if it were just" (559–60). Klytaimnestra's killing of Agamemnon, even if justified (and it is not), is shameful because it entails the breach of one of the ethically most important relationships, the conjugal tie. What Elektra cannot escape and what constitutes her tragedy is this one undeniable fact that she herself points to—the irreparable breach of a *philos* relationship remains shameful, no matter how justified it is ethically. What we witness on stage while Orestes' kills his mother off stage is the horror of the deed, represented in the response of Elektra. Her words, "strike a second blow, if you have the strength", is the expression of the utter disregard for Klytaimnestra as a *philos*, all the more horrifying in that it breaks the closest *philia* ties of all, those of blood. To understand the force of this we should remember that Elektra's strong sense of *aidos* always entailed the recognition of

her mother as one who is owed filial piety. She may reject Klytaimnestra as a person, but she never rejects the moral basis upon which
her claim for piety rests. That she expresses her shame to a woman
whom she plainly despises is confirmation of this. What we see during
the matricide, however, is the complete rejection not just of Klytaimnestra, but of the ties of kinship: her words are meant to underscore
the shameful aspect of the killing and mark the deed as *aischron* in
this respect. Her behaviour on stage then hearkens back to the tragic
nature of her circumstances: filial piety is as valid as ever, but cannot be complied with. There can be no final reconciliation between
the demand for justice and the terrible breach of blood-ties involved
in this; it is a deed inescapably just and unavoidably shameful. The
matricide does not resolve the conflict; it merely ends it.

Those who argue that Elektra in the end is no better than her
mother generally seek support for this view in her behaviour during
both the debate with her mother and the matricide. What distinguishes Elektra from Klytaimnestra in the first confrontation is her
strong sense of *aidos*, the moral awareness that her own behaviour
was by some standards wrong. What separates her from her mother
in the end, is simply the justice of the deed. If there is any sense
of reciprocity in the carrying out of the vengeance, it exists not at
the level of the punishment, that is, blood for blood, but at the level
of emotion; yet even here there remains a distinction between the
two. Klytaimnestra receives no pity because she has none herself.
Elektra shows no pity, not because she has none, but because her
mother has forfeited pity. This does not make the refusal of pity any
less ugly, but it does justify it. What we witness during the matricide is an act that is neither honourable nor glorious, only just, but
is, for all its justice, *aischron*, vividly expressed through Elektra's
embrace of the μὴ καλόν.

Equally significant for understanding the nature of the killings is
the response from the Chorus. Its support of Elektra has never been
the blind loyalty of partisan sympathizers. Its reaction to the killing
confirms the dual nature inherent in this deed. The Chorus is horrified
by Klytaimnestra's cry (ἤκουσ' ἀνήκουστα δύστανος, ὥστε φρῖξαι.
1407–8) but it also recognizes that with her death comes the *soteria*
of the family and the city (ὢ πόλις, ὢ γενεὰ τάλαινα, νῦν σοι μοῖρα
καθαμερία φθίνει, φθίνει. 1413–14). When Orestes comes out, the
words of the Chorus give expression to the horror of the deed but
also to its justice: φοινία δὲ χεὶρ στάζει θυηλῆς Ἄρεος, οὐδ' ἔχω

ψέγειν. (1422–23).[33] That he has the blood of his kin on his hand is the ugly *factum brutum*, but the Chorus cannot fault him for this.

The exchange between the two siblings after the killing is also important in ascertaining how we are to judge the deed. When Orestes emerges from the house, he is asked by Elektra, how things are and he replies: ἐν δόμοισι μὲν καλῶς, Ἀπόλλων εἰ καλῶς ἐθέσπισεν. (1424–25). The precise meaning of Orestes' words and, in particular, how we are to take the conjunction εἰ has been one of the main sources of disagreement between the two camps. Critics of the optimistic persuasion see only calm certainty while the pessimistic opponents sense doubt and uncertainty in these words.[34] The dark interpretation isolates the verse and has to attribute to εἰ an undue exegetical weight. But it seems unlikely that if Sophokles wishes to show Orestes filled with doubt about the oracle, he would leave something of such importance to εἰ to carry all the weight.[35] We arrive at a more satisfactory understanding of Orestes' words, if we connect them with his earlier attitude. We remember the point at which he did express doubt when he perceived this deed as an act that would win him *kleos* and *time*. Now having gained a greater

---

[33] It should, however, be pointed out that ψέγειν is a (generally accepted) conjecture, while λέγειν is the reading of all codices.

[34] Jebb *ad* 1425 sees only a "calm confidence" in Orestes' words, taking the εἰ to mean "as surely as". Kamerbeek *ad* 1424, 5 on the other hand detects a note of anxiety while Kells sees the words as heavily ironic. Others who detect a similar doubt include Kirkwood 1958: 241 who thinks that there can be no doubt that Sophokles wishes to "create an atmosphere of shadow and questioning"; Johansen 1964: 27, although conceding the justice of the deed, similarly sees doubt and ambiguity: "An der *Gerechtigkeit* des göttlichen befehls wird nicht gezweifelt; aber, wie wir gesehen haben, sind die Begriffe "Gerecht" and "Schön" in dieser Tragödie nicht ohne weiterest vertauschbar. Schon Kaibel hat bemerkt, wie hier die Zweideutigkeit der Vergeltungstat im Bewusstsein des Orestes auftaucht." See also Linforth 1963: 121 and 124 and Schein 1995: 133. Kitto 1958: 34 points out that the Greek supports either (but he also admits that his earlier judgement that Orestes expresses misgivings here was wrong). The external reader pointed out that if we compare this clause with 773–5, 799, 864–9 in the *Elektra* and 664–5 in *Oidipous at Kolonos*, we see that all the εἰ clauses follow the main clause; none of them have any modifying particles or word such as ἀληθέως; and none expresses any real doubt. I am grateful to the reader for this point.

[35] March 1996: n. 33. To see doubt here, as March points out, requires the rewriting of Orestes' part in the play both before these lines and after. As for Aigisthos' words at 1497–9 ("must this house of necessity see the evils of the Pelopidae, now and to come?"), March argues that the calm certainty of Orestes' reply as well as the final words of the Chorus are enough to negate any ominous hints here. Burnett 1998: 131 n. 33 also fails to see the doubt so many other critics have seen. She suggests that the "if" clause is a "form of asservation".

awareness of the nature of the deed, he uses the conditional as a way of expressing his caution and restraint.[36] There is no victorious boasting or exultation in the death of his mother, but only a prudent expression that he has acted in accordance with the oracle of Apollo.

There is no gloating from Elektra either, but only the desire for assurance that Klytaimnestra is dead (1426–27). Elektra is able to act the way she does during the matricide because for her Klytaimnestra has simply ceased to be her mother. For Orestes, it is not that she has ceased to be his mother that allows him to kill her, but that pity for his sister's pain prevents him from feeling pity for his mother as she was the cause of Elektra's suffering. In other words, pity for Elektra hardens Orestes to his mother; indeed pity for his sister is precisely what ensures his ability to carry out the deed. It is Elektra who enables Orestes to kill his mother as he learns from her what properly constitutes a *philos*, and this allows him to understand who is properly worthy of pity and who is not.

7.4.2 *The killing of Aigisthos*

For Aischylos, the killing of Aigisthos had posed no real moral problems. He is dispatched first and his death passes without fanfare; instead, all the dramatic weight falls upon the confrontation between mother and son, and the play ends with the pursuit of Orestes by the Furies. Sophokles, however, has significantly reversed the order of the killings, a modification which in itself seems to preclude the appearance of the Erinyes as well as placing all the dramatic weight on the debate between Aigisthos and Orestes. Critical focus in this last scene then has generally settled upon ascertaining the reason for the extended debate between Orestes and Aigisthos with the pessimists arguing that it is devised with a view to suggesting either pursuit by the Furies or some sort of future retribution.[37] The focus on Aigisthos, however, is not only expected but also necessary. With regard to the villainy of the tyrants, the play has focused almost exclusively on Klytaimnestra: her adulterous union with Aigisthos, her killing of Agamemnon, her complete lack of *aidos*, her hybristic

---

[36] I am in agreement with Horsley's 1980: 27 n. 29 reading of this line although I do not agree with his overall reading of the play.

[37] The best case for the Furies is made by Winnington-Ingram 1980: 231–239. See Stinton 1986: 75–84 for a good refutation of his argument.

behaviour at hearing of Orestes' death. Because the play establishes her guilt so clearly, her death is treated swiftly with the focus falling not on the murderous deed, but on the response of her daughter. Aigisthos has thus far been absent from the stage; while reference has been made to his tyranny, we have seen nothing of him and thus his guilt has still to be made clear. This is the final test through the *dolos*, and Elektra and the Chorus act in concert in deploying the deception against Aigisthos. There are two important points to consider here: Elektra's role and her behavior, which is hardly that of a bitter and twisted woman; second, the significance of the extended debate between Orestes and the tyrant. Placed as it is between two killings, this exchange draws attention to the manner of Aigisthos' killing, not in order to suggest future retribution for the avengers, but to confirm the nature of justice operating in the play.

Elektra's announcement of the approach of Aigisthos has Orestes and Pylades hurry back inside the palace. The Chorus, who for the most part remained quiet in the last scene, and only reacted to the killing of Klytaimnestra, now becomes more directly involved in the action. This is quite appropriate: as the representatives of the *polis*, its involvement in assisting to topple the tyrant and his oppressive rule is warranted. The Chorus offers the advice that it would be good to "utter in his ear a few gentle words, so that he may rush into the hidden ordeal Justice has ready for him" (1437–41). Elektra takes this advice to heart and adopts a role more suited to Chrysothemis than her own usual defiant behaviour and her exchange with Aigisthos is laced with irony, apparent to all but him.

When Aigisthos enters, he has already heard of the story of Orestes' death in a chariot race. His utter disregard for Elektra is evident from the contemptuous repetitions of σέ in his address to her: σέ τοι, σὲ κρίνω, ναὶ σέ (1445). Elektra does not respond to the personal antagonism evident in his words but adopts the subservient behaviour and arguments of her sister. However, unlike her sister whose obedient actions endorsed the tyranny of the rulers, Elektra's use of this behaviour is part of the *dolos* strategy which will bring liberation from it. Here the function of the *dolos i*s to trap Aigisthos into revealing his *hybris*. Delighted at the pleasure her words have given him (1456), and secure in the thought that Elektra is no longer a threat, the tyrant allows himself a brief moment of exultation in his good fortune:

οἴγειν πύλας ἄνωγα κἀναδεικνύναι
πᾶσιν Μυκηναίοισιν Ἀργείοις θ' ὁρᾶν,
ὡς εἴ τις αὐτῶν ἐλπίσιν κεναῖς πάρος
ἐξῆρετ' ἀνδρὸς τοῦδε, νῦν ὁρῶν νεκρὸν
στόμια δέχηται τἀμά, μηδὲ πρὸς βίαν
ἐμοῦ κολαστοῦ προστυχὼν φύσῃ φρένας. (1458–63)

I order you to open the gates and show
to all the Myceneans and Argives to see
so that if anyone of them was excited by empty hopes
before about this man, now seeing him a corpse,
he may accept my bridle and not by violence,
having met me as punisher, learn wisdom.

These words convict Aigisthos not just of tyranny, but of *hybris* as well, for he exploits Orestes' death as a means of intimidation of the people. He supposes that, at the sight of the corpse, the citizens will be so cowed that they will accept his "bridle", a striking metaphor that attests to his hybristic tyranny. Like Klytaimnestra, he exults in the death of a man whom he sees as a political rival and takes it as an occasion to celebrate his own good fortune. Elektra shows that she understands the proper moment for feigned submission, and thus her obedient behaviour as part of the *dolos* strategy helps achieve their moral and political freedom. Thus after Aigisthos reveals his *hybris*, Elektra says: "See, my part is being accomplished. In time I have acquired sense, so as to serve the interests of the stronger" (1464–65). Those who suppose that since the return of Orestes, Elektra has been increasingly marginalized and her voice silenced, fail to acknowledge what an active part she takes in the *dolos* stratagem. Previously a victim of it herself, she has now become an agent of it, and it is her deceptive behaviour (along with the lie) which causes Aigisthos to reveal his *hybris*.

Once Aigisthos sees the body publicly displayed, he dons a veil of hypocritical piety. Unlike Klytaimnestra, Aigisthos understands the importance of maintaining at least the appearance of piety:[38]

ὦ Ζεῦ, δέδορκα φάσμ' ἄνευ φθόνου μὲν οὐ
πεπτωκός· εἰ δ' ἔπεστι νέμεσις οὐ λέγω.

---

[38] Kells *ad* 1469 oddly thinks that Sophokles wishes us to see that Aigisthos is capable of "generous emotions"; Kamerbeek has a much more sensible reading of these lines: Aigisthos is being hypocritical.

χαλᾶτε πᾶν κάλυμμ᾽ ἀπ᾽ ὀφθαλμῶν, ὅπως
τὸ συγγενές τοι κἀπ᾽ ἐμοῦ θρήνων τύχῃ. (1466–69)

> O Zeus, I see a vision that has fallen, not without the envy
> of the gods; whether there is any *nemesis* in it I do not say.
> Remove all covering from the eyes, so that
> my relation may meet with laments from me.

Aigisthos supposes that he is looking upon the corpse of a man who has fallen from some divine envy, but he refuses to speculate further whether there is some *nemesis* at work. *Nemesis* would mean that Orestes' death is deserved, and while Aigisthos' use of the word seems to imply he would like to believe this, he refuses to say it. Yet *nemesis* and *phasma* both take on an underlying significance when we remember their earlier occurrences: *phasma* was used to describe Klytaimnestra's vision in her dream (501, 644) while Elektra invoked *nemesis* in response to her mother's hybristic reaction to the report of Orestes' death.[39] Although Aigisthos does not realize this, he is looking upon what the meaning of Klytaimnestra's dream foretold and what the warning of the messenger *rhesis* was: the return of Orestes and the downfall of Klytaimnestra. His reaction to the death of Orestes is as revealing as Klytaimnestra's. Her initial fear and momentary pang was easily quenched by a much stronger desire to glory in her own success. Aigisthos initially exults, but then in public assumes a mask of hypocritical piety. What should have provoked fear and pity in both does neither, but becomes an occasion for celebration and joy, behaviour that is hybristic.

When Aigisthos realizes that he is speaking with Orestes, he recognizes the imminence of his death—ὄλωλα δὴ δείλαιος (1482)—so he asks to speak briefly. As she had denied Klytaimnestra's claim for pity, now Elektra denies Aigisthos' right to speak (μὴ πέρα λέγειν ἔα, πρὸς θεῶν, ἀδελφέ, μηδὲ μηκύνειν λόγους. 1483–84). Remembering the words of her brother that superfluous speech would only deprive them of the right time (1292), she counsels her brother to carry out the punishment immediately:

ἀλλ᾽ ὡς τάχιστα κτεῖνε καὶ κτανὼν πρόθες
ταφεῦσιν ὧν τόνδ᾽ εἰκός ἐστι τυγχάνειν,
ἄποπτον ἡμῶν. ὡς ἐμοὶ τόδ᾽ ἂν κακῶν
μόνον γένοιτο τῶν πάλαι λυτήριον. (1487–90)

---

[39] See the perceptive remarks of Kamerbeek on these lines. He points out that φάσμα "has an ominous ring since it is often used of spectral appearance, vision in a dream, portent, omen."

> But kill him as quickly as possible and having killed
> him lay him out before the buriers whom
> it is fitting for this man to meet as this would be
> the only release for me of those ancient woes.

Elektra's words here have always sparked disagreement. For some, they mean that she wishes his body to be thrown to dogs and birds, a grave violation of the rights of burial.[40] Others prefer to read the words as they stand, "having killed him, throw him to the grave-diggers as he deserves" (1487–88).[41] To interpret ταφεῦσιν as to imply "dogs and birds" would need as support a specific denial of burial rites as in *Aias* and *Antigone*, but there is only a wish that Aigisthos receive what he deserves.[42] Indeed there is an open-endedness to her words which allows the audience to draw its own conclusion as to the burial he deserves, but no explicit denial of rites comes from Elektra.[43] Certainly the Chorus does not think that there is anything impious in her words, and this reaction is important, as the Chorus has never been silent on any troublesome aspects of Elektra's behaviour. Segal makes an important point when he writes:

> [Elektra] does not openly taunt Aegisthus with threats of dogs or birds, but leaves the reference to his burial (or non-burial) so vague that it is quite possible that she actually means to give his body proper care.[44]

Moreover, as Segal rightly notes, she uses the verb πρόθες, a word that is regularly used to refer to the ritual laying out of a corpse.[45]

---

[40] Thus followed by Campbell, Jebb, and Kamerbeek *ad loc.*; Kitto 1955: 136; Seale 1981: 77.

[41] Bowra 1944: 254–55; Johansen 1964: 28 n. 34; Segal 1966: 520–521.

[42] Gardiner 1986: 167 points out that in *Aias* and *Antigone* there is a clear attempt to stop others from burying the corpse, while Elektra does not forbid anyone. She further suggests that the words could just as easily be taken to mean "his other relatives" or even "anyone who cares to pick up the body."

[43] There is a reference in Pausanias (Book 2.16.7) to the burial which Klytaimnestra and Aigisthos actually received: Κλυταιμνήστρα δὲ ἐτάφη καὶ Αἴγισθος ὀλίγον ἀπωτέρω τοῦ τείχους· ἐντὸς δὲ ἀπηξιώθησαν, ἔντα' Ἀγαμέμνων τε αὐτὸς ἔκειτο καὶ οἱ σὺν ἐκείνῳ φονευθέντες.

[44] Segal 1966: 520–521 does not think Elektra has "softened" in her attitude towards vengeance, but he thinks there is a hint that "the revenge is perhaps not so fulfilling as she expected." Although he sees a "release" here, for him the whole play moves between life and death and the contradiction inherent in the deed, necessary but grim and ultimately more tied to death than rebirth.

[45] Segal 1966: 521. He goes on to suggest that it would be odd for Elektra at this stage (especially in light of her words to her mother) to be reticent about referring to the fate of Aigisthos' body. Rather she passes over it quickly with little emphasis and the whole force of the scene for Segal suggests that Elektra wants the whole thing over with as quickly as possible.

There is, however, a certain parallel with the matricide, for her "strike a second blow" seems to provide her with the emotional satisfaction she needs which comes from being able to participate in the punishment to some degree, a satisfaction which no impartial court of law could ever provide. We get the sense that she needs to partake in Aigisthos' punishment too, but we should recognize that, just as after the matricide, there is no savoring of the victory, no final taunting of Aigisthos: she simply wants him dead and out of her sight. Moreover, as Elektra's final words suggest, there is a kind of emotional release for her in the killings of her mother and Aigisthos. Their deaths will be the deliverance from her ancient woes, her λυτήριον τῶν πάλαι κακῶν (1489–90). Whether we are to forecast a bright or dark future for Elektra is not the point for Sophokles;[46] rather, it is that the house has been saved, the tyrants killed, and justice and order restored. Any speculations about a grim future for Orestes and Elektra have the weakness of referring to something ἔξω τοῦ δράματος. There is nothing to suggest the moral or psychological fission of her psyche which we witness in Euripides' version. Instead, during the reunion scene, we see a woman whose capacity for love far outweighs her capacity for hatred, a woman whose grief for her brother is stronger than her desire for vengeance. After the killings, we see a woman who does not exult in the death of her enemies, but desires only the liberation from her sufferings. Significantly, λυτήριον is Elektra's final word in the play.

Turning to the confrontation of Aigisthos and Orestes, we shall see a similar tension between what is just but unheroic. According to dramatic conventions, Orestes cannot kill Aigisthos on stage. Yet rather than having the tyrant depart quietly to his death, Sophokles draws attention to the fact that it is to take place inside the palace. This drawn out scene in the final moments of the play is usually interpreted as the poet's way of alluding to future punishment for Orestes and Elektra. Winnington-Ingram has argued that it refers specifically to the Furies' pursuit of Orestes.[47] As Stinton points out, such an interpretation completely alters the moral framework of the

---

[46] See remarks by March 1996: 81 who similarly suggests that this is a question which should not be asked of the play. She argues that Sophokles deliberately ends the play before the mythical plot is completed, i.e. before Aigisthos is killed.

[47] Winnington-Ingram 1980: 205–247.

play, an odd move for the poet at this stage of the game.[48] Moreover, the Erinyes in this play have been aligned with Orestes and Elektra and have been associated with the punishment of adultery.[49] Elektra invokes them early on in the play (110–18) asking them (along with other gods) to send Orestes home; she describes her mother as living with Aigisthos and not fearing any Erinys (276). The Chorus sings an ode which links the Furies with deception and stealth that will come against the adulterers (488–503). Orestes and Pylades (or perhaps Orestes and Elektra) are imagined as twin Erinyes entering the house. The Furies are continually invoked in the play, but they are associated with the punishment of adultery, not the spilling of kindred blood. They are not opposed to Apollo; rather the underworld gods are aligned with Olympian gods against those in the palace. Finally, the staging of the last part of the play, as Taplin observes, seems to preclude any idea of exile, for it ends with the entrance of Orestes inside the palace.[50]

When we regard this scene in relation to the whole dramatic action, it seems to confirm the moral reasoning established by the arguments of Elektra as well as the oracle of Apollo. Aigisthos attempts three times to suggest that there is something wrong with killing him. First is the question why, if the act is noble, should it be committed in darkness:

τί δ᾽ ἐς δόμους ἄγεις με; πῶς, τόδ᾽ εἰ καλὸν
τοὔργον, σκότου δεῖ, κοὐ πρόχειρος εἶ κτανεῖν; (1493–94)

Why do you lead me into the house? If this act is noble
why must it be in darkness, and you are not ready to kill me?

Orestes only replies that he must go to where he killed Agamemnon so that he will die in the same place (1495–96). The second question is a further attempt to suggest that something is wrong with killing inside the palace:[51]

---

[48] Stinton 1986: 84. See also the remarks of Gardiner 1986: 172 note 7.

[49] As Scodel 1984: 84 and others point out, this is the only place where the Furies are specifically associated with adultery.

[50] Taplin 1983: 163 nevertheless still forecasts a dark future: "the stage topography seems purposefully to reject exile; but the future of Orestes and Elektra *within* this ancestral palace does not look bright either."

[51] Those who take 1498 as hint of future ills for Orestes include: Sheppard 1927b: 164f; Alexanderson 1966: 95–7; Winnington-Ingram 1980: 226; Blundell 1989: 176–77. Johansen 1964: 29 discerns here "der tiefe Schatten von Ungewissheit über wahre Bedeutung und rechte Beurteilung der Rachetat." Against this view stand

Aι. ἦ πᾶσ᾽ ἀνάγκη τήνδε τὴν στέγην ἰδεῖν
τά τ᾽ ὄντα καὶ μέλλοντα Πελοπιδῶν κακά;
Oρ. τὰ γοῦν σ᾽· ἐγώ σοι μάντις εἰμὶ τῶνδ᾽ ἄκρος. (1497–99)

Aι. Is it necessary that this house see the
present and future evils of the Pelopids?
Oʀ. Yours at any rate: I am a good prophet in this regard.

Orestes brushes Aigisthos' question aside by confirming his intention (1499). The tyrant's third remark is an attempt to goad the young man by mocking his father who could not foresee his own death. Orestes still refuses to be baited; when he forces the tyrant to lead the way into the house and Aigisthos responds with a mocking "in case I escape?" we finally get an answer from Orestes:

μὴ μὲν οὖν καθ᾽ ἡδονὴν
θάνῃς· φυλάξαι δεῖ με τοῦτό σοι πικρόν.
χρῆν δ᾽ εὐθὺς εἶναι τήνδε τοῖς πᾶσιν δίκην,
ὅστις πέρα πράσσειν γε τῶν νόμων θέλοι,
κτείνειν· τὸ γὰρ πανοῦργον οὐκ ἂν ἦν πολύ. (1503–7)

No, so that you don't die at your leisure:
I must take care that this is bitter for you
This should be the just punishment for everyone,
who wishes to act outside the laws,
to die, for there would not be much villainy.

This rather odd scene at the end, which seems to delay needlessly the entrance into the palace, is, as noted, thought to allude to future retribution. The extended exchange, however, is quite necessary not only that we see the sharp contrast between the behaviour of Aigisthos and Orestes, but the marked difference in the young man himself.[52]

Owen 1927: 51–52 and Bowra 1944: 257. Too many scholars interpret this vague hint as if it *must* mean future punishment. Owen 1927: 50 points out that the phrase τά τ᾽ ὄντα καὶ μέλλοντα also occurs in Euripides (*Ion* 7 and *Helen* 14) where there is no special emphasis on μέλλοντα which is tied closely to ὄντα by the absence of a second definite article. Moreover, as Scodel 1984: 86 remarks, "the hints are hints along Aeschylean lines and the *Oresteia* has a happy ending to long suffering." See also remarks by Linforth 1963: 122–123 and March 1996: 76 n. 33. We should remember that this vague hint is put into the mouth of Aigisthos, who facing death, would quite naturally foretell evil consequences for his killer.

[52] Alexanderson 1966: 96–97 points out that the quoted lines can be interpreted in a number of different ways: (i) as referring to Aigisthos' impending death; (ii) future evils because of the killing of Klytaimnestra and Aigisthos, either from the Furies or friends of Aigisthos; (iii) a broader significance not directly connected to the slayings. He prefers a vague interpretation of vague words. Sophokles raises the possibility of retribution and then dismisses it.

Immediately noticeable is his refusal to be drawn into any debate with Aigisthos: he responds with only a few curt words until his final words of the play. All his answers suggest caution and restraint, and he confines himself to the terms laid down by the oracle. To Aigisthos' question about the present and future woes of Pelopids, Orestes focuses on the present woe of one Pelopid: Aigisthos' imminent death. His reference to being a good prophet in this regard explicitly associates his punitive act with Apollo and his oracle which decreed a just slaughter. The jibe about his father, designed to provoke Orestes into some sort of quarrel, shows the tyrant's nastiness in contrast to Orestes' restraint. That even now, facing impending death, Aigisthos acts with such "impudence" as Kamerbeek puts it, only highlights his tyrannical *hybris* throwing into sharp relief Orestes' greater awareness of the nature of his deed.

If we remember at this point Orestes' initial perception of his deed, we see what a marked difference there is in his behaviour. Earlier Orestes had spoken about falling upon his enemies in terms strikingly reminiscent of the Homeric hero: "So I boast that I too from this report shall shine forth still living as a star upon my enemies" 65–66). To vaunt as Orestes does here, is, as Segal remarks, "a dangerous thing to do in Greek tragedy."[53] He goes on to point out that "Orestes' simile recalls the baleful stars of the *Iliad* to which the warrior in his most murderous moment is compared."[54] Segal is correct to draw attention to these words and their resemblance to those of the Iliadic hero, but what he fails to note is that this is Orestes' initial perception of his deed. Now faced with his enemy, there is no boasting and no taunting words on his part: he takes no pleasure in the death of Aigisthos or in his victory. The restrained atmosphere at the end of the play is largely due to the *sophrosyne* displayed by Orestes who recognizes the inappropriateness of boasting over a defeated enemy.

---

[53] Segal 1966: 491.

[54] Segal 1966: 491 sees a dark shadow cast by Orestes' words in that they also suggest "the *return* of night from which he and his companions have emerged ("the black night of stars," 19). The prologue already contains in small the play's large movement from light to darkness". Segal, however, fails to note the stark contrast between the Orestes of the prologue and the Orestes of the exodos. The whole point in the prologue is to suggest that there is something wrong with Orestes' perception of the deed in order that we may see a development in his character.

That Orestes understands that the death of Aigisthos should be treated as just punishment rather than a heroic deed worthy of *kleos* comes out even more plainly in Orestes' final speech. It is in this context that we should understand the reason for Orestes' demand that the tyrant be killed inside.[55] Aigisthos cannot die καθ' ἡδονήν, that is, he cannot choose the manner in which he dies. His death must be bitter for him, as Orestes says (1504), for it is a form of just punishment (*dike* 1505) rather than an act of personal revenge (*tisis*). Punishment is generally thought to embody certain elements: it must be painful or unpleasant to the offender; it is done because the offender has offended against the norms of society; and it should be carried out by an independent and impartial authority.[56] Revenge on the other hand is not directed at the punishment of the offender, but at the satisfaction of the victim derived from the harm done to the offender; the source of authority is not the law or any public institution, but the subjective interpretation and beliefs of the victim. In other words, revenge is generally personal and motivated by some sort of ill-will. Orestes, however, carries out a just punishment and shows himself a dispassionate agent of Apollo's justice who acts in the interest of the *polis*. Aigisthos' failure to provoke Orestes shows that there is no personal animosity or hostility on the part of Orestes. His punishment will benefit the κοινωνία πολιτική in that it serves as a deterrence for all who wish to act, as Aigisthos did, beyond the laws (πέρα πράσσειν τῶν νόμων 1506). Orestes, now motivated by *dike* rather than glory and honour, has Aigisthos' death exemplify the fitting punishment for tyrannical πανουργία.

As to Aigisthos' first question (if the ἔργον Orestes is about to perform is καλόν, why must it be conducted in darkness?) we see that

---

[55] Sri Pathmanathan 1965: 12 in his study on death in Greek tragedy suggests that there are two reasons for the killing of Aigisthos inside the palace: first, Orestes is aware of the appropriateness of killing Aigisthos in the same spot in which Agamemnon was killed; second, "that a swift, clean death is too good for Aegisthus. Orestes means to make him suffer up to the hilt." He concludes that we are left to imagine what this means. Orestes does say that it must be bitter (πικρόν) for him, but this should not be taken to mean torture or extended suffering in the way Pathmanathan's words appear to imply.

[56] Aristotle draws the distinction between revenge and punishment in the *Rhetoric* 1369b12 in this way: "Revenge and punishment are different things. Punishment is inflicted for the sake of the person punished; revenge for that of the punisher, to satisfy his feelings." See also MacKenzie 1981: 10–12; Nozick 1981: 366–370 for discussions on the distinction between revenge and punishment.

it touches upon the central problem in the play: the tension between τὸ αἰσχρόν and τὸ δίκαιον. Orestes' insistence that the punishment take place within the palace should be understood in the light of this tension. Justice demands that Aigisthos be killed, but the unheroic or shameful nature of the deed demands that he be killed inside. In other words, this is not an act which should be celebrated as a glorious or heroic deed, but an act, which, for all its justice, is still not *kalon*.[57] By killing him inside, Orestes removes the death from the public sphere, an acknowledgement that his dispatch should not be treated in a celebratory fashion. When we remember how Aigisthos treated the 'death' of Orestes, we see the sharp contrast in the behaviour of the two men. Aigisthos ordered the gates of the palace to be opened so that all could look upon the body of Orestes; in other words, Aigisthos uses the public exhibition of his corpse as a form of intimidation and demonstration of his power. Orestes, on the other hand, proves his *sophrosyne*, the restraint and prudence he has learned. His awareness of the less admirable aspect of his deed has him prevent it from becoming a public spectacle; and so he keeps it out of the public eye.

The final words of the Chorus effectively sum up what Elektra and Orestes' have won through their actions—their freedom:[58]

> Ὦ σπέρμ' Ἀτρέως, ὡς πολλὰ παθὸν
> δι' ἐλευθερίας μόλις ἐξῆλθες
> τῇ νῦν ὁρμῇ τελεωθέν. (1508–10)

---

[57] I am in agreement with much of Stinton's 1986: 84 argument, which sees a similar tension within an act which is just but shameful. He, however, has a slightly different perspective of the play. In his words "the avengers are cheated of their triumph by the bitterness of success: all is not well within the house."

[58] The final words of the Chorus have sparked disagreement in regard to who precisely it is addressing. Some argue that Ὦ σπέρμ' Ἀτρέως refers exclusively to Elektra (Segal 1966: 530; March 1996: 78) while others prefer to render the words in plural form or more generally as 'House of Atreus' (Jebb) or 'race of Atreus' (Grene). Schadewaldt renders it as "Same des Atreus". Calder 1963: 215–216 who unfairly ridicules these translations argues that Elektra remains onstage until 1510 and then exits into the palace while the Chorus exits down the *parodos*. While March is correct to point out that 'freedom' is more applicable to Elektra than Orestes, it would seem odd for the Chorus now to exclude Orestes. Everything from the reunion onwards has pointed to the alliance between the two siblings. It is only by their union that the two are able to achieve freedom. Like Kamerbeek *ad* 1508–10 and others, I take these lines to indicate the descendants of Atreus, both Orestes and Elektra, even though Elektra is, no doubt, on stage alone.

> Offspring of Atreus, how, after suffering many things
> you have come with difficulty to freedom,
> by this day's enterprise brought to the end.

Against the desire of some critics who wish to remove these words from the play, on the grounds that they are "intolerably flat"[59] or a meaningless tag which adds nothing to the play, we should recognize that the Chorus' words here are as significant for what they do not say as for what they do. The unspeakable nature of the deed has already been made evident as has its justice and the Chorus needs to say no more about either. Like Orestes and Elektra who show no exultation in the deed, the Chorus is neither jubilant nor triumphant but instead offers only a subdued expression of what the siblings have won by their actions. The Chorus too recognizes that the killings are not something in which to rejoice. The last word of the play, τελεωθέν suggests a finality to the action. That Sophokles ends the play before the mythical plot is actually complete, that is, before the killing of Aigisthos actually takes place, prevents any speculation as the future fates of Elektra and Orestes. Instead, the audience is left only to anticipate the death of the tyrant and the final words of the Chorus confirm what it will bring—the restoration of freedom.

---

[59] Kamerbeek *ad* 1505–07 thinks that the final "moralizing words form perhaps the lines about whose absence in Sophocles' works an admirer of the poet would mind least." See also Johansen 1959: 152 n. 5 and Kells *ad* 1508ff who thinks that the final choral tag is generally meaningless and trite. Yet Kamerbeek, like L-J & W[2], can find no good reason to. There is nothing in the syntax to suggest that they are spurious and, as L-J & W[2] remark "there is no strong objection to them on the score of style or language."

CONCLUSION

Sophokles' *Elektra* is an unusually difficult play, partly because of its deviation from the traditional version of the myth, but chiefly because of its subtle treatment of the vengeance as a phenomenon that is at once a *dikaion* and an *aischron*. One of the main problems for commentators of this play has been how to understand Sophokles' presentation of the vengeance. The failure of the siblings to express the doubt of their Aeschylean and Euripidean counterparts when it comes to carrying out the matricide, and the absence of the Furies or any other element to suggest future retribution or punishment have made it particularly difficult to detect the attitude of the poet. In very general terms, critics fall into two opposing camps according to how they have responded to and interpreted the apparent lack of moral conflict. For the affirmative camp, there is no need for doubt, as the vengeance is a clear-cut case of just retribution; while those of the pessimistic persuasion have interpreted these same elements as part of Sophokles' strategy of casting the whole affair in a dubious light. The justifiers have a number of strong points in their favour: the oracle seems to provide divine sanction of the vengeance; the tyranny and crimes of Klytaimnestra and Aigisthos are emphasized to such a degree that there seems to be little reason to doubt that their punishment is anything but warranted; and the overall movement of the plot is towards *dike*. These elements all support their exegesis of the vengeance as an act of justice which in the end restores order and makes freedom possible. Nevertheless, the affirmative reading fails to be persuasive because it glosses over the darker aspects of the action: the recurring emphasis on *dolos*, and the disquieting and disturbing features in the behaviour and actions of the siblings. The refusal to give these elements the necessary weight in their overall interpretation of the play renders their optimistic readings one-sided and incomplete. It certainly does not do justice to Sophokles' subtle and complex treatment of the relationship of vengeance and justice. It is to the credit of the pessimists to have forced the dark and disturbing features of the play into the centre of the debate and thus given them the weight they deserve. In this respect the ironic approach is a welcome antidote to and corrective of the unreflective

optimism of the affirmative reading. However, the ironists, in seiz-
ing upon the darker aspects, went to the other extreme and turned
them into a coherent pessimistic reading of the play that is as one-
sided and incomplete as that of the other camp. This had led to the
current dilemma in Sophoclean scholarship with regard to *Elektra*:
two opposing exegetical camps, each having captured an important
truth about the play, but in either case it was only a partial truth;
and in this sense there seemed to be no way of bridging them. The
purpose of this study was to find a way to transcend this division
in Sophoclean scholarship.

The most striking feature in Sophokles' treatment of the vengeance
theme is the apparently paradoxical union of *aischron* and *dikaion*, and
related to this the union of *dolos* and *dike*. The one-sidedness of both
schools stems from their inability to recognize that the two elements
of these unions go together: the optimistic reading glosses over *aischron* and *dolos* and the ironic interpretation has the *aischron* and *dolos*
engulf and efface the *dikaion* and *dike*. Yet to understand the nature
of a justice whose vehicle is vengeance requires that we grasp the
tension-laden union of both pairs. Both sides in this respect suffer
from a similar weakness: they fail to see the connection between *dolos*
and *dike*: the role of *dolos* in the pursuit of justice. Given that the
dolos is most pronounced when it is translated into the dramatic
action in the form of the messenger report of Orestes' fictitious death,
it is not surprising that this *rhesis* was also the blind spot of Sophoclean
scholarship. Second, both camps share the view that *Elektra* turns
altogether on the *oikos* and its ethics, and that the *polis* and its civic
ethics have no presence in this play. Yet the frequent use of ethical
terms, often with heavy political overtones, point to the weakness of
this view.

The key element to the exegesis of this play is the understanding
of the role of the *dolos* and the *aischron* in the pursuit of a just
vengeance; this necessitated that much critical attention had to be
paid to the messenger *rhesis* and the ethical concept of *aidos*. This,
however, has resulted in the demonstration that *dolos* and *dike*, and
the *aischron* and the *dikaion* go together in the dramatic constellation
of this play—not by way of paradox, but by way of tension; and it
is the oracle of Apollo and the civic ethics of the *polis* which function to resolve these apparent paradoxes. The *dolos* instigated by
Apollo is not a blanket endorsement of deception but the sanction
of a *dolos* which will secure "just killings", hence the necessity for

narrative and rhetorical elaboration of the report of Orestes' death by the *paidagogos*. The behaviour of Elektra on the other hand, as *aischron* as it is, is sanctioned by the civic ethical code of the *polis* in that it upholds the virtues of *eusebeia* and *sophrosyne* and is in pursuit of a *dike* which will restore order and freedom to *oikos* and *polis* alike. Thus in the first case, the *dolos* shows the operation of divine justice through the agents of Apollo; and in the second case, the *aischron* in the conduct of Elektra is the vehicle through which the civic ethics of the *polis* are upheld. These two themes, the *dolos* and the *aischron*, thus show the parallel movement of a divine and human justice, the agents of which are finally brought together in the reunion scene. Through the dramatic action of this play we are made to understand how inherently discreditable acts such as the telling of a lie and the shameful conduct of Elektra can be in certain constellations also understood as *dikaion*. In this fashion the moral framework for the vengeance is laid and we are brought to the understanding of it as an *aischron* act which is simultaneously *dikaion*. This study then has sought to deepen and enrich the justifiers' claim that the vengeance is an act of justice by giving it the ethical support it requires; while at the same time acknowledging and appropriating the strengths of the pessimistic exegesis which has shown the dubious side of the vengeance. To understand Sophokles' presentation of the vengeance requires that we recognize both sides of its nature: the *aischron* and *dikaion*.

The final result of this study is essentially an affirmative reading of the play which is made complete by integrating the insights and results of the ironic reading: the understanding of how *aischron* and *dikaion*, *dolos* and *dike* cooperate in this play to achieve order and freedom in family and polity without suppressing the natural tension which exists between them. This is the achievement of Sophokles' dramatic art in this play: to sustain this difficult tension in the understanding of justice which has to balance the often conflicting claims of *polis* and *oikos* and of the conflicting loyalties of individuals which flow from their obligations as family-members and citizens.

BIBLIOGRAPHY

Adams, S.M. 1933. "The Sophoclean Orestes." *CR* 47: 209–210.
—— 1957. *Sophocles the Playwright*. Toronto.
Adkins, A.W.H. 1960. *Merit and Responsibility*. Oxford.
Alden, M.J. 1987. "The Role of Telemachos in the *Odyssey*." *Hermes* 115: 129–137.
Alexanderson, B. 1966. "On Sophocles' *Electra*." *C&M* 27: 79–98.
Alexiou, M. 1974. *The Ritual Lament in Greek Tradition*. Cambridge.
Anderson, M.J. ed. 1965. *Classical Drama and Its Influence*. London.
Apostle, H. 1975. *Aristotle The Nicomachean Ethics*. Dordrecht.
D'Arms, E.F. and K.K. Hulley, 1946. "The Oresteia-Story in the *Odyssey*." *TAPA* 77: 207–213.
D'Arms, J.H. and J.W. Eadie. 1977. *Ancient and Modern: Essays in Honor of Gerald F. Else*. Ann Arbor.
Arnhart, L. 1981. *Aristotle on Political Reasoning: A Commentary on the "Rhetoric."* Dekalb.
Arthur, M.B. 1982. "Women and the family in ancient Greece." *YR* 71: 532–547.
Bambrough, R. 1983. "Aristotle and Agamemnon." *Philosophy & Literature* 7: 29–40.
Batchelder, A.G. 1995. *The Seal of Orestes: self-reference and authority in Sophocles' Electra*. London.
Belfiore, E.S. 1992. *Tragic Pleasures: Aristotle on Plot and Emotions*. Princeton.
Bell, C. 1992. *Ritual Theory, Ritual Practice*. Oxford.
Benardete, S. 1961. "Sophocles *Electra* 1087." *RhM* 104: 96.
Benedict, R. 1946. *The Chrysanthemum and the Sword: Patterns of Japanese Culture*. Boston.
Benveniste, E. 1973. *Indo-European Language and Society*. Trans. E. Palmer. London.
Bers, V. 1984. *Greek Poetic Syntax in the Classical Age*. New Haven.
—— 1994. "Tragedy and Rhetoric." In Worthington 1994: 176–195.
Betts, J.H., J.T. Hooker and J.R. Green. eds. 1988. *Studies in Honour of T.B.L. Webster*. Bristol.
Bierl, A. and P. von Möllendorff. 1994. *Orchestra: Drama, Mythos, Bühne. Festschrift für Hellmuth Flashar*. Stuttgart.
Blok, J. and P. Mason eds. 1987. *Sexual Asymmetry: Studies in Ancient Society*. Amsterdam.
Blundell, M.W. 1989. *Helping Friends and Harming Enemies*. Cambridge.
Blundell, S. 1995. *Women in Ancient Greece*. Cambridge.
Booth, N.B. 1976. "Sophocles *Electra* 1082–1089." *RhM* 119: 127–133.
—— 1977. "Sophocles *Electra* 610–611." *CQ* 27: 466–467.
—— 1986. "Arguments against *ameinon* in Sophocles' *Electra* 1085–6." *BICS* 33: 103–106.
Bouvrie, S. 1990. *Women in Greek Tragedy*. Oslo.
Bowersock, G., W. Burkert, and M.C.W. Putnam. eds. 1979. *Arktouros: Hellenic Studies Presented to Bernard M.W. Knox*. Berlin-New York.
Bowman, L. 1997. "Klytaimnestra's Dream: Prophecy in Sophokles' *Elektra*." *Phoenix* 51: 131–151.
Bowra, C.M. 1944. *Sophoclean Tragedy*. Oxford.
Brann, E. 1957. "A Note on the Structure of Sophocles' *Electra*." *CP* 52: 103–104.
Bremer, J.M. 1969. *Hamartia: Tragic Error in the Poetics of Aristotle and Greek Tragedy*. Amsterdam.
—— and A.M. van Erp Taalman Kip. 1994. "Review of *Sophoclis Fabulae*." *Mnemosyne* 47: 236–245.
Bremmer, J.N. 1994. *Greek Religion*. Oxford.

Brown, F. 1956. "Notes on Sophocles' *Electra*." *CQ* 6: 38–39.

Bryant, J.M. 1996. *Moral Codes and Social Structure in Ancient Greece*. Albany.

Burkert, W. 1966. "Greek Tragedy and Sacrificial Ritual." *GRBS* 7: 87–121.

—— 1983. *Homo Necans: The Anthropology of Ancient Greek Sacrificial Ritual and Myth*. Berkeley.

—— 1985. *Greek Religion*. Oxford.

Burnett, A.P. 1998. *Revenge in Attic and Later Tragedy*. Berkeley.

Burton, R.W.B. 1980. *The Chorus in Sophocles' Tragedies*. Oxford.

Buxton, R.G.A. 1982. *Persuasion in Greek Tragedy: A Study of Peithô*. Cambridge.

Bywater, I. 1909. *Aristotle on the Art of Poetry*. Oxford.

Cairns, D.L. 1991. "Shaming Friends: Sophocles' *Electra*." *Prudentia* 23: 19–30.

—— 1993. *Aidos. The Psychology and Ethics of Honour and Shame in Ancient Greek Literature*. Oxford.

—— 1996. "*Hybris*, Dishonour, and Thinking Big." *JHS* 116: 1–32.

Calder III, W.M. 1963. "The End of Sophocles' *Electra*." *GRBS* 4: 213–16.

Canterella, E. 1991. "*Moicheia*. Reconsidering a Problem." In Gagarin 1991: 289–296.

Carey, C. 1989. *Lysias Selected Speeches*. Cambridge.

Carpenter, T.H. and C.A. Faraone, eds. 1993. *Masks of Dionysos*. Ithaca.

Case, J. 1902. "Apollo and the Erinyes in the *Electra* of Sophocles." *CR* 16: 195–200.

Cheyns, A. 1967. "Sens et valeurs due mot *aidos* dans les contextes homériques." *Recherches de Philologies et de Linguistique* 1: 3–33.

Clark, G. 1989. *Women in the Ancient World*. *G&R. New Surveys in the Classics*. No. 21. Oxford.

Claus, D.B. 1974. "*Aidos* in the Language of Achilles." *TAPA* 105: 13–28.

Cohen, D. 1984. "The Athenian Law of Adultery." *RIDA* 31: 147–65.

—— 1989. "Seclusion, separation and the status of women in Classical Athens." *G&R* 36: 3–15.

—— ed. 1991. *Law, sexuality, and society: the enforcement of morals in classical Athens*. Cambridge.

Cole, S.G. 1984. "Greek Sanctions against Sexual Assault." *CP* 79: 97–113.

Conacher, D.J. 1967. *Euripidean Drama: Myth, Theme, and Structure*. Toronto.

—— 1974. "Interaction between Chorus and Characters in the *Oresteia*." *AJP* 95: 323–43.

—— 1987. *Aeschylus' Oresteia: a literary commentary*. Toronto.

Conradie, P.J. 1981. "Contemporary Politics in Greek Tragedy: a critical discussion of different approaches." *AC* 24: 23–35.

Cooper. J.M. 1996. "An Aristotelian Theory of Emotions." In Rorty 1996: 238–257.

—— 1999. *Reason and Emotion: Essays on Ancient Moral Psychology and Ethical Theory*. Princeton.

Corrigan, R.W. 1955. "The *Electra* of Sophocles." *Tulane Drama Review* 1: 36–66.

Coy, J. and J. de Hoz. eds. 1984. *Estudios sobre los géneros literarios II*. Salamanca.

Creed, J.L. 1973. "Moral Values in the Age of Thucydides." *CQ* 23: 213–231.

Cropp, M.J. 1988. *Euripides Electra*. Warminster.

——, E. Fantham, S.E. Scully. eds. 1986. *Greek Tragedy and its Legacy*. Calgary.

Crotty, K. 1994. *The Poetics of Supplication: Homer's "Iliad" and "Odyssey."* Ithaca.

Culham, P. 1986. "Ten Years after Pomeroy: Studies of the Image and Reality of Women in Antiquity." In Skinner 1986: 9–30.

Dain, A. 1958. *Sophocle, tome II*. Trans. P. Mazon. Paris.

Davidson, J.F. 1988. "Chorus, Theatre, Text and Sophocles." In Betts *et al.* 1988: 69–78.

—— 1989. "Homer and Sophocles' *Electra*." *BICS* 35: 45–72.

—— 1990a. "The Daughters of Agamemnon (Soph. *El.* 153–163)." *RhM* 133: 407–409.

—— 1990b. "The Sophoclean Axe." *RhM* 133: 410.

Davies, M.I. 1969. "Thoughts on the *Oresteia* before Aischylos." *BCH* 93: 214–216.

Dawe, R.D. 1976. "Sophocles, Electra. Commentaries by Kamerbeek. Part V." *Gnomon* 48: 228–234.

—— 1978. *Studies on the Text of Sophocles Vol. III*. Leiden.

—— 1985. *Sophocles, Tragoediae I: Ajax, Elektra, Oedipus Rex*. Leipzig.

—— ed. 1996. *Sophocles: The Classical Heritage*. New York and London.

Del Corno, D. 1982. "Dreams and their Interpretation in Ancient Greece." *BICS* 29: 55–62.

Denniston, J. 1939. *The Plays of Euripides. Electra*. Oxford.

—— and D. Page. 1957. *Aeschylus. Agamemnon*. Oxford.

Devereux, G. 1976. *Dreams in Greek Tragedy*. Berkeley.

Dickie, M.W. 1984. "*Hesychia* and *Hybris* in Pindar." In Gerber 1984: 83–109.

Dodds, E.R. 1951. *The Greeks and the Irrational*. Berkeley and Los Angeles.

Dover, K.J. 1974. *Greek Popular Morality in the Time of Plato and Aristotle*. Berkeley.

Dunn, F.M. ed. 1996a. *Sophocles' "Elektra" in Performance*. Drama Beiträge zum antiken Drama und seiner Rezeption. Band 4. Stuttgart.

—— 1996b. "The Urn Revisited." In Dunn 1996a: 150–153.

Easterling, P.E. 1977. "Character in Sophocles." *G&R* 24: 121–9.

—— 1984. "Kings in Greek Tragedy." In Coy and de Hoz 1984: 33–45.

—— 1987. "Women in Tragic Space." *BICS* 34: 15–26.

—— 1989a. "Tragedy and Ritual." *Métis* 3: 97–109.

—— 1989b. "Electra's Story." In Puffet 1989: 10–16.

—— ed. 1997. *The Cambridge Companion to Greek Tragedy*. Cambridge.

Ellendt, F.T. 1872. *Lexicon Sophocleum*. Berlin.

Erbse, H. 1978. "Zur *Elektra* des Sophokles." *Hermes* 106: 284–300.

Erffa, C.E. von 1937. αἰδώς *und verwandte Begriffe in ihrer Entwicklung von Homer bis Demokrit. Philologus Supplement* 30. Leipzig.

Erp Taalman Kip, A.M. van 1996a. "Truth in Tragedy: When are We Entitled to Doubt a Character's Words?" *AJP* 117: 517–536.

—— 1996b. "Sophocles *Electra* 197–200: Who is the θεός?" *Hermes* 124: 282–289.

Euben, J.P. ed. 1986. *Greek Tragedy and Political Theory*. Berkeley.

Ewans, M. 1984. "Elektra: Sophokles, Von Hofmannsthal, Strauss." *Ramus* 13: 135–54.

Falk, E.H. 1955. "Electra." *Tulane Drama Review* 1: 22–30.

Ferrari, G. 1990. "Figures of Speech: The Picture of *Aidos*." *Métis* 5: 185–204.

Fisher, N.R.E. 1976. *Social Values in Classical Athens*. London.

—— 1992. *Hybris. A Study in the values of honour and shame in Ancient Greece*. Warminster.

Fitzgerald, J.T. ed. 1997a. *Greco-Roman Perspectives on Friendship*. Georgia.

—— 1997b. "Friendship in the Greek World Prior to Aristotle." In Fitzgerald 1997a: 13–34.

Foley, H.P. ed. 1981a. *Reflections of Women in Antiquity*. New York.

—— 1981b. "The Conception of Women in Athenian Drama." In Foley 1981a: 127–168.

—— 1985. *Ritual Irony: Poetry and Sacrifice in Euripides*. Ithaca.

—— 1993. "The Politics of Tragic Lamentation." In Sommerstein *et al.* 1993: 101–43. Bari.

—— 1995. "Tragedy and Democratic Ideology: The Case of Sophocles' *Antigone*." In Goff 1995: 131–150.

Fortenbaugh, W.W. 1975. *Aristotle on Emotion*. New York.

Foxhall, L. 1989. "Household, Gender and Property in Classical Athens." *CQ* 39: 22–44.

—— 1991. "Response to Eva Cantarella." In Gagarin 1991: 297–304.

Fraenkel, E. 1950. *Aeschylus. Agamemnon. Vol. 1, II, & III*. Oxford.

Fränkel, H. 1975. *Early Greek Poetry and Philosophy*. Oxford.

Friedrich, R. 1983. "Drama and Ritual." In Redmond 1983: 159–223.

—— 1996. "Everything to do with Dionysos? Ritualism, the Dionysiac and the Tragic." In Silk 1996: 257–283.

—— 2000. "Dionysus among the Dons: The New Ritualism in Richard Seaford's Commentary on the *Bacchae*." *Arion* 7: 115–152.

Furley, D. and A. Nehamas eds. 1994. *Aristotle's Rhetoric: Philosophical Essays*. Princeton.

Gardiner, C.P. 1986. *The Sophoclean Chorus*. Iowa City.

Gagarin, M. 1979. "The Athenian Law Against *Hybris*." In Bowersock *et al.* 1979: 229–36.

—— 1991. ed. *Symposion 1990. Vorträge zur griechischen und hellenistischen Rechtsgeschichte*. Köln.

Gantz, T. 1993. *Early Greek Myth. A Guide to Literary and Artistic Sources*. Baltimore.

Garland, R. 1985. *The Greek Way of Death*. Ithaca.

Garner, R. 1990. *From Homer to Tragedy: the Art of Allusion in Greek Poetry*. London.

Garvey, E. 1994. *Aristotle's Rhetoric: An Art of Character*. Chicago.

Garvie, A.F. 1986. *Aeschylus. Choephori*. Oxford.

Gellie, G.H. 1972. *Sophocles. A Reading*. Melbourne.

Gennep, van A. 1960. *The Rites of Passage*. London. First published in French, 1909.

Gerber, D.E. ed. 1984. *Greek Poetry and Philosophy*. Chicago.

Gill, C. 1984. "The *Ethos/Pathos* Distinction in Rhetorical and Literary Criticism." *CQ* 34: 149–66.

—— 1986. "The question of character and personality in Greek tragedy." *Poetics Today* 7: 251–73.

—— 1990. "The Character-Personality Distinction." In Pelling 1990: 1–31.

—— 1995. *Greek Thought. G&R. New Surveys in the Classics*. No. 25. Oxford.

—— 1996. *Personality in Greek Epic, Tragedy, and Philosophy. The Self in Dialogue*. Oxford.

Goff, B.E. ed. 1995. *History, Tragedy, Theory*. Austin.

Golden, M. 1990. *Children and Childhood in Classical Athens*. Baltimore.

Goldhill, S. 1986. *Reading Greek Tragedy*. Cambridge.

—— 1987. "The Great Dionysia and Civic Ideology." *JHS* 107: 58–76.

Gomme, A.W. 1925. "The position of women in Athens in the fifth and fourth centuries BC." *CP* 20: 1–25.

Gould, J. 1980. "Law, custom and myth: aspects of the social position of women in classical Athens." *JHS* 100: 38–59.

—— 1983. "Homeric Epic and the Tragic Moment." In Winnifrith *et al.* 1983: 32–45.

Gregor, D.B. 1950. "Sophocles *Electra* 610–11. *CR* 64: 87–88.

Grene, D. and R. Lattimore. ed. 1957. *Sophocles II*. Chicago.

Griffin J. 1999. "Sophocles and the Democratic City." In Griffen 1999: 73–94.

—— ed. 1999. *Sophocles Revisited: Essays Presented to Sir Hugh Lloyd-Jones*. Oxford.

Grote, D. 1988. *Sophocles' Electra: social document of late fifth century Athens*. Dissertation: University of Wisconsin-Madison.

—— 1993. "Review of Symposium on Sophocles' *Electra*." *BMCR* 4: 228–232.

Hall, E. 1997. "The sociology of Athenian tragedy." In Easterling 1997: 93–126.

Halliwell, S. 1987. *The Poetics of Aristotle*. London.

Hansen, M.H. 1989. *Was Athens a Democracy? Popular Rule, Liberty and Equality in Ancient and Modern Political Thought*. Copenhagen.

—— 1991. *The Athenian Democracy in the Age of Demosthenes: Structures, Principles, and Ideology*. Oxford.

Harder, M.A. 1995. "'Right' and 'Wrong' in the *Electra's*." *Hermathena* 159: 15–31.

Harris, E.M. 1990. "Did the Athenians Regard Seduction as a Worse Crime than Rape?" *CQ* 40: 370–377.

Harrison, A.R.W. 1968. *The Law of Athens*. Oxford.

Harsh, P.W. 1944. *A Handbook of Classical Drama*. Stanford.

Hartigan, K. 1996. "Resolution without Victory/Victory without Resolution: The Identification Scene in Sophocles' *Elektra*." In Dunn 1996a: 82–92.

Haslam, M.W. 1975. "The Authenticity of Euripides, *Phoenissae* 1–2 and Sophocles, *Electra* 1." *GRBS* 16: 149–74.

—— 1976. "'O Ancient Argos of the Land': Euripides, *Electra* 1." *CQ* 26: 1–2.

Hawley, R. and B. Levick. 1995. *Women in Antiquity: new assessments*. London.

Heath, M. 1987. *The Poetics of Greek Tragedy*. Stanford.

Hertz, R. 1960. *Death and the Right Hand*. Aberdeen. First published in French, 1907.

Hester, D.A. 1973. "Very Much the Safest Plan or Last Words in Sophocles." *Antichthon* 11: 22–41.

—— 1975. "Review of Kamerbeek." *Mnemosyne* 28: 210–5.

—— 1981. "Some Deceptive Oracles: Sophocles, *Electra* 32–7." *Antichthon* 15: 15–25.

—— 1995. "Ironic Interaction in Aeschylus and Sophocles." *Prudentia* 27: 14–44.

Hinds, A.E. 1980. "Binary Action in Sophocles." *Hermathena* 129: 51–57.

Holst-Warhaft, G. 1992. *Dangerous voices: women's laments in Greek literature*. Routledge.

Hooker, J.T. 1975. "The Original Meaning of *Hybris*." *Archiv für Begriffsgeschichte* 19: 125–37.

—— 1987. "Homeric Society: A Shame-Culture?" *G&R* 34: 121–5.

Horsley, G.H.R. 1980a. "Sophokles' *Elektra* 1361." *CR* 75: 300.

—— 1980b. "Apollo in Sophokles' *Elektra*." *Antichthon* 14: 8–29.

Humphreys, S.C. 1986. "Kinship Patterns in the Athenian Courts." *GRBS* 27: 57–91.

—— 1993. *The Family, Women and Death*. 2nd ed. Ann Arbor.

Ierulli, M. 1993. "A Community of Women?" *Métis* 8: 217–229.

Johansen, H.F. 1959. *General Reflection in Tragic Rhesis: A Study of Form*. Copenhagen.

—— 1962. "Sophocles, 1939–1959." *Lustrum* 7: 94–288.

—— 1964. "Die *Elektra* des Sophokles: Versuch einer neuen Deutung." *C&M* 25: 8–32.

—— 1967. *Vergleichende Studien zur sophokleischen und euripideischen Elektra*.

Johnson, S.K. 1928. "Some aspects of dramatic irony in Sophoclean Tragedy." *CR* 42: 209–14.

Johnstone, C.L. 1980. "An Aristotelian Trilogy: Ethics, Rhetoric, Politics, and the Search for the Moral Truth. *Philosophy & Rhetoric* 13: 1–24.

—— ed. 1996. *Theory, Text, Context: Issues in Greek Rhetoric and Oratory*. Albany.

Jones, J. 1962. *On Aristotle and Greek Tragedy*. Stanford.

Jones, W.H.S. 1918. *Pausanias: Description of Greece. Vol. 1*. London.

de Jong, I.J.F. 1987. "The Voice of Anonymity: *tis*-speeches in the *Iliad*." *Eranos* 85: 69–84.

—— 1994. "Πιστὰ τεκμήρια in Soph. *El*. 774." *Mnemosyne* 47: 679–681.

—— and J.P. Sullivan eds. 1994. *Modern Critical Theory and Classical Literature. Mnemosyne*: Supplementum 130. New York.

Juffras, D.M. 1988. *Friendship and faction in Sophocles: Greek political thinking and the Ajax, Antigone and Oedipus at Colonus*. Dissertation: University of Michigan.

—— 1991. "Sophocles' *Electra* 973–85 and Tyrannicide." *TAPA* 121: 99–108.

Just, R. 1975. "Conceptions of women in classical Athens." *JASO* 6: 153–170.

—— 1989. *Women in Athenian Law and Life*. London.

Kassel, R. 1976. *Aristotelis. Ars Rhetorica*. Berlin.

Katz, M.A. 1994. "The Character of Tragedy: Women and the Greek Imagination." *Arethusa* 27: 81–103.

—— 1995. "Ideology and 'the status of women' in ancient Greece." In Hawley and Levick 1995: 21–43.

Kells, J.H. 1986. "Sophocles' *Electra* Revisted." In Betts *et al.* 1986: 153–160.

Kirkwood, G.M. 1942. "Two Structural Features of Sophocles' *Electra*." *TAPA* 73: 86–95.

—— 1958. A *Study of Sophoclean Drama*. Ithaca.
—— 1991. "Review of *Sophoclis fabulae* and *Sophoclea*." *BMCR* 2: 22–31.
Kitto, H.D.F. 1957. *The Greeks*. Middlesex.
—— 1958. *Sophocles: Dramatist & Philosopher*. London.
—— 1960. *Form and Meaning in Drama*. New York and London.
—— 1966. *Greek Tragedy*. London.
Kitzinger, R. 1991. "Why Mourning Becomes Elektra." *CA* 10: 298–327.
Knox, B.M.W. 1964. *The Heroic Temper: Studies in Sophoclean Tragedy*. Berkeley.
—— 1982. "Sophocles and the *Polis*." In de Romilly 1982: 1–27.
—— 1996. "Author, Author." *Philosophy & Literature* 20: 76–88.
Kokolakis, M.M. 1986. "Greek Drama: The Stirring of Pity." In Betts *et al.* 1986: 170–178.
Konstan, D. 1985. "*Philia* in Euripides' *Electra*." *Philologus* 129: 192–201.
—— 1996. "Greek Friendship." *AJP* 117: 71–94.
Kopff, E.C. 1993. "Review of *Sophoclis Fabulae* and *Trachinae*." *AJP* 114: 155–180.
Lacey, W.K. 1968. *The Family in Classical Greece*. Ithaca.
Lamb, W.R. 1930. *Lysias*. London.
Lefkowitz, M. 1995. "Women and Freedom." *Arethusa* 28: 107–111.
Leighton, S. R. 1996. "Aristotle and the Emotions." In Rorty 1996: 206–237.
Lesky, A. 1965. *Greek Tragedy*. Trans. H.A. Frankfort. London.
Lilley, D.J. 1975. "Sophocles, *Electra* 610–611." *CQ* 25: 309–311.
Linforth, I.M. 1963. "Electra's Day in the Tragedy of Sophocles." *UCPCP* 19: 89–126.
Lloyd, A.B. ed. 1997. *What is a god?* London.
Lloyd-Jones, H. 1954. "Sophoclea." *CQ* 4: 91–95.
—— 1975. "J.H. Kells, *Sophocles, Electra*." *CR* 25: 10–12.
—— 1990a. *Greek Comedy, Hellenistic Literature, Greek Religion, and Miscellanea*. Oxford.
—— 1990b. "Honour and Shame in Ancient Greek Culture." In Lloyd-Jones 1990a: 253–254.
—— 1993. "*OMMA* in Sophocles, *Electra* 902 and *Oedipus Tyrannus*." In Most 1993: 300–304.
—— and N.G. Wilson. 1997. *Second Thoughts*. Göttingen.
Lombard, D.B. 1992. "The Suffering of Elektra." *Akroterion* 37.2: 46–60.
Lord, Carnes. 1981. "The Intention of Aristotle's *Rhetoric*." *Hermes* 109: 326–339.
MacDowell, D.M. 1976. "*Hybris* in Athens." *G&R* 23: 14–31.
—— 1978. *The Law in Classical Athens*. London.
—— 1989. "The *Oikos* in Athenian Law." *CQ* 39: 10–21.
Macintosh, F. 1995. *Dying Acts: Death in Ancient Greek and Modern Irish Tragic Drama*. New York.
MacLeod, C.W. 1982. *Homer: Iliad XXIV*. Cambridge.
Maitland, J. 1992. "Dynasty and Family in the Athenian City State: A View from Attic Tragedy." *CQ* 42: 26–40.
Mantziou, M. 1995. "The palace door in Sophocles' *Electra*. In Rybowska and Witczak 1995: 189–195.
Markantonatos, G. 1977. "On the Main Types of Dramatic Irony as used in Greek Tragedy." *Platon* 29: 79–84.
—— 1979. "Dramatic Irony in the *Electra* of Sophocles." *Platon* 31: 147–150.
—— 1980. "On the Concept of the Term 'Tragic Irony'." *Platon* 32: 367–373.
March, J.R. 1987. *The Creative Poet. Studies on the Treatment of Myths in Greek Poetry*. *BICS Supplement* 49. London.
—— 1996. "The Chorus in Sophocles' *Electra*." In Dunn 1996a: 65–81.
Mastronarde, D.J. 1979. *Contact and Discontinuity: Some Conventions of Speech and Action on the Greek Tragic Stage*. Berkeley.
McAuslan, I. and Walcot P. eds. 1993. *Greek Tragedy. G & R Studies*. No. 2. Oxford.

McDevitt, A.S. 1974. "Sophocles' *Electra* 495–7." *RhM* 117: 181–182.

—— 1983. "Shame, Honour and the Hero in Sophocles' *Electra*." *Antichthon* 17: 1–12.

McDonald, M. 1994. "Elektra's *Kleos Aphithiton*." In de Jong and Sullivan 1994: 103–126.

McIntyre, A. 1984. *After Virtue*. Notre Dame.

McKeon, R. 1941. *The Basic Works of Aristotle*. New York.

Meier, C. 1990. *The Greek Discovery of Politics*. Trans. D. McLintock. Cambridge.

—— 1993. *The Political Art of Greek Tragedy*. Trans. A. Webber. Baltimore.

Minadeo, R.W. 1967. "Plot, Theme, and Meaning in Sophocles' *Electra*." *C&M* 28: 114–42.

—— 1994. *The Thematic Sophocles*. Amsterdam.

Monro, D.B. and T.W. Allen. 1920. *Homeri Opera*. Vols. 1–4. Oxford.

Moorhouse, A.C. 1982. *The Syntax of Sophocles*. *Mnemosyne Supplement* 75. Leiden.

Morris, I. 1992. *Death-Ritual and Social Structure in Classical Antiquity*. Cambridge.

Most, G.W., Petersman, H. and Ritter, A.M. 1993. *Philanthropia dai Eusebeia. Festschrift für Albrecht Dihle zum 70. Geburtstag*. Göttingen.

—— 1994. "Sophocles' *Electra* 1086–87." In Bierl and Möllendorff 1994: 129–138.

Murray, G. 1924. *The Rise of the Greek Epic*. Oxford.

Murray, O. 1990. "Cities of Reason." In Murray and Price 1990: 1–25.

—— and S. Price. eds. 1990. *The Greek City from Homer to Alexander*. Oxford.

Musurillo, H. 1967. *The Light and the Darkness*. Leiden.

Nehamas, A. 1994. "Pity and Fear in the *Rhetoric* and the *Poetics*." In Furley and Nehamas 1994: 257–282.

North, H.F. 1947. "A Period of Opposition to *Sophrosyne* in Greek Thought." *TAPA* 78: 1–17.

—— 1966. *Sophrosyne. Self-Knowledge and Self-Restraint in Greek Literature*. Ithaca.

—— 1979. *From Myth to Icon: Reflections of Greek Ethical Doctrine in Literature and Art*. Ithaca.

Nozick, R. 1981. *Philosophical Explanations*. Cambridge.

Nussbaum, M. 1986. *The Fragility of Goodness: Luck and Ethics in Greek Tragedy and Philosophy*. Cambridge.

—— 1990. "Tragedy and Self-Sufficiency: Plato and Aristotle on Fear and Pity." In Rorty 1992: 261–90.

—— 1996. "Compassion: The Basic Social Emotion." *Social Philosophy and Policy* 13: 27–58.

Opstelten, J.C. 1952. *Sophocles and Greek Pessimism*. Amsterdam.

Owen, A.S. 1927. "Τὰ τ'οντα καὶ μελλόντα, The End of Sophocles' *Electra*." *CR* 41: 51–52.

—— 1936. "The Date of the *Electra* of Sophocles." In *Greek Poetry and Life*. 1936: 145–157. Oxford.

Pakaluk, M. ed. 1991. *Other Selves: Philosophers on Friendship*. Indianapolis.

Parker, R. 1983. *Miasma. Pollution and purification in early Greek religion*. Oxford.

Parry, H. 1979. *The Lyric Poems of Greek Tragedy*. Sarasota.

Pelling, C. 1990. *Characterization and Individuality in Greek Literature*. Oxford.

Peradotto, J. and Sullivan, J.P. eds. 1984. *Women in the Ancient World: The Arethusa Papers*. Albany.

Petropoulou, A. 1979. "The Attribution of Sophocles' *Electra* 1015–16. *AJP* 100: 480–486.

Podlecki, A, 1981. "Four *Electras*." *Florilegium* 3: 21–46.

Pomeroy, S.B. 1975. *Goddesses, Whores, Wives, and Slaves: Women in Classical Antiquity*. New York.

—— 1997. *The Family in Classical and Hellenistic Greece*. Oxford.

Poulakis, J. 1995. *Sophistical Rhetoric in Classical Greece*. Columbia.

Puffett, D. ed. 1989. *Richard Strauss: Elektra. Cambridge Opera Handbooks*. Cambridge.
Race, William H. 1981. "The Word Καιρός in Greek Drama." *TAPA* 111: 197–213.
Redfield, J.M. 1994. *Nature and Culture in the Iliad*. Chicago and London.
Redmond, J. ed. 1983. *Themes in Drama V: Drama and Religion*. Cambridge.
Rehm, R. 1994. *Marriage to Death*. Princeton.
——— 1996. "Public Spaces, Private Voices: Euripides' *Suppliant Women* and Sophokles' *Elektra*." In Dunn 1996a: 49–59.
Reinhardt, K. 1979. *Sophocles*. Trans. H. and D. Harvey. Oxford.
Ringer, M. 1996. "Reflections on an Empty Urn." In Dunn 1996a: 93–100.
Roberts, D.H. 1987. "Parting Words: Final Lines in Sophocles and Euripides." *CQ* 37: 51–64.
——— 1988. "Sophoclean Endings: Another Story." *Arethusa* 21: 177–96.
de Romilly, J. ed. 1982. *Sophocle: Entretiens sur l'antiquitè classique. XXIX*. Genève.
Roisman, H. 1984. *Loyalty in Early Greek Epic and Tragedy*. Königstein.
Ronnet, G. 1969. *Sophocle poète tragique*. Paris.
Rorty, A.O. 1980. *Essays on Aristotle's Ethics*. Berkeley.
——— 1992. *Essays on Aristotle's Poetics*. Princeton.
——— 1996. *Essays on Aristotle's Rhetoric*. Berkeley.
Rosenmeyer, T.G. 1977. "Irony and Tragic Choruses." In D' Arms and Eadie 1977: 31–44.
Rybowska, J. and K.T. Witczak. 1995. *Collectanea Philologica II in honorem Annae Mariae Komornicka*. Lodz.
Salkever, S.G. 1986. "Tragedy and the Education of the *Dêmos*: Aristotle's Response to Plato. In Euben 1986: 274–303.
Sandbach, F.H. 1977. "Sophocles, *Electra* 77–85." *PCPS* 23: 71–3.
Saxonhouse, A.W. 1992. *Fear of Diversity: The Birth of Political Science in Ancient Greek Thought*. Chicago.
Schadewaldt, W. 1926. *Monolog und Selbstgespräche*. Berlin.
Schein, S.L. 1982. "*Electra*: A Sophoclean Problem Play." *Antike und Abendland* 28:69–80.
——— 1988. "φιλία in Euripides' *Alcestis*." *Métis* 3: 179–206.
——— 1997. "Divinity and moral agency in Sophoclean tragedy." In Lloyd 1997: 123–138.
——— 1998. "Verbal Adjectives in Sophocles: Necessity and Morality." *CP* 293–307.
Schlegel, A.W. von 1876. *Lectures on dramatic art and literature*. Trans. J. Black. London.
Schmitt Pantel, P. 1990. "Collective Activities and the Political in the Greek City." In Murray and Price 1990: 199–214.
Scodel, R. 1984. *Sophocles*. Boston.
Scott, M. 1979. "Pity and Pathos in Homer." *AC* 22: 1–14.
——— 1980. "*Aidos* and *Nemesis* in the works of Homer, and their relevance to Social or Co-operative Values." *AC* 23: 13–35.
——— 1982. *Philos, Philotês* and *Xenia. AC* 25: 1–19.
Seaford, R. 1985. "The Destruction of Limits in Sophokles' *Elektra*." *CQ* 35: 315–323.
——— 1993. *Dionysos as Destroyer of the Household: Homer, Tragedy, and the City-State*. In Faraone and Carpenter 1993: 114–146.
——— 1994a. *Ritual and Reciprocity: Homer and Tragedy in the Developing City-State*. Oxford.
——— 1994b. "Sophokles and the Mysteries." *Hermes* 122: 275–288.
——— 1996. "Something to do with Dionysos—Tragedy and the Dionysiac: Response to Friedrich." In Silk 1996: 284–294.
Seale, D. 1982. *Vision and Stagecraft in Sophocles*. London.
Segal, C.P. 1966. "The *Electra* of Sophocles." *TAPA* 97: 473–545.
——— 1980. Visual Symbolism and Visual Effects in Sophocles. *CW* 74: 125–42.
——— 1981. *Tragedy and Civilization: An Interpretation of Sophocles*. Cambridge, Mass.
——— 1983. "*Kleos* and its Ironies in the *Odyssey*." *L'Antiquité classique* 52: 22–47.

—— 1995. "Review of *Ritual and Reciprocity*." *BMCR* 6: 651–657.

Segal, E. ed. 1983. *Oxford Readings in Greek Tragedy*. Oxford.

Seidensticker, B. 1995. "Women on the Tragic Stage." In Goff 1995: 151–173.

Shaw, M. 1975. "The female intruder: women in fifth century drama." *CP* 70: 235–66.

Sheppard, J.T. 1918. "The Tragedy of Electra according to Sophocles." *CQ* 12: 80–3.

—— 1927a. "Electra: A Defense of Sophocles." *CR* 41: 2–9.

—— 1927b. "Electra Again." *CR* 41: 163–5.

Silk, M. ed. 1996. *Tragedy and the Tragic*. Oxford.

Sinos, D.S. 1980. *Achilles, Patroklos and the Meaning of Philos*. Innsbruck.

Smith, C.S. 1990. "The meanings of Καιρός in Sophocles' *Electra*." *CJ* 135: 341–343.

Snell, B. 1928. *Aischylos und das Handeln im Drama. Philologus Supplement 20*. Leipzig.

—— 1975. *Die Entdeckung des Geistes*. Göttingen.

Solmsen, F. 1967. "Electra and Orestes: Three Recognitions in Greek Tragedy." *Mededelingen der koninklijke Nederlandse Akademie van Wetenschappen*. 30: 31–62.

Sorum, C.E. 1982. "The Family in Sophocles' *Antigone* and *Electra*" *CW* 75: 201–211.

Sri Pathmanathan, R. 1965. "Death in Greek Tragedy." *G&R* 12: 2–14.

Stanford, W.B. 1954. *The Ulysses Theme. A Study in the Adaptability of a Traditional Hero*. Oxford.

—— 1983. *Greek Tragedy and the Emotions: An Introductory Study*. London.

Stevens, E.B. 1941. "Some Attic Commonplaces of Pity." *AJP* 65: 1–25.

—— 1948. "Envy and Pity in Greek Philosophy." *AJP* 69: 171–189.

Stevens, P.T. 1978. "Sophocles: Electra, Doom or Triumph?" *G&R* 25: 11–20.

Stinton, T.C.W. 1986. "The Scope and Limits of Allusion in Greek Tragedy." In Cropp *et al.* 1986: 67–99.

Stokes, M.C. 1979. "Sophocles, *Electra* 1087; Text and Context." In Putnam 1979: 134–43.

Strauss, B. 1986. *Athens after the Peloponnesian War*. London.

Stuart, D.C. 1918. "The Recognition Scene in Greek Tragedy." *AJP* 39: 268–290.

Swart, G. 1984. "Dramatic Function of the 'Agon' Scene in the *Electra* of Sophocles." *AC* 27: 23–29.

Synodinou, K. 1977. *On the Concept of Slavery in Euripides*. Ioannina.

Szlezak, T.A. 1981. "Sophokles' *Elektra* und das Problem des ironischen Dramas." *MH* 38: 1–21.

Taplin, O. 1978. *Greek Tragedy in Action*. 1974.

Taylor, G. 1985. *Pride, Shame and Guilt*. Oxford.

Taylor, M.W. 1981. The Tyrant Slayers: The Heroic Image in the Fifth Century B.C. New York.

Thomson, G. 1941. *Aeschylus and Athens*. London.

Torrance, R.M. 1965. "Sophocles: Some Bearings." *HSCP* 69: 307–14.

Vellacott, P. 1979. "Woman and Man in Ancient Greece: The Evidence from Tragic Drama." *The Carleton Miscellany* 18: 7–33.

Verdenius, W.J. 1945. "αἰδώς bei Homer" *Mnemosyne* 3: 47–60.

Vernant, J.P. 1983. *Myth and Thought among the Greeks*. London.

—— 1991. *Mortals and Immortals*. Princeton.

Vickers, B. 1982. *Towards Greek Tragedy*. London.

Viketos, E. 1987. "Sophokles, Elektra 1508–10." *Hermes* 115: 372–3.

Voigt, C. 1972. *Überlegung und Entscheidung: Studien zur Selbstauffassung des Menschen bei Homer*. Beiträge zur klassischen Philologie 48, Meisenheim am Glan.

Waldcock, A.J.A. 1951. *Sophocles the Dramatist*. Cambridge.

Walton, J.M. 1996. "Sophocles' *Electra*: Actors in Space." In Dunn 1996a: 41–48.

Webster, T.B.L. 1936. *An Introduction to Sophocles*. Oxford.

West, M.L. 1979. "Tragica III." *BICS* 26: 104–117.

—— 1991. "The New OCT of Sophocles." *CR* 41: 299–301.

de Wet, B.X. 1977. "The *Electra* of Sophocles—A Study in Social Values." *AC* 20: 23–36.

Whitelaw, R. 1883. *Sophocles*. London.

Whitman, C.H. 1951. *Sophocles: A Study of Heroic Humanism*. Cambridge.

—— 1958. *Homer and the Heroic Tradition*. Cambridge.

Wiersma, S. 1984. "Women in Sophocles." *Mnemosyne* 37: 25–55.

Wilamowitz-Moellendorff, T. von. 1917. *Die dramatische Technik des Sophokles*. Berlin.

Williams, B. 1993. *Shame and Necessity*. Berkeley.

Willink, C.W. 1997. "Sophokles' *Elektra* 137–9." *CQ* 47: 299–301.

Wilson, J.R. 1979. "ΚΑΙ ΚΕ ΤΙΣ ΩΔ᾽ ΕΡΕΕΙ: An Homeric Device in Greek Literature." *ICS* 4: 1–15.

—— 1980. "*Kairos* As 'Due Measure'." *Glotta* 58: 177–204.

Winkler, J.J. and F.I. Zeitlin eds. 1990. *Nothing to do with Dionysos?* Princeton.

Winnifrith, R., P. Murray, and K.W. Gransden eds. 1983. *Aspects of the Epic*. London.

Winnington-Ingram, R.P. 1979. "Sophoclea." *BICS* 26: 1–12.

—— 1980. *Sophocles: An Interpretation*. Cambridge.

—— 1983a. "The *Electra* of Sophocles: Prolegomena to an Interpretation." In Segal 1983: 210–7.

—— 1983b. "Sophocles and Women." In de Romilly 1983: 233–37.

Woodard, T.M. 1964. "*Electra* by Sophocles: the dialectical design, Part 1." *HSCP* 68: 163–205.

—— 1965. "*Electra* by Sophocles: the dialectical design, Part II." *HSCP* 70: 195–233.

Worthington, I. ed. 1994. *Persuasion: Greek Rhetoric in Action*. London and New York.

Zaidman, L.B. and Schmitt Pantel, P. 1992. *Religion in the Ancient Greek City*. Trans. P. Cartledge. Originally published in French as *La Religion grecque* 1989. Cambridge.

Zak, W.F. 1995. *The Polis and the Divine Order. The Oresteia, Sophokles and the Defense of Democracy*. Lewisburg.

Zeitlin, F.I. 1970. *The Ritual World of Greek Tragedy*. Dissertation: Columbia.

—— 1978. "The dynamics of misogyny: myth and mythmaking in the *Oresteia*." *Arethusa* 11: 149–194.

—— 1985. "Playing the Other: theater, theatricality, and the feminine in Greek drama." *Representations* 11: 63–94.

GLOSSARY OF TERMS

agathos good, noble
agon debate, argument (in tragedy); contest (in athletics or battle);
aidos respect, shame
aischos disgrace, moral ugliness
aischros shameful, disgraceful, morally ugly
andreia courage, 'manliness'
arete excellence
asebes impious, disrespectful

deileia cowardice
dikaios just
dike justice, judgement, lawsuit
dolos deceit, trickery, deception

echthros (pl. *echthroi*) enemy
eleos pity
eleutheria freedom
eleutheros free
ergon (pl. *erga*) deed
eros passion, passionate desire
eusebeia reverence, piety
eusebes respectful, law-abiding, reverent

homilia intercourse (social or sexual)
hybris arrogance, insolence

kairos the right or proper time (for action)
kakos bad, base, cowardly
kalos fine, noble, beautiful
kerdos gain, profit
kleos fame, reputation
kommos sung exchange between actor(s) and chorus
kudos glory, renown
kurios male guardian of an Athenian woman

lex talionis law of revenge

nemesis righteous indignation
nomos convention, law

oikos household, family

paidagogos tutor/slave who accompanied children
patrios nomos ancestral custom, tradition
philia friendship
philos (pl. *philoi*) friend, dear one
phugas an exile, one who is exiled

physis nature
polis city-state
prohairesis choice

rhesis a long set speech by an actor

sebas respect, reverence, awe
sophron sound mind, sensible, temperate, wise
sophrosyne moderation; restraint; self-limitation
soteria safety, salvation, deliverance, preservation
stichomythia rapid single line by line exchange between two actors

talio revenge
telos end, fulfilment, completion
time honour

GENERAL INDEX

adultery (moicheia)   71–2, 87, 89–90,
    95–7, 96n39, 179
aidos   13, 19, 41–2, 48–60, 80–1,
    84, 90–102, 144, 152, 173, 185–7;
    see also shame
    Cairn's view of   42, 49–53, 49n17
    and conscience   42, 50–3
    definitions of   48–9, 48n12
    and Elektra   62, 64–6, 68–9, 90–1,
        93, 99–102, 140, 145, 148, 151,
        160–1, 170–1
    and eusebeia   53–7
    and hybris   128–9
    and nemesis   129–30, 132
    and sophrosyne   57–60
Aigisthos   2, 9, 10, 12, 13, 15, 26, 32,
    39, 43–4, 46, 54, 57, 71, 74, 84,
    89–90, 95, 96–7, 126, 131, 135,
    136, 140–3, 145, 146, 152, 154,
    155, 163, 166–7, 173–84
aischron   14, 16, 20, 55n28, 93,
    93n31, 94, 161, 162, 171, 183,
    185–7
Aischylos   1, 9, 19, 29, 58, 64, 72,
    153, 173
    Agamemnon   85–6
    Choephori   72, 107
    treatment of Orestes legend   3–4, 7
Amphiaraos   134
andreia   66, 144–5, 144n10; *see also*
    courage
Apollo   3, 7, 11, 17, 20, 23, 23n5,
    25, 28–38, 46, 74, 79, 102–5, 107,
    108, 111, 112, 120, 138, 153,
    159–60, 161, 165, 173, 179, 181,
    182, 186–7
arete   64, 67, 155

Blundell, M.W.   12–3, 16, 80–1, 83,
    90, 93–4, 97, 101–2, 108
Bowra, C.M.   8–9, 126

Cairns, D.   13, 16, 42, 49–53, 55–7,
    80–1, 91–3, 95, 99–102, 128–9
Chrysothemis   45, 59, 61–71, 74–8,
    79, 102, 103, 105, 133, 134,
    135–48, 155, 160, 174
Chorus   8, 9, 18, 25, 33, 39, 40, 41,

42–8, 53, 57, 61, 62, 68, 71, 77–8,
    89, 102, 103, 131, 132–4, 148–52,
    153, 154, 155, 158, 162, 165–6,
    167, 170, 171–2, 174, 177, 179,
    183–4
Creon   43
courage   51n21, 58, 144n10; *see also*
    andreia

dikaion   14, 16, 20, 55n28, 63, 93n31,
    183, 185–7
dike   19–20, 37, 40, 47, 71, 80, 81,
    82–3, 93, 102, 137, 145, 146, 163,
    182, 185; *see also* justice
    and dolos   20, 22, 23–4, 31, 33–4,
        37, 38, 46, 108, 111, 125,
        159–62, 186–7
dolos   20, 102, Ch. 5, 137, 139, 146,
    155, 156, 159–62, 163, 165, 167,
    174–5, 185–7; *see also* dike
    and Klytaimnestra   10, 19, 24, 33,
        46, 104, 160
    and Orestes   10, 13, 19, 22, 24, 30,
        33–8, 46, 157–9
    and the oracle   19, 23, 30–4
    and the paidagogos   111, 112–4,
        120, 123–6, 160
dreams, interpretation of   70

eleos   68; *see also* pity
eleutheria   18, 19, 63, 137, 142;
    see also freedom
eros   46–7, 89
Erynes see Furies
eusebeia   19, 41, 48, 53–7, 56n32, 59,
    60, 65, 66, 69, 78, 90–1, 93, 100,
    130, 132, 137, 141, 142, 145, 146,
    151, 170, 186–7
Euripides   9, 51, 178
    Elektra   1, 107, 153
    treatment of Orestes legend   3–4, 5,
        12, 17, 29
exile (phugas)   31–3, 97, 112, 120–1,
    122, 179

fear   33, 44, 48, 71, 77, 78, 103, 104,
    111, 114, 116, 122, 130, 131, 176
    Aristotle's treatment of   114–7

SUPPLEMENTS TO MNEMOSYNE

EDITED BY H. PINKSTER, H.W. PLEKET

C.J. RUIJGH, D.M. SCHENKEVELD AND P.H. SCHRIJVERS

Recent volumes in the series:

190. Hout, M.P.J. van den. *A Commentary on the Letters of M. Cornelius Fronto.* 1999.
ISBN 90 04 10957 9
191. Kraus, C. Shuttleworth (ed.). *The Limits of Historiography.* Genre and Narrative in
Ancient Historical Texts. 1999. ISBN 90 04 10670 7
192. Lomas, K. & T. Cornell. *Cities and Urbanisation in Ancient Italy.* ISBN 90 04 10808 4
In preparation
193. Malkin, I. *History of Greek Colonization.* ISBN 90 04 09843 7 *In preparation*
194. Wood, S.E. *Imperial Women.* A Study in Public Images, 40 B.C.-A.D. 68. 1999.
ISBN 90 04 11281 2
195. Ophuijsen, J.M. van & P. Stork. *Linguistics into Interpretation.* Speeches of War in
Herodotus VII 5 & 8-18. 1999. ISBN 90 04 11455 6
196. Tsetskhladze, G.R. (ed.). *Ancient Greeks West and East.* 1999. ISBN 90 04 11190 5
197. Pfeijffer, I.L. *Three Aeginetan Odes of Pindar.* A Commentary on *Nemean* V, *Nemean* III,
& *Pythian* VIII. 1999. ISBN 90 04 11381 9
198. Horsfall, N. *Virgil*, Aeneid 7. A Commentary. 2000. ISBN 90 04 10842 4
199. Irby-Massie, G.L. *Military Religion in Roman Britain.* 1999.
ISBN 90 04 10848 3
200. Grainger, J.D. *The League of the Aitolians.* 1999. ISBN 90 04 10911 0
201. Adrados, F.R. *History of the Graeco-Roman Fable.* I: Introduction and from the Origins
to the Hellenistic Age. Translated by L.A. Ray. Revised and Updated by the Author and Gert-Jan van Dijk. 1999. ISBN 90 04 11454 8
202. Grainger, J.D. *Aitolian Prosopographical Studies.* 2000. ISBN 90 04 11350 9
203. Solomon, J. *Ptolemy* Harmonics. Translation and Commentary. 2000.
ISBN 90 04 115919
204. Wijsman, H.J.W. *Valerius Flaccus Argonautica, Book VI.* A Commentary. 2000.
ISBN 90 04 11718 0
205. Mader, G. *Josephus and the Politics of Historiography.* Apologetic and Impression
Management in the *Bellum Judaicum.* 2000. ISBN 90 04 11446 7
206. Nauta, R.R. *Poetry for Patrons.* Literary Communication in the Age of Domitian.
2001. ISBN 90 04 10885 8
207. Adrados, F.R. *History of the Graeco-Roman Fable.* II: The Fable during the Roman
Empire and in the Middle Ages. Translated by L.A. Ray. Revised and Updated by
the Author and Gert-Jan van Dijk. 2000. ISBN 90 04 11583 8
208. James, A. & K. Lee. *A Commentary on Quintus of Smyrna*, Posthomerica V. 2000.
ISBN 90 04 11594 3
209. Derderian, K. *Leaving Words to Remember.* Greek Mourning and the Advent of Literacy. 2001. ISBN 90 04 11750 4
210. Shorrock, R. *The Challenge of Epic.* Allusive Engagement in the *Dionysiaca* of Nonnus.
2001. ISBN 90 04 11795 4

211. Scheidel, W. (ed.). *Debating Roman Demography*. 2001. ISBN 90 04 11525 0
212. Keulen, A.J. *L. Annaeus Seneca* Troades. Introduction, Text and Commentary. 2001. ISBN 90 04 12004 1
213. Morton, J. *The Role of the Physical Environment in Ancient Greek Seafaring*. 2001. ISBN 90 04 11717 2
214. Graham, A.J. *Collected Papers on Greek Colonization*. 2001. ISBN 90 04 11634 6
215. Grossardt, P. *Die Erzählung von Meleagros*. Zur literarischen Entwicklung der kalydonischen Kultlegende 2001. ISBN 90 04 11952 3
216. Zafiropoulos, C.A. *Ethics in Aesop's Fables: The* Augustana *Collection*. 2001. ISBN 90 04 11867 5
217. Rengakos, A. & T.D. Papanghelis (eds.). *A Companion to Apollonius Rhodius*. 2001. ISBN 90 04 11752 0
218. Watson, J. *Speaking Volumes*. Orality and Literacy in the Greek and Roman World. 2001. ISBN 90 04 12049 1
219. MacLeod, L.. *Dolos and Dike in Sophokles' Elektra*. 2001. ISBN 90 04 11898 5
220. McKinley, K.L. *Reading the Ovidian Heroine*. "Metamorphoses" Commentaries 1100-1618. 2001. ISBN 90 04 11796 2